AGAINST THE WORLD

A Behind-the-Scenes Look at the Portland Trail Blazers' Chase for the NBA Championship

Kerry Eggers
Dwight Jaynes

SAGAMORE PUBLISHING
Champaign, Illinois

Production Manager: Susan M. Williams
Cover and photo insert design: Michelle R. Dressen
Proofreader: Phyllis L. Bannon

Library of Congress Catalog Card Number:92-82549
ISBN:0-915611-67-8

Printed in the United States.

For Dad: I know you'd have been proud.

— Kerry Eggers

For my bright and wonderful children, Willie and Beth, who are nearly ready to take on the world. The world, by the way, has no chance.

— Dwight Jaynes

CONTENTS

ACKNOWLEDGMENTS

First and foremost, the authors wish to thank John Lashway and John Christensen of the Trail Blazers' public relations staff. Their patient assistance over the years has been invaluable, as was John White's in previous seasons.

There are other unsung heroes in the Trail Blazer organization, too — people who work tirelessly behind the scenes for a company that really does seem to try to be a good corporate citizen. This is an appropriate place to thank some of those people for their kindness over the years. With a sincere apology to anyone unintentionally omitted, thanks to Joe Bashlow, Dan Burke, Chuck Charnquist, Sandy Chisholm, Dr. Robert Cook, Brian Drake, Neil Gomes, Berlyn Hodges, Karl Kellner, Pat Lafferty, Tom McEnry, Traci Rose, Lori Ryan-Spencer, Roger Sabrowski, Wally Scales, Mike Shimensky (and Ron Culp before him), Christee Sweeney, Jim Taylor, and George Wasch.

Thanks, too, are expressed to the Blazer coaching staff and players, who were gracious enough to give up a small slice of their summer to relive some memories of last season.

Most of all, though, gratitude must be expressed to Trail Blazer fans everywhere, without whom this book would not have been possible. It's for those fans — the ones who recognize that vivid, close-up looks at their heroes often reveal small blemishes — that this book is written.

INTRODUCTION

There is a time and a place to celebrate, and for the Chicago Bulls and their legions of fans, this was it. New Year's Eve and Mardi Gras, rolled into one.

Up on the playing floor of venerable Chicago Stadium, the Bulls players were gleefully answering a collective curtain call after claiming their second straight National Basketball Association championship. Minutes before, Chicago had rallied from a 17-point deficit late in the third quarter to win Game 6 of the 1992 NBA Finals and polish off the Portland Trail Blazers with stunning deliverance.

Michael Jordan was toting the championship trophy courtside, then leading his teammates in a giant line dance on top of the scorer's table as their supporters screamed in delight. Pandemonium prevailed as photographers tripped over each other trying to capture the moment, fans pressed in to touch or give a back pat to their heroes while overmatched security guards and police struggled to maintain control of the situation.

Downstairs, in the area of the visitors' dressing room of the old, decrepit arena, there was a much different scene. A small number of media — mostly television camera crews and reporters from Portland — waited outside in the hall, speaking only in hushed tones. Bert Kolde, the Blazers' vice chairman and second in command to owner Paul Allen, managed a smile as he held 3 1/2-month-old daughter Sasha in his arms. Soon, a grim-faced Geoff Petrie, the team's senior vice president/operations, pushed his way inside the dressing room, and Allen followed.

Inside, a trash can lay horizontal, compliments of a fierce kick from Buck Williams. Clyde Drexler had taken a swat at it, too. Cold chills hit Drexler as he sat on the bench by his locker near the entrance. Sweat beads trickled down the arms and legs of his sinewy body. His sore right knee ached. He stared at the floor for the longest time, seeing nothing but the end of a long season, thinking about what had happened and what he could have done to prevent it. "Torn," he said to himself. "I feel torn." Finally, he grabbed a towel, wiped himself off and started to undress.

The players sat mostly in silence for several minutes. Danny Ainge kicked at his locker in frustration. Jerome Kersey was almost inconsolable, and his sobs brought waves of teammates over to try to comfort him. Wayne Cooper, the respected veteran who had played his last game in a Trail Blazer uniform, also wept openly. He realized it might have been his final shot at being a member of a championship team. He felt a sense of loss, both from a personal standpoint and for the way he felt about the players sitting with him in the locker room. To lose a chance at a championship always hurt. To lose the way the Blazers had, by blowing a 15-point lead after three quarters, was worse. Much worse.

Rick Adelman entered the room. His sports jacket was removed, his necktie loosened, his white dress shirt untucked, his hair askew, his face drawn. This was one of the most difficult moments of his 3 1/2-year reign as coach of the Blazers. Expectations for his team had run high everywhere, but nowhere were they higher than with the 13 players and their coaches. Anything but a title would mean they had fallen short of their ultimate goal. Now, they had fallen short, and despair filled the room.

Adelman, almost nonpareil in the coaching field in terms of drawing the most from each of his players, was crestfallen, especially with the way the Blazers had lost — blowing the big lead in the fourth quarter. But that wasn't the message he wanted to deliver on the evening of June 14, 20 minutes after John Paxson tossed the basketball high into the rafters as the final horn signaled the end of Game 6 and the long NBA season.

"We should have won this game tonight," Adelman began, his hoarse voice cracking with emotion, "but we didn't. And I know everyone in this room feels we should have won (a title) this season. You're disappointed, I'm disappointed, because it was there for us to win.

"I'm very proud of every one of you. You didn't quit tonight. We lost because we flat-out ran out of gas. I'm not happy about that, and it hurts. But you did not quit, and I'm proud of you for that. We won't be champions, but you guys have the hearts of champions. You played your asses off. You had a great season ... a great three seasons, and nobody can take that away from you. Our dream is not dead yet. This team has a lot of character.

"This team has a great future. I don't think it has to be broken up. Right now, you don't believe it. Maybe next week, you won't believe it. But we're still the team that came out of the West two of the last three years. We're still the best in the West until somebody knocks us off. I think we'll be back here next year — and maybe it will be our turn to win it."

Adelman worked the room, shaking hands with the players, thanking them for their contributions and trying to lift their spirits. In his three full seasons as Portland's head man, the Blazers had averaged nearly 60 regular-season wins, running up a win-loss record of 179-67. Twice they had reached the NBA Finals. They were working on back-to-back Pacific Division crowns.

They had climbed the mountain but had failed in their bid to plant their flag at the top. And there was really very little Adelman could say to soften the blow for his disconsolate players.

Moments later, the media entered and the Blazer regulars were forced to deal with the harsh realities of losing a championship series they had their chances to win.

Petrie looked on the scene with empathy. He had never played for a championship, but he had been an All-Star player and he knew the enormous commitment each of the players had made to make the Blazers a winner. He had great admiration for the group.

"I don't think most people realize what a toll it takes on guys both physically and mentally when you get as far as we've gone the last three years," Petrie said. He had watched Drexler and Kersey and Porter and Kevin Duckworth grow up as players, and as people, and wished they could have been rewarded with a championship. "Guys you used to know as bright-eyed kids look like guys coming back from eight years of war. They're grizzled, they're worn down physically, they have bumps and bruises ... but they continued to push themselves as hard and as far as they could."

"Maybe it just wasn't meant to be," said Buck Williams, the rock of a man who had been so instrumental in the Blazers going from also-rans to contenders in the 1989-90 season. There was a resigned tone to the familiar husky voice that would have fit so neatly into one of the old-time westerns. He was icing a sore foot that he wouldn't have played on under normal conditions. The veteran power forward was struggling to come to grips with the fact that shouting "We're No. 2" is nowhere near as fun as being fitted for a championship ring.

For the past two seasons, the Blazers had been among the best in basketball at rebounding, at 3-point shooting, at running the fast break. They had also been among the league leaders in technical fouls and run-ins with referees. What they had developed was a reputation as whiners, both with the officials, and with the league's media and fans. And appropriately, a string of calls early in the fourth quarter had played a big part in Chicago's surge and impending triumph in Game 6.

"We had four or five plays that really hurt us in the fourth quarter," Williams said. "This has not been a season of getting calls."

It was a familiar refrain among the Blazers. The way they saw it, respect was something they didn't get enough of.

"The officiating was not the way it should have been," center Kevin Duckworth said. "I seen other guys get calls, the nobodies, and they get calls over you. I hate to put the blame on one thing, but whew . . ."

Kersey, distraught and uncommunicative, refused an interview with a couple of TV types, then grudgingly opened up to a newspaper beat reporter.

"I thought we played very well tonight — the fourth quarter, too," said the Blazers' ultra-competitive small forward. "It's hard to play against eight people." To him, Hugh Evans, Mike Mathis and Ed Rush might as well have been suited up in Chicago Bulls uniforms.

The Blazers' antagonism extended to the Bulls, too, who had fueled the "Blazers-are-a-dumb-team" theory by questioning their court intelligence after a win over the Blazers at midseason. In the finals, the Bulls and their eccentric coach, Phil Jackson, had lamented "giving away" Games 2 and 4, and had made no secret they felt they should have won the series with a sweep, a source of irritation with the prideful Blazers.

"Chicago's players have a certain arrogance about them," Williams said. "They have a lot of confidence in themselves, and they said some things that didn't show too much respect for us.

"But you have to hand it to them. They're a fine team. They came out and showed the world they're the best team. They know how to get the big plays when they need them most."

Across the room, Terry Porter was being asked if this was a great Chicago Bulls team.

"I don't know if I'd call them a great team," Porter said. "They have one great player. Outside of Michael, they really have a bunch of role players."

If that seemed an ungracious response, and unfair to Jordan teammate Scottie Pippen, it reflected the mood of the Blazers. Without Jordan, the Portland Trail Blazers are champions of the world. That's like saying that without Julia Roberts, "Pretty Woman" is a bomb. Roberts starred in "Pretty Woman," and the movie was a smash. The Bulls have Michael Jordan, and they're the best team on the planet.

And soon Drexler was dressed and marching along the back halls of the arena toward the Bulls' dressing room, his everlasting devotion to political-correctness on automatic pilot. "I thought we had it, but they took it away from us," he said, managing a smile. "Give them credit." And then he was shaking hands with the Bulls players, his internment as the star of the second-best basketball team in the world not yet over.

The Blazers had blown this golden opportunity to cast away all the doubters who had questioned their heart and their intelligence and their mettle. Just before the playoffs began, Ainge distributed t-shirts to all his teammates with "Us Against the World" emblazoned across the front. It became a slogan that symbolized the feeling held by the Blazer players and management and fans alike.

The feeling was something like this: Portland is a small city located far from the major metropolitan areas. Because of it, the Blazers never get their just due, not from the national media or the television networks, or the schedule-makers or those prejudiced broadcasters or, especially, from the referees.

"Our philosophy was it was the 12 guys in this room, along with the coaches, against the rest of the world," Ainge said. It was a Three Musketeers approach — One for All and All for One — together with a little Martin Luther King: We Shall Overcome.

In the end, they couldn't overcome the Bulls. "In time, I still think they will look at this as a great experience," Petrie said. For now, they were facing the long, solemn bus ride through the celebrating streets of Chicago, and, the following day, a long flight home to Portland, where it had begun with such promise and hope some 8 1/2 months earlier.

1

"Walter Could Still Play, But He Screwed Up My Whole Game."

Right from the start, it was obvious that this would be a different kind of season.

The previous two years, training camp had been held at Salem's Willamette University, as Coach Rick Adelman took his team out of town in an effort to find solitude and a good working environment.

Evidently Adelman felt those things weren't necessary or important any longer. The 1991-92 Blazers gathered on October 4 on the campus of Lewis & Clark College, a small NAIA school tucked away on a wooded hill in the southwest corner of Portland. It was a much different base for the team — but just one of many fundamental changes that greeted the Portland players at the onset of the season.

The college would continue to be the team's practice site throughout the season, ending a long-time run at the Mittleman Jewish Community Center. The team's uniforms would be modified—"updated" as the marketing people would say — even though traditional wisdom in sports dictates that you don't mess with success. The good guys were still wearing black, but the lettering was now all upper-case rather than the familiar lower case, and the team's pinwheel-like logo had been tilted. Home games would be moved, too — from 7:30 to 7:00.

Walter Davis showed up without his trademark mustache. Danny Young, who had shaved his upper lip during the summer, grew his mustache back by popular demand. Alaa Abdelnaby flashed his familiar smile through braces on his teeth. Change was everywhere.

"Everybody tells me I look 10 years younger," the 37-year-old Davis said on the eve of his 15th season of professional basketball. "Wish I felt like it inside."

Adelman came to camp with real on-court changes in mind for his team. The Blazers' six-game loss to the Los Angeles Lakers in the 1991 Western Conference finals had left the team, the coaches, and the entire state of Oregon in alternating stages of bewilderment and despair. Coaches and players recover more quickly than fans, however. And Adelman had plans.

"We like a lot of things we did last year," he said. "But there are things we'd like to improve on."

Most of that improvement involved the team's offense. A running team that scores a lot of points off its transition game, the Blazers would often struggle in the slow-paced, halfcourt-oriented style that dominates the playoffs. In fact, the Lakers whipped Portland the previous spring by hustling all five players back on defense, shutting down the Blazers' fastbreak baskets and then clogging up the middle to handcuff Portland's slashers. The Blazers, with rare exception, didn't move the ball or their own bodies quickly enough to exploit the Lakers' strategy.

"We were inconsistent," Adelman said. "And it was our lack of patience sometimes. We have to pay more attention to how we execute, to have better spacing on the floor, things like that. We need to take it one or two more passes at times."

But the Blazers have basic faults that prohibit them from ever functioning as well in the halfcourt game as other teams. Their front court—Buck Williams, Kevin Duckworth, and Jerome Kersey—features solid offensive players, but only Duckworth is a dependable shooter from beyond 10 feet. None of the three is much of a passer.

The team's best outside shooter is Terry Porter, its point guard. Its next-best outside gunner is its center, Duckworth. And the team's best passer is probably Clyde Drexler, the off-guard. It's a team of paradoxes, a funky blend of players with marked strengths and weaknesses that seems to provide unique matchup problems for teams with less-versatile players.

But as is his wont, Adelman tends to spend more time

thinking about what his players can do, rather than lose sleep over what they can't.

He planned to introduce an important wrinkle into his team's halfcourt game, one that would help maximize the strengths of his guards. Adelman's plan often sent Drexler to the low post — where he could score over smaller defenders and make slick passes to teammates when double-teamed — and allowed Porter to spot up on the outside for jump shots.

But it wasn't Portland's starting guards in the spotlight as training camp opened. It was the third man, Danny Ainge, who was getting the attention.

The Blazers feared for a while that Ainge wouldn't even show up for the camp. He had said a few days beforehand that he was "considering" becoming a holdout. Ainge was playing the final season of a $725,000-per-year contract that served as a monument to the idiocy of signing a long-term contract in the National Basketball Association. It was the final season of a contract that must have, to Ainge, seemed to be a life sentence — a six-year deal that Ainge originally signed during his days with the Boston Celtics. A sweet deal at the time, perhaps, but inflation in the NBA had made Ainge's contract look embarrassing in an era when $1 million was the league average and nearly $2 million per year was the going rate for decent guards.

Ainge had asked the Blazers to extend his contract two or three seasons, with terms that would call for him to make an average of $1.7 million annually. He would have settled for a little less. The Trail Blazers had extended contracts for Drexler, Williams, Kersey, and Cliff Robinson. But they didn't seem at all interested in offering Ainge any real money. Ainge, who said he was told when he arrived in a trade with Sacramento that his contract would be taken care of, felt rejected and betrayed. But the Blazers claimed they had promised no such thing.

"We did not promise to redo his contract," Geoff Petrie said. "We told him we would sit down and discuss it at season's end."

"That's just a matter of semantics," Ainge said. "To me, it's the same thing. They told me the same thing they told Buck, and they took care of Buck."

But Williams hadn't struggled the season prior to signing his contract extension. The fact of the matter is that Ainge dropped off to 44.8 percent shooting from the field in the playoffs the previous year, averaging only eight points and fewer than 17 minutes per game. The coaches had lost confidence in his ability to play the point, and a swing guard who can't handle the ball against pressure isn't worth much.

On top of that, he may have offended some of his teammates the previous spring. Ainge was asked about the Blazers' demise against the Lakers, and the player responded by questioning the team's leadership.

"Verbally, Danny is his own worst enemy," Williams would say some months later. "He made some statements about (lack of) leadership on our team. I think it kind of betrayed some people. It separated him from some of the other players after that. I don't think it was wise of him to do that."

In general, though, Ainge's teammates liked him a lot. They just learned to take some of the things he said with a grain of salt.

"He's so opinionated," Porter said. "Every time we'd lose, he had about 80 different opinions about why it happened. But he's been through everything in this game and he still brings an excitement to it. We all used to ask him, 'You're not really 32, are you?' He was in his 30s, but he acted like he was 18 all the time. I wanted to see his birth certificate."

At 32, was Ainge still a player who could command $1.7 million? The Blazers' braintrust, quite frankly, didn't think so — and wasn't about to be bullied into offering such a deal. Ainge, by the same token, felt he deserved the same treatment others on the team got. After all, he was going to give the team two seasons of hard work at much less than market value. Why couldn't they give him the benefit of the doubt over the next two years?

"They haven't shown any sense of making this a priority," Ainge said before camp. "It frustrates me because I see players in the league who do a lot of negative things image-wise for their organization, who don't play hard every night, who don't play injured, who complain about contracts and hold out . . . These guys get rewarded.

"Maybe they think I've been a nice guy my whole career and they've got a fish. They're taking advantage of the situation instead of being fair. The dollars we're asking would make me the seventh-highest paid player on the club."

Ainge would report to camp on time, but bring his disgruntlement with him, where it would fester all season. In his mind, he had been screwed. And he is too much of a competitor to take it lying down — as the Trail Blazers would discover several months later.

Ainge felt Davis' arrival the previous season did a lot to change his role on the team.

"One of the biggest mistakes we made was trading Drazen Petrovic for Walter Davis," Ainge said long after Davis was gone. "I love Walter Davis, but we should have gotten future draft picks for (Petrovic). Walter could still play, but he screwed up my whole game. We were playing great the first half of last season, with me and Danny Young coming off the bench. But from the point we got Walter, everything changed. And everybody played worse. I didn't see why we needed another guy. If we could have gotten a backup center or a fast point guard, I could have seen it.

"The problem is, outside shooters are [needed] to complement Clyde's driving or Duck's inside game. You don't get outside shooters to set picks, double downs. Walter and I would come into the game and we'd run our 4-strong and have him come off a double pick and we'd be on the floor with Wayne Cooper and Mark Bryant. They didn't have to guard those guys. They'd switch out on me or Walter. When I'm handling the ball, the one shooter is taken out of it. The combinations weren't working. If you were to bring Walter in for Jerome Kersey and left Clyde and Terry out there with him, he might have been a great player for us. A lot of the time we came into the game together, and we're the same type of players.

"I think Rick felt pressure to play Walter when they got him and he tried to figure out a way. But he didn't have a training camp to figure it out."

But Adelman had Davis in camp this year and still couldn't find a way to make use of him. At one time in his brilliant career, Davis could defend small forwards, making it possible to use him at that position. But during the previous season, each time Adelman used Davis in Kersey's spot, the opposing team would immediately isolate him and capitalize on his defensive liabilities.

It appeared that Davis would probably just sit quietly, an expensive insurance policy against an injury to Drexler or Ainge. But as camp opened, it quickly became apparent that Davis would have trouble even making the team. There were hungry youngsters on hand and a front office very interested in keeping the team from aging all at once.

Out of USC and out of the draft, too, came free-agent point guard Robert Pack, a tightly wound 6-2 package of quickness and guts who seemed to thrive on the impossible dream of making the veteran-laden roster. In camp, too, was rookie Lamont Strothers, a second-round draft pick, and free-agent veteran Ennis Whatley, another roster longshot.

Adelman's wish was to stand back, give everyone an equal chance and then see who emerged. It made for an interesting camp — as did the physical preparedness of the team's enigmatic center.

Duckworth came into camp at somewhere between 275 and 300 pounds. His actual weight is more of a secret than the number on George Bush's red telephone, but there was little question that Duckworth didn't spend the summer in serious training. Oh, but he did, he said. It's just that Duckworth didn't have time for a lot of physical exertion during the offseason, because he was "getting the mental part taken care of."

And on the first day of practice he hauled his body up and down the court well enough to be the leading scorer in the team's scrimmages. "Duck played very well," Adelman said. "He was very active."

That's one thing he wasn't during the summer — active. The sensitive big man spent much of the summer back home in Chicago, inside the protective cocoon of his family and away from criticism he was getting in Portland for his play in the playoffs.

"I didn't want to have anything to do with the team or anybody," Duckworth said. "I just wanted to be alone. I got to the point where I really didn't care, and that's pretty bad. That's why I stayed in Chicago as long as I did. I felt more comfortable there, around my relatives and people who love me. Family always loves you, no matter what."

Adelman had spent a part of the first day of camp in a meeting with his players, during which he talked about their on-court demeanor. By the end of last season, Portland was known as much for its whine as its roses. Adelman himself made a big point of trying to alter his stance with officials — who often thought of him as a crybaby.

But it was certainly a team-wide problem.

"We've talked a lot about that as a team," Drexler said after the meeting. "We have more experience on this team now, and we have to realize you must leave the officials alone and concentrate on the game. I think you'll see us make tremendous strides in that area this season without losing our intensity."

Adelman came up with a unique approach to regulating behavior that he hoped would also increase unity. He suggested the team use a kangaroo court — similar to the ones baseball teams have used for years — to allow players to bring cases in a lighthearted way against each other for various transgressions. In a narrow balloting, Duckworth won a vote of his teammates over Wayne Cooper and Buck Williams for the key position of judge.

Fines were scheduled for missed free throws, technical fouls, and poor decorum on the playing floor. Then there were the usual amount of what Duckworth called "crazy rules."

"Passing gas in a concentrated area, like on the airplane or in an elevator," Duckworth said.

"We're just wondering how Duck plans to prove it," Ainge said.

"You're a very important man now, Duck," Robinson said. "You're the judge."

Alas, Duckworth was probably not the right choice. He was too lenient, too moody, and didn't really get into the spirit of the thing. As the season went on, it collapsed. Ainge, who during his professional baseball career had seen kangaroo courts work well, admitted he made a mistake when he nominated Duckworth for the position.

"I thought he'd be one of the most just judges," Ainge said. "It turns out he is very soft."

Later, when the season ended, Ainge looked back at the ill-fated idea and said, "We made Duck our judge and that was a horrible mistake."

At the same time he set up the court, Adelman also let the team know that he was going to tighten the reins a little.

"I don't think I'll change that dramatically," said Adelman, who would, indeed, do that very thing late in the season. "I am going to be demanding of the players. For two years, we've been finding out about ourselves. Now we know how we can play. I'm going to do what I have to do to make sure we improve in certain areas."

The emotional improvement actually went better than the basketball improvement. The team started sluggishly.

The first exhibition game seemed to set a tone for most of the first part of the season. Drexler stepped in and became a one-man rescue squad. He scored 11 points in the final 7 minutes and 15 seconds, including a game-winning three-point play with 9.6 seconds to go as the Blazers held off Indiana 97-94. The biggest news of the day was sad, though, as Porter was informed his father, Herman Porter, died of a heart attack in his sleep.

Porter returned to Milwaukee for the funeral and eventually missed about a week of training camp, something that would contribute to a decrease in his physical condition and an ensuing slow start. Porter's mother had passed away early in the 1989-90 season, and the death of his father seemed to be even more of a blow. His parents had been divorced, and Porter had lived with his father throughout his high school years. Since the passing of his mother, the father and son had become even closer.

"When you lose one parent, it makes you appreciate the other parent a little more," Porter said. "After my mother died, we got closer and closer. I'm so thankful that within the last year I was able to spend a lot more time with him. I got a lot of pictures of him and have a lot of moments, a lot of good times to think about. I just have to think he's in a better place now."

There was another subtle change that was picked up only by a few writers right from the first exhibition game. The coaching staff wasn't even aware that prior to the first game, it was Drexler — not co-captains Kersey and Porter — who met with officials in the customary mid-court captain's meeting.

There was no new election. There was no mandate.

"I just felt the inclination to become the captain," Drexler said when asked about it. "On our team, four or five guys are leaders, so it's not that big a deal. But I just thought I'd take a more active role. Since I've been here the longest, it's only fitting that I be the captain."

Kersey deferred to Drexler.

"He started going out there," Kersey said. "He's always had the leadership ability on this team. It doesn't matter to me."

Coaches in the NBA usually don't arrive at courtside until just before the national anthem, and Adelman admitted he didn't know anything about Drexler meeting with the officials until a reporter asked him about it. Adelman handled the situation in an interesting way. In the end it was the right way, too. A situation that could have resulted in some hurt feelings just kind of went away.

"Rick came over to Terry and I and said Clyde wants to be captain — all three of you guys can be captain," Kersey said. "I said, 'I'm not hung up on being captain. It's a nice honor, but if Clyde wants to be captain, that's great for the team.' Clyde can probably get away with a lot more stuff talking (with the referees) than me or Terry can."

Said Adelman: "I had discussions with Terry and Jerome about it. We had never had an election since I took over as coach. Terry and Jerome were elected prior to that, and I just kind of left it that way. Clyde said he wanted to be more vocal and talk to the officials, and I had no problem with that.

"But I was not going to take Terry and Jerome away from the captaincy. I just let the whole thing ride. I don't think it was a big deal. I kind of look at those four guys — Terry, Clyde, Jerome, and Buck — as the same, anyway. If I'm thinking about doing something, I always talk to all four of those guys, anyway."

But Drexler would blossom in the captain's role. As the season progressed, he would become more and more vocal in leadership situations — something that seemed impossible just a couple of seasons earlier, when Drexler showed no affinity for the captaincy.

Portland captured wins in three of its first four exhibition games, before dropping a 120-108 loss at Chicago to the defending world champion Bulls. Then with Kersey resting a sprained ankle that would become a season-long problem, and Williams visiting his critically ill mother in North Carolina, the Blazers were blown out 131-116 at Indiana.

Adelman feels that eight exhibition games are two too many and got his way this season. Portland returned home 3-3 in its non-counting schedule and faced the big decisions.

Pack had played so well in the exhibition games that it was obvious he'd earned a roster spot. The player personnel types — Bucky Buckwalter and Brad Greenberg — weren't about to let their only draft pick, Strothers, go. It was an early sign of problems to come, a split between the front office and the coaching staff, with Geoff Petrie in the middle.

David Kahn, who formerly covered the NBA for *The Oregonian* and who now works as a pro basketball expert for NBC, recognized immediately that the Adelman/Petrie relationship would be threatened.

"A lot of the problems that haunted that organization in the down years seemed to resurface in the front office," Kahn said. "It wasn't so much the backstabbing, although there was some of that. It was more a case of certain people trying to take credit for everything that turned out positive and similarly trying to distance themselves from everything that turned out to be negative. That's what I like so much about the Petrie/Adelman faction — for the most part, they're stand-up guys who don't pride themselves on seeing their name in national columns, and they don't run away from errors in judgment."

There were other decisions, too. Whatley had shown enough savvy that the team didn't want to ship him out, either. And what about the veterans, Young and Davis, whose experience made them much more valuable than the youngsters to a team seeking a championship?

Then providence, or at least the NBA's version of it, played a hand. What is the injured list for, if not to use? The Blazers leaned on it heavily throughout the season, constantly putting off what once seemed an inevitable decision of which player to keep and which to send home.

Whatley suffered a chipped bone in an ankle and would be out of action for months. Strothers, showing amazing instincts for a rookie, came up with back spasms that he said began during the final exhibition game, and was placed on the injured list — a place that would prove to be his home away from home during much of the season.

But that still left the team to decide between Davis and Pack, with youth being served. Unable to make a deal, Portland placed Davis on waivers prior to the opening of the regular season. After clearing the process, he would end up back in Denver, from whence he came.

It was an agonizing decision for the coaches, mostly because of their warm feelings for Davis, a classy veteran with strength of character unbroken by his history of drug problems. To its credit, the coaching staff also had respect for Davis' long and productive NBA career and didn't feel it would be fair to ask him to spend what would probably be his final season in the league as a benchwarmer. Davis' credentials had earned him at least a chance to compete for playing time with another team.

"It was the hardest decision I've made since I've been here," Adelman said. "Walter is a class person and a real professional, and we hated to let him go. The guy we kept was going to be our 12th man. You don't expect a lot of minutes at that spot, unless an injury occurred. We were concerned that if Walter sat for a long time, his effectiveness would be hampered.

"Robert gives us a younger player with potential. He has grown from the first day we had him. We feel we can use his quickness in spots and can bring him along slowly."

But no one expected Pack to contribute as quickly as he did.

2

"'Fat Boy.' Wish I Had a Nickel for Every Time I Heard That."

Everyone was anxious to see how the Blazers would come out against Cleveland in their opener, a November 2 date in Memorial Coliseum. Most national publications, including *Sports Illustrated*, were predicting a Chicago-Portland matchup in the NBA Finals, and several were forecasting the Blazers as champions.

The Blazers weren't quite sure what to expect against Cleveland because the preseason had been more fragmented than either of the previous two. The only starter to play in each of the six exhibition games was Kevin Duckworth, and the regulars' time together as a unit was limited.

Clyde Drexler saw that as a positive.

"I think it's good for us," he said during the final days of preparation for the 1991-92 debut. "The coaching staff did a great job of resting guys who are going to get a lot of minutes, and we're all pretty fresh as we go into the season. I think everybody is game ready, I really do."

Any team singled out by prognosticators as a team to beat carries a burden, but the pressure on the Blazers didn't come merely from their favorite's role. There was the failure to get back to the finals and the hangover from that. And there was the incredible start of the previous season, when they had blasted from the blocks 11-0 and 19-1 en route to a 63-19 regular season.

It was a difficult standard to live up to, and Rick Adelman was trying to downplay any suggestions the Blazers might duplicate the uncanny early record this time around.

Cleveland presented Portland with an interesting first test. The Cavaliers were 33-49 during the 1990-91 season but injuries had decimated their regular group, and all-star point guard Mark Price was still out of commission after undergoing reconstructive knee surgery the previous December.

The Cavs, under one-time Blazer coach Lenny Wilkens, were expected to be one of the East's better teams this time, if they could just stay healthy. The massive front line featured 7-foot Brad Daugherty, 6-11 Larry Nance and 6-10 John Williams, and the Blazers were admittedly a little wary of opening against such a strong club.

"They're a very good passing team and everyone shoots the ball well," Adelman said. "If you don't get after them defensively, they'll pick you apart."

The Blazers had little to worry about. The only thing that went wrong all night was the soundtrack to the video that was shown on the scoreboard replay screen as part of the pre-game pageantry. First time around, it was a silent picture. Finally, embarrassed engineers got the sound going, and soon the Blazers were on their way to a resounding 117-106 victory.

Portland shot .511 from the field and ran out for 24 fast-break points. Daugherty and Nance had big games, but the Blazers put on enough defensive pressure to help force 19 Cleveland turnovers, which resulted in 21 Blazer points.

Criticism of their halfcourt offense the previous year had left an impression, and Adelman had stressed ball and body movement during the preseason. Adelman liked what he saw against the Cavs. "We thought if we moved the ball quickly they'd have a hard time guarding us," Adelman said. "We did a nice job finding the open man most of the time."

Danny Ainge thought he saw a difference in the offensive execution from that of the previous year. "In the past," he said, "we've kind of set up the play and taken the shots regardless. Tonight we worked hard at finding the open man and taking what the defense gives us. Against a good team, we have to go to the third and fourth options at times."

Drexler opened with a flourish, spinning out these numbers in a boffo 37-minute show: 31 points on 14 of 20 from the field, seven rebounds, seven assists. Clyde did heavy damage around the basket with layups and dunks, but it was his six jump shots from the perimeter that left Craig Ehlo, Steve Kerr and Jimmy Oliver immobilized.

"When Clyde has the jumper rolling," Ainge said, "you can't stop him. And he's capable of that. He's been doing it all through training camp."

Terry Porter was only three of seven from the field but made 12 of 13 foul shots en route to an 18-point game. Buck Williams, the NBA field-goal percentage leader the previous season, took up where he left off by making seven of nine shots and contributing 17 points and eight rebounds. Cliff Robinson came off the bench for 15 points and eight rebounds. The only Blazer to struggle was Duckworth, who made four of 14 shots and finished with nine points and four rebounds in 24 minutes.

All in all, it was a pleasant way to open the season, and the Blazer fans enjoyed the performance immensely, rising from their seats for ovations several times and waving the red and white pompoms that had been handed out to all those in attendance.

Memorial Coliseum was the smallest arena in the league. Built in 1960, it had been the home of the Blazers since their inception in the 1970-71 season. Fans began buying all the 12,666 seats during the championship 1976-77 season and, with capacity now at 12,884, the sellout string was to reach 683 by season's end for regular-season and playoff games, longest in professional sports history.

For years, the coliseum had been as noisy as any arena in the NBA. In recent years it had become a mellow, almost serene place to play. Part of the reason was that the same season ticket-holders kept their seats year after year. Had there been more turnover and new, enthusiastic fans gotten a chance to cheer on their team, it might have been different. But these fans had seen it all, and except for games against name opponents such as the Lakers or Boston, they pretty much waited until the playoffs to get rowdy.

Adelman's oft-scratchy voice was the only thing that didn't make it happily through the opener. "I took my son (David) trick-or-treating last night," he said. "He got the candy, and I got a cold."

Game 2 swept across the Blazers' faces like a cold, biting wind the following evening. The Phoenix Suns came to town representing one of the major threats to the Blazers in their quest for the division title, but for the second night in a row, Portland would be facing a team without its all-star point guard. Kevin Johnson had sprained an ankle in the Suns' opener at Seattle and would not be available for duty.

So how to explain a stunning 100-76 Phoenix victory, marking the second-lowest scoring total in Portland's 22-year club history and the worst home loss since a 140-104 blowout against the Los Angeles Lakers in January 1987?

For the bumbling Blazers, the game could have fit nicely into a Johnny Carson monologue. How bad were they?

They were so bad they shot only .357 from the floor, including .286 in the first half. They were so bad they were a ghastly four of 21 in a second quarter that saw them match an all-time franchise low of nine points. They were so bad that the Suns won the rebound battle 53-34, including 44-23 over the final three periods.

"That's the worst game I've seen us play in a long time," said Drexler, who managed to score a game-high 27 points. "Phoenix did a great job, but the way we played tonight, I don't think we could have beaten an expansion team."

"The worst game we've played as long as I can remember," agreed Porter, who had a grand total of four points and three assists playing against Johnson's backup, Negele Knight. "I'd rather get it out of our system now, I guess, than have it happen later in the season. But to have it happen in the second game? At home? That's frustrating."

Duckworth rebounded from his poor opening night by making seven of 11 shots and contributing 18 points and eight rebounds. But the only cause for much cheer for the Blazer fans was the debut of Robert Pack. Pack Man put in 10 creditable minutes and was rewarded with a huge ovation.

Jeff Hornacek was brilliant for Phoenix, tossing in 26 points to go with a career-high 14 rebounds and seven assists. The Suns were terrific defensively, blocking 10 shots — even Tom Chambers had three — and limiting Portland to six fast-break points.

"I grew up in California and used to run on the beach," Adelman said. "That's how I felt tonight. We were running in sand. You're going to have games like that. One game does not a season make. We just have to go back to work."

The first road trip was a Texas swing with stops at Houston and San Antonio, and the Blazers knew it wouldn't be an easy one. Along with Utah, the Rockets and Spurs were widely regarded as the teams to beat in the Midwest Division. For Duckworth, it meant facing Hakeem Olajuwon and David Robinson on successive nights.

Duckworth spent the 3 1/2-hour flight to Houston reading a lawn bag full of fan mail. It had been a very difficult summer for the XXXL-sized center of the Blazers, who bore a lion's share of blame from media and fans for his poor play in the playoffs, particularly in the loss to the Lakers in the Western Conference finals.

There are few professional athletes who are as sensitive to criticism as Duckworth. Some players let it slide like water off a duck's back. It sticks to Duck like sandpaper. Kids are cruel, and Duckworth has spent a lifetime hearing taunts about his immense size. "I wasn't skinny from the day I was born," he said. "'Fat boy.' Wish I had a nickel for every time I heard that."

He'd heard it in the NBA, too. He came to San Antonio out of Eastern Illinois as a 330-pound project who had spent part of his high school years working at Burger King and looked the part. He worked himself into shape, dropped in the neighborhood of 50 pounds and, after a trade to Portland during his rookie year, became a starter, 18-point scorer and two-time all-star for the Blazers.

But Duck appeared to have put back on some of the poundage during the 1990-91 season, and when he floundered during the Laker series, complaints about him being out of shape ran rampant. He heard them in the newspapers, on the radio talk shows, and even at the supermarket. Plenty of things went wrong in the Laker series, and Duck was one of them, but he became the scapegoat. "An easy target," as Adelman put it.

Duckworth hardly worked out at all during the summer. He picked up a basketball only a few times and lifted weights sporadically. Getting away from it all was the important thing — mental reconditioning, so to speak.

"I fished mostly," he said. "Even in Portland, I spent most of my time fishing with my friends. It was what I call a relaxed summer. I needed to air out."

Duckworth arrived in training camp refreshed in spirit, and while his play was inconsistent, he seemed to have a better handle on his emotions.

"I just have to learn to not be so sensitive about things," he said. "But sometimes that's not easy."

During the exhibition season, an article in *The Oregonian* detailed Duckworth's inner turmoils and feelings about the public's perception of him. As he read his fan mail on the flight to Houston, he was touched by how many of those in Blazerland really did care.

"I can't believe how many letters I got," he said. "Some people said they read the article and it made them cry a little bit. I got a letter from a housewife who said she and her kids started watching basketball two years ago and she just wanted me to know they supported me.

"These people weren't asking for autographs. They were writing just to tell me they care, to keep up the good work and to hang in there. There are some great people out there."

The Blazers arrived in Houston and went through a quick workout at the Summit. Adelman's practice sessions are among the briefest in the league. His philosophy is to get in, do the necessary work and get out; that a fresh body and a fresh mind will pay off down the line. His players appreciate that, particularly Drexler, who is not an all-out practice player but can never be questioned for his effort in games.

Clyde and Adelman's predecessor, Mike Schuler, didn't see eye to eye on a lot of things, and one of their differences was in quality and, in particular, quantity of practice time.

"In my opinion, I've always practiced hard," Drexler said. "One of the great things about Rick is he knows when you need to give the guys a rest. Schuler never understood that. I'd play 45 minutes two nights in a row, and the next day he'd want me to practice two hours. I had a problem with that, and any guy with any kind of sense would agree with that."

The Blazers talked as if they were out to prove the Phoenix game was an aberration. "One thing we all agree on is we were awful against Phoenix," said Drexler, who always enjoys his returns to Houston, his hometown. "Hopefully we can rebound and prove it was just a fluke that happens to everybody."

"Whenever we've lost a game the last two years, it's been important to prove ourselves the next game," Duckworth said. "We don't want to get a losing streak started. The Houston game is important for us to get some momentum going. I know everybody is hungry."

But there was a feeling that things weren't quite right.

"If we win both of these games, it won't make us a great team, and if we lose them, it won't make us a poor team," assistant coach Jack Schalow said. "There's a lot of season left. But this team has always responded well after a bad game."

This time, the Blazers didn't. The Rockets, who had lost seven in a row to Portland, rallied from a 17-point first half deficit and outscored the Blazers 12-2 over the final 2:10 to win 106-99. It marked the first time Portland had dipped below .500 since the 1988-89 season.

The following night, the Blazers went from bad to brutal in a 119-93 loss to San Antonio, dying on the vine down the stretch to fall to 1-3.

Owner Paul Allen flew in to watch both games, and he couldn't have enjoyed what turned out to be a pair of eyesores.

Portland controlled the game much of the way against Houston, seizing a 46-29 lead midway through the second quarter. Robinson, Ainge, and Mark Bryant were outstanding off the bench, and the Rockets were cold as a mint julep, making 10 of 33 shots from the floor to that point.

Houston rallied to get to within 56-49 at the half and, with small forward Matt Bullard bombing in 3-pointers, drew even at 77-77 late in the third quarter. Portland still led 97-94 when the final collapse began, triggered by a Houston trap that helped force six turnovers in the final 4 1/2 minutes. The new emphasis on posting Clyde down low and letting him deal the ball to cutters didn't work well at all in the clutch.

"We took the ball out of their key people's hands, especially Drexler," said Don Chaney, the 1990-91 NBA coach of the year, but a man destined to be fired as the Rockets' coach before season's end. "We made sure he had to give the ball up. They had to make the extra pass to get a shot."

The Blazers didn't do that at the end, and Adelman wasn't of the opinion that Houston's defense had a lot to do with it.

"We really played poorly the last six minutes," Adelman said as he sipped at his ritual post-game beer. "We didn't take care of the ball. There's no reason for it. There wasn't a lot of defensive pressure, just some really poor decisions on our part.

"They were double-teaming Clyde. You make two passes, and Terry has a wide-open shot. We couldn't get the ball over there. Something's wrong when we can't do that. Disappointing."

Houston won the game at the foul line, sinking a spectacular 39 of 43 to only 14 of 24 for the Blazers. And the Rockets, with Olajuwon leading the way with 27 points and 20 rebounds, won the backboard battle 55-45.

Through it, Adelman was trying to maintain a positive outlook.

"I'm not concerned," he said. "It's only three games into the season. We had a lot of good minutes tonight, playing on the road against a tough team. You have to do better than we did, but I'm not concerned we can't do it."

"It's good to end the streak," Chaney said, referring to the string of losses against the Blazers, "but to beat the best team in basketball, that's even better."

The "best team in basketball" plaudit rang even more hollow after the Blazers' performance in San Antonio. Portland played hard to stay within 83-74 after three quarters, then simply gave up in the final moments.

Open shots simply would not go down. Duckworth was productive, sinking eight of 16 shots on his way to a team-high 20 points, but he had very little help. Portland shot an embarrassing .378 from the floor. Clyde was five for 18, Porter four for 10, Kersey three for 10, Robinson three for nine.

"We just have to shoot the ball better," Adelman said. "I think that's going to happen sooner or later, and it's going to make things a lot easier for us."

The Spurs, one of Portland's biggest rivals over the previous two seasons, were sharp. David Robinson needed only 30 minutes to score 25 points and haul in 10 rebounds and Sean Elliott was on fire, knocking down nine of 11 — three of three from 3-point range — for a game-high 28 points.

Elliott and Robinson passed on an opportunity to shovel dirt on the Blazers when they were down.

"It's probably going to take them a little while to get into sync," Elliott said. "Last year they spoiled their fans and everybody when they got out to such a great start. They're still a talented, explosive team."

"I don't know what's wrong," Robinson said. "It's early in the season and maybe they're just working the kinks out the way we are. I'm sure they'll settle down a little bit."

And Adelman was asked again if he was becoming concerned with the direction of the Blazers.

"I'm being honest when I say I'm not worried about this team," he said. "We're going to break out of it. We have to stay positive and realize what kind of a team we are. It's going to come."

With nine of their next 12 games in the friendly confines of Memorial Coliseum, the Blazers set out to get well. One of the areas in which they were struggling was 3-point shooting. The previous season, Portland had led the league in 3-point accuracy at nearly 38 percent, setting an all-time NBA record for accuracy in a season. In the first four games this season, they were eight of 37 (.216) and were shooting .428 overall from the field.

Porter was zip-for-eight from 3-point land, and was averaging 12.3 points and 4.8 assists. For someone who averaged 17 points and eight assists and was an all-star the year before, it was a comedown. "I haven't been shooting the ball that well," the veteran point guard said. "A lot of the 3s I've missed, maybe last year I would have made them. I went through streaks last year where I didn't shoot 3s well. Right now, I'm not doing it at all."

Herman Porter's death, and the loss of a week of pre-season workouts as a result, didn't help with Terry's preparation, both mentally and physically.

"That would have an impact on anybody," Adelman said. "But Terry is so tough mentally, he'll fight through that. I think it's been timing as much as anything. He missed a lot of work and maybe he's still catching up."

When Porter's mother, Louise, died early in the season two years ago, Terry didn't skip a beat when he returned to action. He wasn't blaming his woes on his father's death this time, either.

"It's been hard to deal with, without a doubt," he said, "but I thought I played well after my mother passed away. When I get on the floor I try not to think about that. All I can do is keep my fond memories of him and try to go out and play hard every night to show him some respect. Hopefully, he can look down with pride from above."

The Blazers came out and laid a 121-96 whipping on Indiana, following that with a 116-90 rout of Boston, and a 120-82 dismantlement of Denver, all at home. All seemed right in Rip City for a change. Porter burst out of his slump by blistering the nets for 13 points in the first quarter and 20 in the first half. He didn't score after intermission, but he didn't need to.

"The demise of Terry Porter," Adelman said wryly, "was greatly exaggerated."

"I was able to get more good opportunities tonight," Porter said. "My offense was definitely important, but the big thing was the way we rebounded and defended. Those two things will be the key to our season."

Portland out-rebounded Indiana 54-40, claimed 22 off the offensive glass and recorded 16 steals that went a long way toward 23 Pacer turnovers, including 11 in a whirlwind third quarter. Indiana coach Bob Hill wasn't around much longer than that, picking up two technicals and an ejection in the final period. "We were embarrassed," said Hill, who kept his players long after for a heart-to-heart team meeting.

Kersey contributed 19 points, 11 rebounds — including seven offensive — and four steals, and Pack, fast becoming the people's choice among Blazer fans, was all over the place with 11 points, three rebounds, five assists and six steals in 18 electrifying minutes.

"He brings in energy," Ainge said. "That's one thing we've been lacking. We've been talking about the need for intensity. Robert supplies some of that. You have to love the guy's energy level."

You had to love the fact that Pack was around at all. The 6-2 rookie out of Southern Cal was so lowly regarded out of college, he not only was bypassed in the draft, but he also wasn't offered a spot in a summer rookie/free agent camp by any of the NBA's 27 teams.

The reasons were three-fold. First, Pack was overshadowed by his flashy backcourt mate at USC, Harold Miner, who in

1992 would be the 12th player taken in the draft. Second, Pack's jump shot was suspect, and his ability to hit an NBA-range 3-pointer virtually nonexistent. Third, his job in George Raveling's controlled system was to get the Trojans into their offense and place the ball in the hands of Miner and forward Ronnie Coleman.

Even so, Pack thought he had played well enough to be noticed by some NBA team . . . any NBA team.

"I was distraught about the draft," Pack said. "I felt I had the talent to at least go in the second round. But even more disappointing to me was not getting invited to anyone's rookie camp. It was like I didn't exist in college at all. I thought my chances were gone. It took me a couple of weeks to get my spirits back up."

Pack decided he just had to get noticed, so he hooked on with a team sponsored by radio station KJLH in the free agent division of the Southern California Summer Pro League. Nearly all of the players with pro potential were involved in the NBA portion of the summer league. There wasn't a lot of hope for those like Pack, but all he needed was a sliver.

And when the league ended, he had played well enough to earn MVP honors of the free-agent division. "I was really loose," said Pack, water-bug quick and hardnosed as a foundry worker. "I didn't let anything bother me and just showed them what I could do. It was kind of loosely structured, which allowed me to just go out and play."

Even so, NBA teams weren't banging on Pack's door. Raveling had attended the Orlando pre-draft camp and became convinced Pack, whom he called the best athlete he'd ever coached, was better than any of the guards there. He told that to Brad Greenberg, Portland's director of player personnel who had played a season for him at Washington State, along with a host of other NBA scouting types. Duly impressed, the Blazers nevertheless opted not to bring Pack to summer camp, casting their lot with such forgettables as Lorenzo Neely, Sterling Mahan, and Pat Greer.

Blazer scouts watched Pack in LA, though, and decided to bring him into Portland for a look prior to fall veterans camp. Pack was so impressive during informal scrimmage sessions at Lewis & Clark College he earned an invitation to camp. The rest is history.

"I came to Portland with a positive attitude," he said. "I mean, I thought about them being a great team, and maybe there would be other teams I'd have a better chance to stick with. But (Brad) mentioned the possibility of looking for younger talent. If I came in, worked hard and made an impression on the coaches, I felt I had a chance to make the team."

Boston came to Portland without injured point guards Dee Brown and Brian Shaw, and the Blazers used strong rebounding, defense, and persistence to pound the Celtics. The Blazers grabbed 22 offensive rebounds for the second straight game and held a 56-43 rebounding edge. Portland, who went into the game 24th in the NBA in field-goal percentage at .433, shot .421 on 40 of 95, but the Celtics were worse at .389 on 36 of 93. Larry Bird and Kevin McHale combined for 10-for-33 mismarksmanship, and the Celtics were out of it after Drexler took over the game with one of his amazing flurries early in the third quarter.

Clyde, who finished nine of 12 from the floor en route to a game-high 26 points in 29 minutes, scored on a drive, nailed a 3, converted a post-up move for a three-point play and capped the two-minute, 40-second spurt with a 15-footer to give Portland a 67-54 lead. Soon it was 86-64, and the coliseum fans were being treated to the Blazers' most one-sided win over Boston since the 1977-78 season.

"That's Clyde," said Adelman, shaking his head at his superstar's flash of brilliance. "He has the ability to take a game over like that."

The other guy with that kind of ability, Bird, never took flight. Bird came into the game averaging 24.2 points, 8.6 rebounds, and 7.2 assists, but he was three for 14 in the first half, and finished five of 18 for 12 points, 12 rebounds, and two assists.

Portland continued to shoot atrociously from the perimeter, making only three of its first 22 from 15 feet and beyond before finishing seven of 27.

"I feel sorry for the team playing us," Williams said, "when we get all of our things together just one time."

3

"I Wanted to Do More With My Life Than Party."

Denver was the unfortunate victim as the Blazers finally played the complete game their fans had grown to expect the previous two seasons. The Nuggets game was memorable not only for the one-sided score, but for a wet coliseum floor causing a 65-minute delay in the start of the game. For a long time, the moist substance — evidently condensation caused by the warm evening and the hockey ice below the playing floor — seemed destined to postpone the game. As it was, the Nuggets took the night off, anyway.

Once the game finally started, Portland jumped to a 16-2 lead and was in front 63-26 at the half — the lowest total a Blazer opponent had ever run up in a half. The late start didn't seem to bother the Blazers at all.

"It was like a rain delay in baseball," kidded Danny Ainge, the former infielder with the Toronto Blue Jays. "We came into the locker room and played cards."

Jerome Kersey was playing on a pair of bad ankles, but packed a game full of activity into 21 minutes. He scored 13 points on five of six from the field, and three of four from the line and had five rebounds, two steals, and a blocked shot. One play in the first quarter typified the Kersey spirit. He dived onto the floor to retrieve a loose ball and somehow got it to Terry Porter, who buried a 3-pointer just before the 24-second clock expired.

Portland shot 50 percent from the floor for the first time since the opener and got double-figure scoring from its first seven players. Nobody played more than 26 minutes as Rick Adelman rested his regulars for a two-game trip to Minnesota and Denver.

Kersey's left ankle sprain was nearly healed, but his right ankle continued to bother him. There was an inflamed joint in the tendons alongside the ankle that gave him varying degrees of pain. Sometimes it felt pretty good. Other times, no relief was in sight.

The one veteran who was a regular participant in the informal pre-training camp scrimmage sessions at Lewis & Clark was Kersey. He enjoyed the games and felt it was a good way to work into shape. But it was there that Kersey aggravated the right ankle, which he first hurt the season before and had evidently not fully healed, even with rest over the summer.

And now, just a few games into the regular season, Kersey was spending more time getting treatment from trainer Mike Shimensky than in practice sessions. The bad ankle hampered his jump shot, but even more important, it limited the activity of the Blazers' starting small forward. And to Jerome Kersey, activity on the court was everything.

"Running around and jumping and hustling — that's my game," Kersey said. His game was being stifled on the bad nights. But he continued to play. And he never talked to the media or in public about the ankle.

"The ankle was constantly bothering me," he admitted long after the season had ended. "Some days it felt fine. Other nights, when I was warming up, I'd be thinking, 'Come on, are you going to loosen up or what?' Usually it was like a dull ache, but something you can constantly feel is there. It was like I was living in the training room.

"Once the ball went up, I forgot about it, but you couldn't help but let it affect the way you play. And there were nights I walked out of there I felt I should have been on crutches."

Kersey wasn't able to practice with the Blazers before they departed for Minneapolis, which irritated him to no end. "I don't enjoy sitting out practices," he said. "I think I'm a practice player. I enjoy competing every day."

So Kersey spent his off day doing a couple of TV spots — one of which he knew nothing about.

Reporter Nicole Watson spent part of the day with Kersey doing an interview that was aired over TNT three weeks later. Then he played a starring role in a segment of a nationally syndicated show called "Basketball's Funniest Pranks."

The show's producer called John Lashway, the Blazers' director of media services, and asked him to suggest a player who would enjoy helping stage a prank. Lashway chose second-year forward Alaa Abdelnaby, who enlisted Ainge for support.

The scenario: Abdelnaby and Ainge were supposed to be going in on the purchase of a prize racehorse. Each had chipped in $50,000 and were looking for a third partner. Abdelnaby, who knew Kersey had expressed an interest in one day owning a stable of horses, figured he'd be the perfect fall guy.

"I knew Jerome would be a total sucker for it," Alaa said.

The three met in the coliseum parking lot to view the horse, which was said to be unbeaten in three races and a young up-and-comer. The truth was, the horse was a nag with one eye and a swayback and looked about 15 years old.

"We're talking about an ugly, ugly horse," Alaa said.

Abdelnaby and Ainge, with the hidden camera rolling, were unbending in their support of the venture.

"You know, Jerome, that one eye might be an advantage for a racehorse, because he could concentrate on the rail," Ainge said with a straight face.

Kersey later admitted his teammates were convincing. He said he had reservations about the horse, but "I was trying to be nice. I was thinking, 'Are you sure you want to invest $50,000 in this?' "

Finally Alaa left to discuss terms with the trainer — an actor for the show — and Ainge, following the plot, changed his story. He pointed out the horse's obvious shortcomings and said he intended to ask for his money back. Then the trainer returned and said he had money from Abdelnaby and Ainge and needed a check from Kersey. Kersey said he needed more time, but the trainer told him he already had Kersey's signature on the contract. When Alaa sheepishly admitted to Kersey he'd forged his teammate's signature, Kersey exploded. "You what?" he said, steaming off back into the coliseum as all those in on the gag yukked it up.

Then Alaa retrieved Jerome and let him in on the stunt. He

took it well, in part because he was relieved he hadn't really blown $50,000. "Yeah," said Jerome, "it was pretty funny."

On the way to Minneapolis on the Blazers' private BAC-111 jet—nicknamed "Blazer One" by veteran radio announcer Bill Schonely—came the first meeting of the new year of the board members of the Championship Fund Group. At the end of the previous season, Ainge, Porter, Clyde Drexler, Buck Williams, Kevin Duckworth, and Wayne Cooper had each contributed $5,000 toward investment in a major stock purchase. Duckworth was a silent partner, choosing not to be involved in the decision-making. "You got my money," Duck said. "Make me some more."

So the other five would talk and argue and debate which stocks to sell or buy. It was fun, it was relaxing. It could take the players' minds off the staggering pressures of the team and their careers. And hey, it could be lucrative. By the end of the 1991-92 season, each player's contribution was worth about $15,000.

"I find myself reading the *Wall Street Journal* and keeping up on trends," Cooper said. "I'm no expert, but neither are the other guys."

They liked to talk like they were, though. It made for some pretty good banter.

"We abuse each other on the losing stocks," Ainge said. "We have a lot of fun with that."

The Blazers needed Kersey, healthy or not, against a surprising Minnesota team. Kersey collected 15 points and 17 rebounds, including 10 at the offensive end, high for a Portland player all season. But the story of the Miracle in Minnesota was the little rookie with the jets, Robert Pack, who turned on a national TNT audience and tuned out the Timberwolves in an astounding 117-112 Blazer win.

Minnesota entered the game 1-6 and as the poorest-shooting and lowest-scoring team in the NBA. Portland held a career 32-1 record against the four expansion franchises (Minnesota, Charlotte, Orlando, and Miami), a mark they were to improve to 39-1 at season's end, the best in the NBA. Even if this one was in the Target Center, it seemed inconceivable that the Blazers could lose.

And so when the Blazers rallied from a 21-point deficit in the second half to pull out the victory, there were a lot of collective brows being wiped dry.

"Is there anything bigger than a miracle?" Kersey asked. "That's what it was tonight."

Most of the way, the Blazers were awful, but a pulp mill would have smelled like a rose garden in comparison to the way they played to open the second half. They started the third quarter one for 15 from the field and one for eight from the line, and the only surprise was that the Wolves led only 75-54 with four minutes remaining in the third period. Adelman was thoroughly disgusted and those on hand and watching on TV were wondering why anyone would be considering Portland a championship contender.

So the comeback was quick and remarkable. Drexler finished with 35 points, including 15 in a row at the end of the third quarter as Portland began to draw back. But Pack, harassing Minnesota's Pooh Richardson and scoring 13 of his 15 points in the fourth period, was the point man for the Blazer rally.

Late in the third quarter, Adelman went to a three-guard lineup and a pressing, trapping defense that clicked the production at the other end into gear. Portland scored on seven of its last 11 possessions in the third quarter, then was almost flawless in the fourth period, scoring on 18 of 21 possessions — including the last 11 in a row — and committing only one turnover.

Pack was sensational, pestering Pooh at the defensive end and driving to the basket to hit seven of 10 shots and dish off four assists in 19 minutes. He came up with the game's two biggest plays at the end. First he scored on a running 10-footer from the middle with 26.2 seconds remaining and the shot clock near zero to give Portland a 104-102 lead. After a timeout, a pressing Pack tipped the ball away from Sam Mitchell in the Wolves' backcourt. Drexler fed Pack for a layup with 6.4 seconds left, and the improbable win was secure.

"Pack was their most valuable player tonight," said Minnesota's Tony Campbell. "He played some outstanding basketball. He surprised me. I thought he was going to come in and be a role player. He came in to be a game winner."

"Robert won the game for us, no doubt about it," Clyde said. "He defended, he made shots, he penetrated — he did it all."

It was a shining hour for Pack, the point guard nobody wanted just three months earlier. Here he was, playing a critical role for a team expected to battle for the NBA championship. It was a long way from his boyhood in the Fisher Housing Projects on the wrong side of the tracks in New Orleans.

The second oldest and only son of four children to Robert Pack, Sr. and his wife, Wilda, Robert learned early to fend for himself. Dad was a taxi driver and Mom was a desk clerk, and they both worked long hours to put food on the table.

New Orleans' Fox playground was Robert's second home. "Growing up in the projects, all my buddies did it," he said. "You played the sport in season, or you were inside watching the soap operas on TV."

His first team was the Fisher football Eagles, where he established himself as one of the best grade school quarterbacks on the West Bank. He was a Little League pitcher and a point guard in basketball. "I always liked to play the leader positions," he said. "I was always the one in charge."

Pack was a fine wide receiver, quarterback, and safety in football, but his principal interest was basketball. He was so fast, so strong, so quick that few could stay with him. And he loved to play.

"I was in the parks 'til 2 in the morning playing basketball," he said. Some of his friends were into drugs or were members of gangs. Robert never had any interest.

"Kids are always bad, but I never got into too much trouble," he said. "I wanted to do more with my life than party."

He was an all-state guard as a senior, and signed a letter of intent to attend Southeast Louisiana, but fell short of the ACT entrance standards by one point, and wound up at Tyler (Texas) JC, where he played in the same league as Charlotte's Larry Johnson, who was at Odessa.

Many teams came calling during his second season at Tyler, including Oklahoma, Florida, Loyola-Marymount, Tulane, Providence, and Baylor, but he wound up at Southern Cal, wooed by the silvery tongue of Raveling. And he had two solid seasons running the attack at SC, averaging nearly 15 points, and leading the team in assists and steals.

"He could have scored a lot more points for us, but that wasn't his role," Raveling said. "He concentrated on running our team.

"I thought he would have a tough time (in Portland) because they had so many veteran guards, but I knew if he got a chance to play he would make their roster. I honestly believed that. His senior year, there was nobody in the country who could take the ball baseline to baseline faster than Robert. Our football coaches thought he would make a great defensive back.

"He was a long shot, but I think that worked in his favor. No one thought he could do it. It's like in boxing; it's always easy to penetrate a guy's defense when he doesn't respect you. He lowers his guard and is more susceptible to the jab."

Pack landed an uppercut, but it took awhile for him to convince Adelman, who had long been a proponent of Danny Young. Young wasn't flashy or a big scorer, but he was dependable, a good position defender, and a nice role player on a team stacked with pretty good talent.

But Pack gave the Blazers a dimension they didn't have — a quicksilver young guard who could apply some pressure at the defensive end and create some opportunities with penetration on offense. And when Young couldn't buy a basket early, missing 12 of 13 shots in the first six games, Adelman was inclined to give Pack his chance.

After the Minnesota game, a lot of TNT viewers were ready to consider Pack for a spot on the league's All-Rookie team. The Pack Man had gobbled up a little notice for himself.

"I got a lot of calls the next couple of days, some from guys I'd played with or against, who didn't even know I was in the league after I didn't get drafted," he said. "I heard from some coaches who were pleased for me. It was fun."

Adelman took the Minnesota game as an opportunity to defend Portland's oft-criticized halfcourt offense, pointing to the near-perfect production at game's end.

"People talk about our halfcourt offense," he said, "but when the game is on the line, we're one of the best teams in the league. We don't lose very many when it's close down the stretch."

It wasn't close down the stretch as the Blazers were losing 122-111 at Denver the following night. It was a 49-point turnaround from the 120-82 Blazer win at Portland four days earlier. And Drexler, who turned in a four-for-15 shooting game, summed up the Blazer performance in one word: "Awful."

Reggie Williams looked like Michael Jordan, lighting up Clyde on 13-of-18 shooting. Dikembe Mutombo (18 points, 12 rebounds, three blocks) and Cadillac Anderson (16 points, 11 rebounds) controlled the middle, and an old friend, Walter

Davis, came off the bench for six straight baskets and 14 points. "Walter gave us an incredible spark," Denver coach Paul Westhead said.

There was little spark to the Blazers. The Nuggets said they were motivated by the way the Blazers had acted in the rout at Portland.

"We didn't like what happened to us," Williams said. "They were cocky. Good teams are cocky. That's how you become good. But we wanted to show we're a lot better than we showed in Portland."

The Blazers, befuddled by the Denver debacle, came back to whip the Clippers in back-to-back games in Portland and Los Angeles that were mirror image in story line. The Blazers, with Drexler running up 39 points, seven rebounds, and nine assists, and Kersey adding 28 points and 10 rebounds, drop-kicked the Clippers 132-112 in Portland, then rallied from a 51-50 halftime deficit to whip the Clips 106-91 in LA. The only unhappy face in the visitors' dressing room in the Sports Arena was Duckworth, who saw 23 minutes of action after playing only 22 the game before. It was growing clear that Adelman intended to use Cliff Robinson, a better defender, and a much more active player, for extended minutes at center.

And Duck didn't like it a bit. He groused to a sportscaster after the Portland game that he never saw the ball anymore and he was being unfairly singled out as the reason the Blazers had been inconsistent thus far. Some of it was real, some of it was imagined. He met with Adelman after practice between games, but after the second game he was still in a dark mood.

"When we do well, everybody gets the credit except me," he said. "When things turn bad, I get the blame. I'm tired of people getting on me about something I have no control over. This is the best I've felt in the last two years, and I'm not involved in the offense. Give me a chance to do something. Get me involved."

In a way, Duck's pleas were falling on deaf ears. The patented pick-and-roll play that had been so effective the previous two seasons — Porter driving off the screen, then dropping the ball off to Duck on the left baseline for a 10-to-15 foot jumper — was being used only sparingly. Duckworth would still set screens, especially early in games, but when Porter rolled off he would either go to the basket or find someone on the other side of the court. Part of it was opponents were defending it better, and often two players would close off the passing lane between Porter and Duckworth. But part of it seemed to be that Porter had lost confidence, either in Duck, or in his ability to get the ball to him without turning it over.

The Blazers returned home and lost 116-112 to Golden State in a game they never should have lost. Portland rampaged to a 41-point second quarter to go into intermission with a 74-62 advantage. The Blazers still led 94-87 going into the fourth quarter, but blundered numerous times down the stretch, committing two 24-second violations, going two for six from the foul line, calling an ill-advised timeout, and then allowing Chris Mullin an open look at a 17-foot jumper with 1.2 seconds remaining to break a 112-112 tie.

Adelman was bitterly disappointed to see his team drop to 7-5 in such a disheartening manner. He struggled to gain his composure afterward, much as his players had in the closing minutes of the game. "It was our game to win," he said, "and we didn't do enough to win it."

Clyde, as usual, was sensational with 31 points, 10 rebounds, and seven assists in 44 minutes. He was plain mad at his team's showing. "What we did tonight wasn't indicative of a veteran team," he said. "If we make our free throws, if we defend, if we play smarter down the stretch, we win. That just doesn't cut it. Golden State played well, but I thought we gave them a lot of help."

Drexler was becoming a little more outspoken in trying to motivate his teammates. To the press, though, he never singled out a player for criticism. It wasn't his style. He considers it bad form to talk about his own considerable skills, too, and will often respond to post-game queries about his brilliant play with white-bread comments about "rebounding and defense won it for us" and "my teammates did a great job of getting me the ball." His selection to the writers' All-Interview team at season's end had everything to do with his cooperation and star status, and little to do with his candid and creative quotes.

Duckworth played 13 minutes in the Golden State game, making one of seven shots and collecting three points and one rebound. Adelman went with Robinson to match up with Don Nelson's small, quick Warriors, and the 6-10 third-year man had a nice game before fouling out with 15 points and 11 rebounds. Duck was unhappy and left the dressing room before the media — required by the league to wait 10 minutes after the game ended for a "cooling-off period"— entered. The next day, Duck admitted he was annoyed by "negative comments" by his teammates at times during the game. "I don't need them bickering at me."

The negative comments were little more than Clyde and Buck and Terry trying to get Duckworth moving and into the game, but with his minutes decreasing, he wasn't in the mood to hear it. Not that he ever liked to hear about what he wasn't doing. "That's one of my faults," he had told a reporter the previous spring. "I never could take criticism, not even as a kid."

The Blazers will pay Drexler $8 million during the 1995-96 season, and he earned a chunk of it with his performance in the next outing, a 116-111 win over San Antonio at home. Clyde scored 48 points — two shy of his career high, and three short of Geoff Petrie's franchise record — to go with six rebounds, six steals, three blocked shots, and three assists. Porter added 22 points and 10 assists, but nobody else was on top of his game, and the two centers, Duckworth and Robinson, combined for an almost unbelievable six-for-32 shooting game.

Clyde was 10 of 13 in the first half, throwing in shots from inside, outside, and everywhere. He rang up 29 points in a 20-minute first-half display that left fans, players and sportswriters searching for adjectives.

"Unconscious," said David Robinson, who had 25 points, 20 rebounds, and nine blocked shots for the Spurs. "Clyde was really something."

Adelman called for Clyde to shoot a 3-pointer in the final minute that would have given him 50 points, but he wound up getting fouled on a drive and making one of two foul shots. Later, he chuckled about the moment. "I thought he was kidding at first. I think it's the first time he ever called a play for me to shoot a 3. He said, 'You need 3 to get 50.' I said, 'All right, let's do it.'"

Larry Brown, still coaching the Spurs, but soon to be piloting the Clippers, was left shaking his head: "Clyde was phenomenal. They've been struggling a little, and he obviously wanted to make a statement tonight."

Portland was fortunate to escape with a 107-98 overtime win over Milwaukee in a game most notable for the reappearance of Abdelnaby. Alaa, inconsistent during the preseason, had been beaten out by Mark Bryant for the backup power forward spot, but Bryant had really struggled through the first 14 games of the regular season, making only 17 of 55 shots (.309).

Adelman gave Alaa some minutes in both halves, and he contributed 10 points and five rebounds in 16 active minutes.

Adelman decided the day before he was going to use Abdelnaby and told the 6-10, 240-pound second-year man from Duke after practice. It was like a "get-out-of-jail-free" card for Alaa, who desperately wanted to play.

His rookie year had been enjoyable on one hand, yet very difficult on another. Alaa liked and respected his coaches and teammates and had become popular with the fans, and he had even grown to like the city, though the gray skies of late fall, winter, and early spring depressed him. The toughest part was collecting dust on the bench behind Duckworth, Williams, Cooper, and Bryant, seeing only 290 minutes of action all season. Blazer coaches liked his offensive skills and agility for a big man, but had reservations about his defense, heart, and work ethic.

Alaa's parents are native Egyptians, and he was born in Alexandria. His father, Abdelhamid, left his wife and young son shortly after Alaa was born to go establish a new life in the United States. He settled in New Jersey, where he worked for a while in a laundry before moving on to a business as a computer engineer. When Alaa was two, his father called for the family to join him and they settled in Harrison before winding up in Bloomfield, where Alaa attended high school.

Alaa became a prep All-American and New Jersey Athlete of the Year. He signed with Duke, where he played for three years in the shadow of the likes of Danny Ferry. That bothered him, because he resented and disliked Ferry, and felt he was Coach Mike Krzyzewski's fair-haired boy. The players argued and fought in practice, and Alaa felt he wasn't given the opportunity to blossom that he deserved. There was plenty of talent at Duke, and Coach K wasn't convinced Alaa was a force yet, and he was only a part-time starter as far along into his college career as his junior year. Then Ferry graduated, and Alaa came into his own, shooting .620 from the floor and playing superbly in the NCAA playoffs, helping the Blue Devils to the NCAA championship game and the Final Four for the third time in four seasons.

Blazer scouts liked his upside enough to take him with the 25th pick in the 1990 draft, and now finally he seemed to be getting his chance, and making the best of it.

———————————

The Blazers ended the month with a showdown against the defending champion Chicago Bulls at home, a highly anticipated matchup in Portland. Michael Jordan was always a top draw, and now the Bulls were the team that achieved what all Blazer fans desperately wanted and thought their team should have — a title.

Chicago prevailed in a 116-114 double-overtime thriller that left a lot of questions about the Blazers unanswered. Jordan scored 40 points and Drexler 38 in their personal duel, but Clyde was only six of 12 from the line, and missed three late in regulation and the overtime sessions that were critical. Of more concern were mental errors, such as Williams taking an inbounds pass with one second on the shot clock and passing the ball to a teammate as time expired. The Blazers led 105-103 and had the ball with 22 seconds to go in the first overtime, but Kersey tried a long outlet pass to Porter, who was called for traveling while trying to control the ball. Jordan came back for a leaning 12-footer with 1.2 seconds to go to force a second extra session, and the Blazers were doomed.

Later in the season, Magic Johnson would refer to the Kersey pass when asked about the Blazers and the "dumb-team" controversy that swept America and so rankled the Blazers. Dumb or not, the Blazers were in a much less envious position than they'd been the previous year, when they opened the season 11-0. They entered December 9-6, hopeful they'd left their poorest basketball behind them.

4

"Sometimes People Don't Understand Why You Try to Keep Your Privacy."

12/1/91 NBA Pacific Division Standings									
	W	**L**	**Pct.**	**GB**		**W**	**L**	**Pct.**	**GB**
LA Lakers	11	4	.733	-	Phoenix	8	9	.471	4
Golden State	9	5	.643	1½	LA Clippers	6	10	.375	5½
Portland	9	6	.600	2	Sacramento	5	10	.333	6
Seattle	8	7	.533	3					

The Blazers didn't exactly take a dive to open December. But Jerome Kersey did. In another kamikaze-type play that has become the hallmark of his career, Kersey went hurtling hard to the floor in the final moments of a game in Memorial Coliseum against the Washington Bullets.

Kersey was attempting to dunk over the Bullets' Pervis Ellison, who was called for a flagrant foul on the play when he bumped Kersey in midair. The Blazer forward landed hard on his right side, but x-rays following the game showed no fracture, only a deep bruise to the ulnar bone in his right forearm.

Ellison claimed he was only trying to get out of Kersey's way, but Kersey objected to Ellison being there in the first place. He felt Never Nervous Pervis never had a chance to block his dunk attempt.

"We got a steal, and I was on the wing racing up court, and they got me the ball, and Pervis was on my side," Kersey said. "I was going to drive in for a dunk, and he wasn't there, I had a good two steps on him. And at the last minute he got there and bumped me and turned his back on me. I landed on my arm and side, and when I hit, it was like everything went numb."

As Kersey fell to the floor, time clicked into slow motion. "You don't realize how far away the floor is until you start coming down parallel. It felt like it took all day. I knew I was going to land hard, and I couldn't do anything."

After laying in a heap for a moment, Kersey got up and let loose a string of profanities at Ellison. "I told him to foul me rather than turn his back and have no chance to grab me and cushion my fall," Kersey said. "I've been undercut big-time four or five times in my career. You don't understand what it's like to have somebody running at your feet like that until it happens to you."

Kersey's biggest fall came the previous year in a game at Los Angeles, where he landed on his neck after going airborne over the Lakers' A.C. Green. It was a frightening play that was shown time and time again on replay by television stations, and everyone breathed a sigh of relief when he was able to get up and walk off under his own power with only minor injuries.

Now, said Kersey, he has reeled in a little of his breakneck style, even if it wasn't readily noticeable. "I probably missed a few shots because of it, but I look now," he said. "If I have a clear lane, I'll dunk it, but if I have a chance to lay it in rather than dunk over somebody who is challenging me, I'll do it."

Portland actually won the game with the flagrant foul call on Ellison, getting three points out of that possession, and holding on for a 91-87 triumph in spite of what looked like a hangover from the home loss to Chicago.

"We just couldn't seem to get anything going," Rick Adelman said. "I don't know why we had such a difficult time getting started. You have games like this, and after that emotional game against Chicago it may have been difficult for us to get up."

Wayne Cooper, the forgotten man who played in only four of the Blazers' first 15 games, came in and gave the team 13 solid minutes, making three of his four shots from the floor, grabbing four rebounds and scoring six points. It was a rare moment in the spotlight for the 35-year-old veteran backup center, who spent much of the season watching from the sidelines.

"Everyone could learn a lesson from watching Wayne Cooper," Adelman said. "He puts the team first. He's done a good job every time I play him, and you could look at me and ask me why I'm such a dummy for not playing him. He deserves to get some minutes, and he'll get more."

That would not prove to be true. Adelman spent minutes on Alaa Abdelnaby and Mark Bryant through much of the season, in an effort to get their games going. When they didn't respond, Adelman responded by cutting his rotation down and using Cliff Robinson even longer. Cooper would finish the season playing a total of only 344 minutes in 35 games.

"Coming into the season I knew from the start the younger guys were going to get the minutes," Cooper said at season's end. "I made up my mind not to worry about it. You can only control what you can control. I knew guys like Alaa were going to get a chance.

"Every player is a competitor, but I pretty much accepted my role. Don't say it was easy, because it wasn't. It was the toughest season I've ever had. I had never been out of a rotation before. I had always played, from my rookie year on. I think not playing built up on me as the season went along."

Cooper's professionalism, though, was probably worth as much to the team as his shotblocking. The example he set for the younger players was perfect. He worked hard, pulled for his teammates, and stayed ready. A quiet and shy man by nature, he worked diligently at coming out of his shell and encouraging others.

That began prior to the season when Cooper was the only player to take advantage of the team's offer to work with a media specialist. Often interview-shy throughout his career, Cooper became accomplished and relaxed during media sessions—forcing his way past what was almost a career of respectful silence.

"I've always watched other guys," Cooper said. "When you don't talk much, you listen more. I listened to the veteran players and learned a lot. You learn how to act. I always watched Dr. J — Julius Erving. I think my biggest idol was always Arthur Ashe."

Hampered at times by injuries, Cooper coaxed more NBA games out of his body — 984 — than most people would have ever expected.

"After my first three years in the league, one general manager — I won't say who it was — called my agent and said they wanted me to sign a waiver," Cooper said. "They said my knees were so bad I wouldn't last another year in the league. That was about 12 years ago."

———————————

What the Trail Blazers needed is exactly what they got. A lot of people go to Florida for vacation, and Portland went there to get well. The Blazers have never lost to the Miami Heat, and on December 3 they romped to a 124-94 win by shooting 54.7 percent — a big improvement over the 45-percent figure they took into the contest.

"Must have been the humidity here," Adelman said. "Maybe I should have (owner) Paul Allen fly in some humidity to use in Memorial Coliseum. That was a really solid effort. For 48 minutes we played excellent basketball. That may have been the best job we've done of following the game plan all year."

The Blazers followed with a 124-115 win at Orlando against the Magic, when Clyde Drexler chalked up a 34-point, 10-rebound, and seven-assist effort. He hit 11 of his first 14 shots, many of them perimeter jumpers.

It was a peaceful two days for Adelman, who was finding this season much different than the previous year. There was no magical 19-1 start like in 1990-91, and Adelman didn't expect one. But there were concerns when the team got out of the gate slowly.

"You're always a little bit concerned," he said. "I felt a good start this year didn't necessarily have to be 14-2. If we got off to a winning record the first month I was going to be pleased. I knew we weren't going to duplicate what we did last year. I was more concerned that as long as we didn't lose faith in what we could do, get into a long losing streak, we'd be OK. I felt we were going to right ourselves."

For Adelman, who grew up in Los Angeles, it was nice to get to the warm weather. After struggling much of the previous season with a cold, he was feeling better and able to do his daily jogging with more verve. His mindset was better, too, than it had been the previous season.

In the midst of what was a marvelous 1991-92 regular season—"the long, hot winter" that became the title of Adelman's book—the coach was tormented by a situation that he was never willing to talk about for local newspapers.

Adelman's oldest daughter, Kathy, a starting point guard for the basketball team at the University of Portland, was being stalked by a man who drifted in and out of the shadows of her life. Phone calls and notes were the early signs, followed by mysterious appearances at her basketball games.

When he finally broke into her dormitory room at the college and waited for her arrival, the Adelman family became desperate. She changed dorms, spent more time at the family home in Tigard, stayed closer to friends, and the man's appearances tailed off.

"They never caught him," the coach said more than a year later. "The team and Paul Allen were terrific during that time. They even hired a private detective to try to help. Sometimes people don't understand why you try to keep your privacy . . ."

Adelman isn't your average NBA coach, immersed in basketball with little time for anything else. He has always found as many creative ways as possible to attend his children's school activities and tries very hard to be the best possible father. That's what made this situation so difficult. How would you like to go out on the road for a week or two at a time, knowing your daughter was in such a vulnerable situation?

For nearly a year, the Adelman family kept an uncomfortable eye over its shoulders before finally relaxing. It now seemed the trouble was over.

Adelman still worried about the situation a little, but it was nothing like it had been during the previous season. Now his concern was the impact of the team's shocking Western Conference finals loss to the Lakers. It was obvious that his team was still dealing with the pain.

At the start, Adelman, at least figuratively, stayed away from his players a little. It was the wrong time to ride them.

"I couldn't demand the same things," he said. "They needed time to get into the season. You can't continually be on the same super-charged high. They weren't going to listen to that. We needed time to forget."

The two wins in Florida weren't any indication of a major turnaround. Portland traveled to Philadelphia and lost to the 76ers in overtime as Johnny Dawkins swished a 27-foot, 3-point goal that resulted in a 105-102 finish. The Sixers didn't even have Charles Barkley, who sat out the game because of bruised ribs. Portland scored only seven points in the second quarter in what Danny Ainge called a "total embarrassment" and "a disgrace."

Just when the team thought it was back on track, it derailed. "That first half must have set basketball back a long way," Adelman said after his team trailed 41-31 at halftime. In the laughable second quarter, Portland made only three of 21 shots from the floor and had 10 turnovers. A team trying to throw the game wouldn't have wanted to look that bad.

"I've never seen anything that bad since I came to this country," said Manute Bol, the 7-foot-7 human javelin from the Sudan who plays center for Philadelphia. "Nobody would believe it."

———————————

Sometimes in any sport, luck, fate, or just circumstances dictate who wins and who loses. Portland pulled into Indiana on December 7 and found a team willing to help it finish off a road trip with its third win in four games.

The Pacers missed six free throws inside the final 3:48 and let themselves get out-rebounded 53-30 — just enough to let the Blazers sneak through with a 115-112 win. "The end of the game was designed for us to win," Indiana coach Bob Hill said. "We just missed free throws."

Cooper, pressed into service because of travel fatigue and the absence of an injured Kersey, again came up big. He made four of five shots, had eight points and four rebounds in 14 minutes. After making just one of his 13 shots from the floor at Philadelphia, Terry Porter came out and made only two of 10 in the first half of this game. But he hit nine of 11 in the second half, many of them from the outside, and had 10 assists and six rebounds.

"I actually felt pretty good in the first half," Porter said. "The shots weren't going down, but I stayed aggressive and got some real good opportunities in the third quarter."

Portland returned home to play Houston and immediately laid another egg. A big, stinky one, at that.

The Blazers blew a 97-85 lead with four minutes to play, allowed the Rockets to score on each of their last 10 possessions and lost a 108-106 decision that left the Portland locker room unable to find words — or an explanation.

For three quarters of the game, Duckworth outplayed Houston center Hakeem Olajuwon. Duckworth made nine of his first 11 shots from the floor while holding the Rocket superstar to three field goals and 10 points through three periods. But when

Adelman went to the bench at the start of the fourth period he opted for Robinson, rather than Cooper, to defend Olajuwon.

Olajuwon suddenly caught fire and scored 15 points in the final quarter to fuel the rally.

"Cliff has done a good job on him in the past," Adelman said. "I wanted to get somebody more active on him.

"It was a game we should have won. We just stopped playing the last five minutes. We thought we had it won. We didn't play smart. It shouldn't have happened."

We didn't play smart, Adelman said. And it wouldn't be the last time. Soon, the team would begin to be known for that characteristic.

Detroit followed Houston into Memorial Coliseum and laid a 113-103 whipping on Portland that wasn't as close as the score might indicate. The Blazers missed their first 13 shots from the floor in the fourth quarter and in spite of the fact that the Pistons, losers of seven of their previous nine road games, were nothing like the team that dominated the league for two seasons, they mopped up the floor with the home team. This was painful deja vu from a Finals past, when the Blazers could have won a championship by winning three straight home games, but instead lost three straight to the Pistons.

"Flashback, Jack," Duckworth said. "I saw Isiah Thomas do his little dance, just like he did on us two years ago."

Adelman shook his head sadly and said, "They picked us apart. They shot the ball as well as any team has against us all year, with the possible exception of Phoenix. They had an answer for everything we tried."

The Blazers were 13-9. Twenty-two games into the 1990-91 season they had been 20-2. They didn't suffer their ninth loss that season until February 6, the game before the All-Star break. At that point, they were 39-9. This was becoming a very different season.

Things didn't get better quickly. Kersey, still bothered by ankle miseries, played, but not effectively so. And the Blazers were without Buck Williams, who had flown to Rocky Mount, N.C., for his mother's funeral. In the next game, a shaky 115-110 win over Sacramento in Memorial Coliseum, Williams was still gone, Ainge sat out due to a sprained right knee, and Porter departed with a sprained right ankle with three minutes left.

Williams had been encouraged to take another game off, but with Ainge and Porter listed as questionable, he returned in time to suit up for a 119-104 win over Minnesota on December 17. It was an appearance that Williams felt was important.

"It was one of the most stressful times ever for me," Williams said later. "I played that one game because of my faith. I felt I had to show the world. It was a public test. You profess to be a Christian; well, part of that is being able to operate during adversity. I had to play. But we're not machines. We're people. It was very difficult."

Kersey understood. Family was very important to the veteran forward. His mother, Dolores Florence, had given birth to him out of wedlock when she was 18, and he was raised by his maternal grandparents, Herman and Elizabeth Kersey, in rural Clarksville, Virginia. He had always called his mother Dolores — "She always seemed like one of my aunts," Kersey said — and his grandparents "Mom" and "Dad." The Kerseys had raised six children of their own, and only now was Jerome beginning to realize the incredible commitment they had made toward giving him an opportunity in life.

When Elizabeth Kersey became ill and needed minor surgery the previous year, Jerome was beside himself with worry. And now he had lived through the deaths of parents of teammates Porter and Williams.

"I saw Terry the day after, and Buck the morning after," Kersey recalled. "It was the first experience I'd had to sit down with Buck and really talk about our feelings. It kind of ran deep with me. Some of the same things he said about his Mom are the same things I feel about my Grandma. It affects you more directly than people might think. It makes you think about family, and you realize basketball is not the most important thing in the world."

Several of the Blazers had experienced not only death but terrible tragedies with family members. When Williams was 12, his 16-year-old brother, Moses Williams Jr., drowned while swimming in a pond. Drexler's half-brother, Michael Prevost, who was eight years older than Clyde, was killed by a policeman in an attempted robbery of a pharmacy. Prevost had gotten involved with drugs. "He'd come home, all doped up, creating havoc around the house," Clyde said. "The other kids would wonder, 'What's wrong with him?' I used to try to help him. He was the kind of guy who was always in trouble. When he died, it was the worst feeling. I was devastated. I don't think my mother ever recovered. She blamed herself."

Ainge had lived through the suicide of his mother, Kay, in 1982. "It was very traumatic," said Ainge, a devout Mormon who used his faith to help him get through the grief. "It made me sit back and think about what life really is about. It made me want to try to be the person I want to be so I will never go through the depression my Mom went through."

Personal pressures were placed on top of external pressures for both Porter and Williams. The disappointment of the season before had led to pressure this season, both from the fans and media, and from within themselves.

"There was a lot of pressure and a lot of stress," Williams said. "It wasn't one of the most enjoyable seasons. You enjoy winning, but it wasn't as much fun as the previous two years. It just seemed to be ingrained in everyone's mind that it was a 'do-or-die' situation. There was tremendous pressure. It was like every game was a playoff game.

"This town lives through our team."

After a stretch of 14 straight games without reaching double figures in rebounds during November, people were beginning to wonder if Williams wasn't heading toward the end of his wonderful career. Williams, though, said he was just pacing himself a little bit.

"I think it's easier for me to play now than ever before," he said. "If I've lost a step physically, I think I've made up for it by getting smarter. I think as I get older, I'll get a lot sharper. After a while, you have to learn a different mental approach. I don't try to run through the wall anymore. I've learned to run around it. I've figured out how to do that."

5

"Clyde Just Carried Us."

12/19/91 NBA Pacific Division Standings								
	W	**L**	**Pct.**	**GB**		**W**	**L**	**Pct.**	**GB**
Golden State	15	7	.682	-	Seattle	13	11	.542	3
LA Lakers	16	8	.667	-	LA Clippers	14	12	.538	3
Portland	15	9	.625	1	Sacramento	7	16	.304	8½
Phoenix	14	10	.583	2					

The Blazers had a chance to pull into a first-place Pacific Division tie with Golden State on December 20, but lost a 123-118 decision to the Warriors at Oakland. Chris Mullin, Tim Hardaway, and Sarunas Marciulionis combined for 86 points to kill Portland— which struggled to defend Coach Don Nelson's small lineup.

Nelson, part genius and part con man, had been the story in the early part of the season. He had swung a deal that sent off-guard Mitch Richmond to Sacramento for the rights to Billy Owens, and his team got off to a terrific start.

"We don't belong in first place," Nelson said after defeating the Blazers. "I don't expect to be there at the end. But it sure feels nice to be there now."

Actually, the Warriors stayed there for a good part of the season, and Nelson's poormouthing sounds cheap in retrospect. His team still needed a big player, sure, and several sources confirmed that the Kings wanted Richmond so badly that Nelson could have swung the trade prior to the draft and had a chance at center Dikembe Mutombo — who eventually went to Denver. But Nelson couldn't bring himself to pull the trigger.

Perhaps it's just easier not to have that big man, anyway, some felt. You get the big man in the middle, and pretty soon everyone expects you to win — rather than just be a bunch of overachieving little guys. At least that's the way a lot of Portlanders figured it. Nelson is not a popular man in Portland — not in light of some very uncomplimentary remarks Nelson made about Drexler a couple of years ago.

Nelson had unloaded some cheap shots about the Blazer guard, designed to get former Portland coach and Nelson aide Mike Schuler off the hook for getting fired by the Blazers. It must have worked, too, because Schuler got hired by the Los Angeles Clippers before his own personality — not Clyde Drexler — got him fired again.

It's interesting in basketball how the attitude and demeanor of the head coach seems to shape the personality of an entire organization. When the fitness-conscious Jack Ramsay roamed the Blazer sideline, everyone in the organization seemed to be on the "Eat to Win" diet. Anyone caught with a french fry was not to be trusted. Under Adelman, the Blazers seemed to be a more relaxed and looser organization, with families an important consideration.

But with Schuler at the helm, it didn't take long before the Blazer organization seemed as edgy and paranoid as the coach — who was actually a charming man when he wanted to be. But often he didn't want to be.

Schuler bragged about not knowing anything about Watergate and other than knowing the words to several country and western songs, didn't have time for anything but basketball. This behavior did nothing to endear him to his players. Professional athletes are often men who fight hard to view their jobs as eight-hour-a-day pursuits. They have the money to isolate themselves from the rest of the sports-wacky world, and don't really want to spend a lot of time thinking about the game when they're not in uniform. They do their best, then try to go home and forget about it. It's not always possible, but it's the goal.

Schuler became known as a man possessed. During his tenure as Portland coach, the team still traveled via commercial airlines, and it used to be fun for the newspapermen traveling with the team to watch Schuler on flights. He was often — especially when things weren't going well — too nervous to sit, and instead roamed the plane soliciting opinions on what could be done with his team or players.

Then-radio analyst Geoff Petrie was respected by Schuler, and was often a target. Schuler would haul Petrie out of his seat and adjourn to the back of the plane for an hour of hushed conversation. Sometimes, if no one else was available, he'd haul a beat reporter to the back for the same purpose. "C'mere, Big Boy," Schuler would say. "I wanna talk to ya."

Normally, reporters relish these kind of intimate conversations with coaches or players. It's a chance to learn a lot, and sometimes if the writer is trusted, it's an opportunity for serious give and take in an off-the-record fashion. But not with Schuler. He took, but never gave. He wanted opinions, but never let his guard down long enough to reveal anything about himself or his situation. He would go off on hypothetical tangents that left the writer wondering what the hell was going on.

That's why the little trips to the back of the plane with Schuler began to become known as trips to the penalty box. Schuler distrusted the media, and soon seemed to carry his suspicions over to his own staff. By the time he was fired on February 18, 1989, he had sealed his own fate. He seemed to create such a feeling of discomfort for those around him that it was inevitable he would have to be cut loose — like an aching tooth that had to be pulled.

Schuler was soon to be fired by the Clippers, and later said that one of the problems was lack of loyalty from his assistant coaches, which he intimated was also the case in Portland. Jack Schalow, who served as a scout and assistant coach while Schuler was with the Blazers, begs to differ.

"We were loyal to him, really did everything he wanted," Schalow said. Schalow regarded Schuler as a friend, and to this day likes him away from the court. But he didn't enjoy Schuler's obsession with work, work, work, or his singlemindedness of objective when it came to the profession.

"He's a really nice guy," Schalow said. "Get him away from basketball and he has a good personality, jokes around, and is a normal guy. But he gets so uptight in coaching, his personality changes. Contrary to what some people think, I never heard him yell and scream at players. But sometimes by that look on his face, players knew he was singling them out, and they didn't appreciate it. He wanted to win so badly, I don't think he ever enjoyed the game. He wanted to watch film by the hour, keep going over it . . . when a game was over, a lot of times the coaches watched films for 3 hours until 2, 3 in the morning. It just makes you start to feel negatively about that person."

Blazer players began feeling negatively about their coach as early as the exhibition season of Schuler's second year in Portland. There was a game at Colorado Springs, Colorado, against the Denver Nuggets, when Schuler flew off the handle and blasted guards Terry Porter and Michael Holton during his postgame news conference. Holton and Porter, to that point, had been among Schuler's biggest boosters and most dependable performers.

There are always players on any team who don't like the coach — but they are usually the borderline players, benchwarmers, or just bad guys who don't even like themselves. When the "good guys" go over to the other side, it's a sign of trouble.

The Seattle SuperSonics came into Portland within a game of the 15-10 Blazers on December 22, and could have pulled even with a win. But the home team rallied in the second half to post a 96-87 win — after an eruption by Mt. Adelman at halftime.

The Sonics were playing on the second night of back-to-back games and were without injured starters Shawn Kemp and Nate McMillan. Yet they led Portland 49-35 late in the second quarter, and 49-42 at intermission.

That's when Adelman threw a fit.

"He blasted us," Williams said. "He was very upset, and he had good reason to be."

Adelman didn't kick over a table, as he had a year earlier during a halftime rage at Los Angeles. Nor did he kick over a chalkboard —"but only because they're secured to the walls," he said.

"I was not happy. I couldn't believe how we came out so flat. We've seen this too many times this season. Seattle played a very solid first half, but we have to come out with more fire at the start. I told them we had to do three things. We had to start defending, we had to get to the boards, and we had to get the ball downcourt and make them do some work at the other end."

Adelman didn't often show a temper. He chose his spots well. Normally, the players knew what to expect. He was . . . well, consistent.

"He is the same all the time," Schalow said. "Well, most of the time. You win, you lose, he's not going to rant and rave. The players have told me that's the thing they really like about him. When he does chew them out, they listen, because they know it really bothers him. He can tell a guy he's not playing hard without having to raise his voice.

"But that's the kind of guy Rick is. He very seldom says a bad word about anybody, he has a great sense of humor, and he'll ride you in a joking way. I've learned a lot from Rick. I think I'm a better coach today than I was before I joined Rick's staff."

The Blazers annihilated the Dallas Mavericks 113-88 in their first game after Christmas. Portland had a 30-12 rebound advantage at halftime, and then captured the first seven boards of the third quarter.

The Mavericks, who chose a few years back to draft Roy Tarpley, have been paying for the move ever since. In and out of trouble and rehab centers, the talented big man helped drag a once-proud franchise right down to the gutter with him. After this loss, Dallas stood at 12-16 for the season. The Mavericks would win only 10 more games.

It's a tough call in professional sports. Do you go with talent or attitude? Do you take a chance on a player with a checkered past, even though his problems are as well-known as his talent? A lot of teams were wondering that same thing at this point of the season when the Philadelphia 76ers began shopping Charles Barkley around.

Barkley, who didn't have the substance-abuse problems of Tarpley, has had his share of other foibles — from spitting on a young girl at courtside to off-court fistfights. He says whatever happens to cross his mind, and it often turns out to be something offensive. A selfish player who has problems getting along with teammates, he's a reporter's delight and a coach's nightmare.

And it was about this time when rumors were flying that he was headed to Portland. When he told a reporter from *The Oregonian* that he'd love to play for the Trail Blazers, those rumors escalated even more.

Sports-talk radio, which seems to have the ability to create and perpetuate unfounded rumors better than a town with six newspapers, was abuzz with Barkley-to-Portland trades. How about Jerome Kersey, Kevin Duckworth, and Danny Ainge for

Barkley and Hersey Hawkins? How about throwing in Mark Bryant and getting Manute Bol in return?

Certainly the NBA's salary cap prohibited most of the possibilities from ever happening, but talk show hosts usually leave such mysteries for their daily paper to interpret, anyway. And Barkley was available for the right price, no question about that.

"He's out there, I wouldn't be surprised to see him moved in the next couple of weeks," said Bucky Buckwalter, the Blazers' vice-president/basketball operations.

Through a scheduling quirk, the Trail Blazers had to wait a long time to get their first look at the Los Angeles Lakers. The game on December 28 at Los Angeles was the first of the five meetings between the teams and Portland's first look at the Lakers without Magic Johnson.

When Johnson announced on the eve of the season that he had tested positive for the AIDS virus, it sent shock waves through the league. Players reacted as if they'd been suckerpunched below the belt. Newspapers and magazines rushed into print with stories about the sex lives and late-night habits of professional athletes, while the players themselves crossed their hearts and promised to be more careful and discriminate in their behavior.

But by late December, it was fairly obvious that things hadn't changed an awful lot. Even though trainers of professional teams had been handing out condoms to their players for years, many players still admitted they didn't bother using them. And while many players promised to be less prolific, it was still hard to pass up some of the tightly wrapped packages that showed up on their doorsteps so willing to please.

For his part, Johnson continued to work out and be a familiar figure around the Forum. He had promised he would fulfill his Olympic commitment, and by this time was getting thousands of votes for the Western Conference all-star team.

The Lakers were a surprising 17-10 without him, before falling 98-88 to the Trail Blazers. Although he had some shooting problems, Drexler led the way yet again with 22 points, nine rebounds, and eight assists. In the next game, a 129-96 whipping of Miami in Memorial Coliseum, Drexler was even more sensational, getting 14 points, six assists, four rebounds, and two steals in the third quarter.

"He just exploded," Adelman said. "That's what you call turning it on. I think he wanted to rest the fourth period."

Portland's record heading into the new year was 19-10 and, in spite of a lot of early problems, the Trail Blazers still stood just a half-game out of first place in the Pacific Division. And whatever the team accomplished, it was mostly due to Drexler, who just seems to get better every season.

"It was a maturity in Clyde," Adelman would say at season's end. "He was a little more vocal. He did a little more talking about what we had to do. It carried out on the floor. He played at a very consistently high level. He just didn't allow us to lose in a lot of those games."

In the past, there had been times when Drexler had become frustrated by the inconsistent play of his teammates. He was known for barking at other Blazer players on the court, sometimes in a nasty way. But this didn't seem to happen anymore.

"He never really got down on anybody," Adelman said. "He just kept playing hard. He was playing well, and some other guys weren't. There was some frustration there, but it never showed. He kept us above water. We might have been below .500 without him."

Ainge didn't qualify it with a "might have been."

"We'd have had a losing record without him there for awhile," Ainge said. "It was unbelievable. Every game he was playing spectacular basketball, and everybody else was struggling. He was just carrying us. He carried us as much as any player can carry a team through most of the first half of the season."

Kersey, who was now beginning to have to play with pain all the time, admitted later that the team was riding Drexler's coattails.

"Nobody seemed to be in a groove but Clyde," he said. "We weren't taking bad shots. It's just nothing was falling. Guys got to the point where they didn't want to shoot the ball. You saw guys like Danny and Terry passing up shots they usually take. You could see the expression on their face — should I shoot or pass? That's the way I felt, too. When I'm in between, there's no telling. Everybody was pressing, wondering what you have to do to make a shot.

"Nobody else was doing anything, really. And Clyde was at the top of his game. If we were having just one or two others playing three-fourths as well as Clyde was playing, we could have pulled a few games out."

To the players' credit, they recognized very quickly that Drexler was their meal ticket. And they punched that ticket as often as they could.

"I knew I wasn't in a good groove, and I looked to get Clyde the ball," Kersey said. "I think everybody else did. Guys recognized right away."

Drexler's improvement has been remarkable throughout his career. His jump shot was still not a thing of beauty, but it was effective. Instinctive and intelligent, he was as skilled at making plays for others as for himself. He was carrying the team the way Magic, Michael, and Larry did it.

"I've played with Clyde eight years," Kersey said. "He can do almost anything out on the court. His jump shot has come a long ways. He still takes some bad shots at times, like anybody does, but he has that ability to make a bad shot into something good a lot of times.

"How many times have you seen Clyde take a shot and say, 'Oh no, don't shoot that,' and he'll make it? He has so much athletic ability and the game seems to flow to him. Clyde plays his best when somebody makes him angry. Jumping, shooting . . . he might have the most athletic ability of anybody in the league. There are some times I find myself watching him and saying, 'God, I cannot believe he did that.' People around the globe don't see him do that the way they see Michael Jordan. Clyde makes some spectacular plays I don't even think Jordan could duplicate."

Kersey noticed, too, that Drexler suddenly began to accept more responsibility for leading his teammates.

"He spent some time trying to inspire the guys," Kersey said. "And that's something new coming from Clyde. Maybe he's been there mentally, but he'd never really voiced it before. He wasn't boisterous, but he wanted people to play well. We were so tired of the negative press and we wanted to get things done."

Kersey and Drexler got on well now, but it wasn't always that way. Clyde and Kiki Vandeweghe, Kersey's predecessor as the Blazers' starting small forward, were close friends. As Kersey developed and eventually became a threat to win Vandeweghe's job, Clyde seemed to ally himself with Kiki.

"There was never any friction between Clyde and me, per se," Kersey said. "It came more about because he and Kiki were friends. They always hung around together, went to movies, and ate out together on the road. I never was in on that. They were more on the same page. I think Clyde leaned toward Kiki in the (debate) between us."

At times, Jerome felt Clyde was showing favoritism on the court. "There was a little pressure there," he said. "Some nights, if I missed a pass from Clyde, or things weren't going well . . . Clyde might give me a little look or say something. He was the main guy, the superstar, and Kiki was an excellent scorer, and they hooked up on a lot of passes. If the superstar goes to the coach and says you need to get somebody else in there . . . I just had the feeling I had to produce."

Kiki was traded in 1988, and any problems between Clyde and Jerome ran their course. "We've had our short little arguments," Kersey said, "but it never got to a thing where it carried off the court."

Now Drexler and Kersey were leaders on a club that had a lot more going for it than the Drexler/Vandeweghe teams of previous seasons. Things hadn't gone smoothly for the Blazers so far, but a new year was approaching. If the calendar changed overnight, though, the Blazers didn't.

6

"Here's a Chance for a Young Guy to Play, and He Didn't Even Have His Uniform On."

	W	L	Pct.	GB		W	L	Pct.	GB
					1/1/92 NBA Pacific Division Standings				
Golden State	19	8	.704	-	Seattle	15	13	.536	$4^1/_2$
Phoenix	19	10	.655	1	LA Clippers	16	15	.516	5
Portland	19	10	.655	1	Sacramento	8	20	.286	$11^1/_2$
LA Lakers	17	12	.586	3					

The Blazers rang in the new year with an old friend, Darell Garretson, in Salt Lake City, of all places. The Blazers' least favorite referee is a unanimous choice, and it's not Garretson. Jake O'Donnell voodoo dolls would sell superbly within the Blazer organization, and Buck Williams would probably buy out the entire supply himself. Buck traces his problems with Jake back to his days in New Jersey, though he can't remember a single incident. "I think he gave me a technical and we had words, and we've had problems since then," Williams said.

The Blazers feel O'Donnell has been out to get them on several occasions, and by the looks of it, they're right, especially in Memorial Coliseum. But they're not alone. Jake loves making the tough call against the home team, and hearing the boos and catcalls rain down on him. His ego loves the attention, just like that of a pro-wrestling bad guy.

During this season, O'Donnell had taken to talking to Williams early in a game, cautioning him against excessive use of hands and body on defense, and Buck had taken exception to what he considers condescending instruction. It had resulted in technicals and a war of words, and on one occasion, Jake telling Buck, "Don't look at me like that."

There is no official in the league who comes across as more pompous than O'Donnell, but some would vote for Garretson, the veteran supervisor of officials. And in the Blazers' first game of the new year, Darell played a role in a 107-103 Utah victory that left the Blazers with a cyanide-like aftertaste.

Salt Lake is always a difficult place for the Blazers to play, and the Jazz were working on a win streak in their brand new Delta Center that would reach 17 games. The Blazers had played well and were in position to win, but it was one of those nights where seemingly every close call made by the officiating crew of Garretson, Lee Jones, and Gary Benson went against them.

Portland led 101-100 inside a minute to go, when Terry Porter reached out for what appeared to be a clean pick of the ball from John Stockton. Porter tapped the ball out toward midcourt, and Stockton, anticipating Porter coming up with the ball and going the other way for an easy layup, appeared to foul Porter in the scramble for the ball.

But Benson whistled a foul on Porter — his sixth — and Stockton went to the line to make one of two foul shots as the Blazers howled their protests in disbelief. Instead of being ahead 103-100, Portland found itself tied at 101-101 without its veteran point guard in the game. Utah gathered itself to steal the very important victory.

Stockton thought the foul was called on the original pick by Porter. "If they'd called me for a foul (on the scramble) for the loose ball, I'd have agreed with that," he said.

But the timing of Benson's whistle indicated the call was made on the scramble, not before that. It was important to find out, and a pool reporter made his way with Jazz public relations director Kim Turner to the officials' dressing room after the game to find out. NBA rules mandate that one member of the media can serve as pool reporter to conduct a post-game interview of an official, then distribute any response to other writers who so desire.

Benson — a medium-to-lower-level official who is a nice guy and cooperative with the press — was requested for a question, but it was Garretson who came out of the dressing room to ask what the question was about. "The timing of the call on Porter," he was told. Garretson said he'd go in to ask Benson about it and return. The reporter asked if he could talk to Benson, since he was the one who made the call. Garretson said he, as lead official, would speak for the crew. Why? "Because I said so." When the reporter voiced his opinion that that was a ludicrous reason, Garretson ordered security to remove the reporter.

Later, Garretson confided he was concerned with what Benson might say. "Some of our younger officials aren't as comfortable in interview situations," he said. "That's why we have lead officials take care of any questions."

It's a rule promulgated by Garretson, but it's not on the books for the officials. And many of the veterans, such as Mike Mathis, Paul Mihalak, Dick Bavetta, and Joey Crawford, are glad to answer questions from reporters about calls that play key roles in outcomes of games. They realize by explaining their actions, they are allowing reporters, fans, and even players and coaches to understand their side of things.

The Benson call wasn't the only one for which the Blazers would have liked an explanation. Jones nailed Rick Adelman with a technical with Portland ahead 95-91 and 5:46 remaining. Adelman jumped in the air in disgust over a Jones call, but didn't say anything. Seconds later, Jones, who had his back turned to the coach, signaled the "T."

Jones told Adelman he got the T for stomping his feet, which the referee saw as the culmination of the coach riding him much of the game. "I reacted to the call and turned and walked the other way," Adelman said. That will work with most officials, who figure the coach is blowing off steam, but not trying to show him up. "I wasn't even looking at him. You just don't give out a T that late in a close game without being pretty certain."

Porter and Garretson also had an interesting exchange in the first half. Porter, out of the game at the time, came off the bench to direct a few words toward Garretson, who was standing near the Blazers' baseline. Garretson looked at Adelman and said, "Rick, tell Mr. Porter he's not captain."

Geoff Petrie was concerned enough to call Rod Thorn, the NBA's vice president/operations, the next day with a complaint. Thorn, who said he would look into the matter, had already been briefed by Garretson on it. Thorn, an affable enough guy and generally cooperative with the media, works with Garretson in instructing, supervising, and rating the 53 officials who call NBA games each season. Garretson, meanwhile, works a near-normal schedule refereeing himself. It's a direct conflict of interest, since Garretson is involved in the grading and advancement of men he is working alongside of, as well as himself. But Garretson insists there is no conflict of interest, and Thorn has no problem with it, either. Many of the NBA's officials would love to see Garretson removed from his position of authority, but the status quo is likely to remain indefinitely.

Thorn oversees a variety of things for the NBA, including player fines and injury-list regulations. Over the previous few seasons, some teams had been taking advantage of lax enforcement of policy regarding the injury list. A year earlier, Phoenix had found itself with 14 or 15 healthy players, and wound up juggling two or three players on and off the injury list with questionable injuries.

This year, the Blazers had 14 players they wanted to retain. That included off guard Lamont Strothers, the second-round draft choice they obtained from Golden State in a deal that gave the Warriors two future second-round picks, and point guard Ennis Whatley, still on the injured list. So there were a few winks among those in the media when on the day before the final roster cutdowns were to be announced in late October, Strothers came down with a back injury that placed him on the injured list to start the season.

Strothers was the odd man out and, without the injury, would have found himself on the waiver wire. The suspicion among cynics was somebody within the Blazer organization had suggested to the rookie from tiny NCAA Division III Christopher Newport (Virginia) College it would be a wise move to get hurt quick. Petrie swore that wasn't the case, and that he'd warned his management staff against it.

Long after the season ended, Strothers was still claiming he'd really been hurt, that he'd injured it during the final preseason game against Indiana.

"Some guy took a cheap shot at me and hit me in the back," he recalled. "It didn't really bother me at the time, but by the next day back in Portland it was killing me. I could hardly walk. I called Mike (Shimensky) and he told me to come in for treatment in the morning."

So Strothers was out with some sort of back spasms that he told reporters were really painful. Not painful enough, though, to keep him from shooting for a half-hour before practice two days after going on the injured list. Nor painful enough to keep him from playing plenty of basketball in the ensuing weeks, at

Riverplace Athletic Club, and Lewis & Clark, and any place that could offer him some competition.

"Everyone questioned I was hurt and thought I was able to play," he said much later, "but no one was inside my body but me. And I was hurt."

Strothers returned to full practice duty on November 25, and it seemed likely that somewhere down the line, a Blazer would suffer an injury serious enough to place him on the injury list, and Strothers would wind up getting activated. It never happened. The Blazers have been very fortunate to avoid major injuries the past three seasons — partly because Adelman often gives days off during the season and is a master at keeping regulars' minutes down — and Strothers was still on the injured list into the new year.

On December 11, Thorn told *The Oregonian*: "We give clubs a chance to work a guy out and get him in shape. It usually takes two or three weeks for a player to get there. I would say they'll have to make a decision within a few days, or maybe another week."

Another week went by, and another, and another, and it became obvious the Blazers were putting off a decision as long as they could. The league's guaranteed-contract day is January 10, after which the contract of every player a team carries must be paid in full for the season. The Blazers intended to wait until just before that date in case an injury should pop up, and Thorn wasn't about to play hardball, just as he wasn't with other teams that had abused the rule in the past.

"They gave up a couple of second-round picks to get him," Thorn said on January 3. "I'm sure they want to take as much time to evaluate him as possible. We're almost down to the cutoff date. If they say next week, that's fine with me. I have no problem with that."

The problem with that was Strothers wasn't injured any-more — if, indeed, he ever had been — and had been practicing for more than five weeks, and if the Blazers hadn't evaluated him by now, they never would be ready to. The decision for the final roster spot, it appeared, would be between keeping Strothers and reserve point guard Danny Young. Strothers had potential, but Adelman, who felt Young was dependable and useful, thought Strothers to be a project at best.

In the meantime, Portland poleaxed Philadelphia 115-102 at home, and there were several sidelights worth remembering. Duckworth went 2-0 in individual confrontations with Charles Barkley, first throwing down a dunk over Barkley on a fast break, then blocking the Round Mound of Rebound as he tried to even the score on the next trip upcourt. Barkley thought he blocked the Duckworth shot into the basket and had been fouled by Duck on his stuff attempt. Duck laughed when told of the comments of Barkley, who had earlier bounced an uncontested dunk try off the back rim and all the way out to midcourt.

"I like Charles as a person, and the way he plays the game, but he has a big ego," Duckworth said. "Maybe it's hard for him to accept things sometimes. I don't take that personally."

Then Manute Bol didn't like a foul call, and tossed the ball toward Alaa Abdelnaby at the Blazers bench. Abdelnaby caught it and threw it back, catching Bol on the back of the neck. Bol had a few choice words for his opponent, whom he called "a damn Egyptian," but it ended there. "We almost needed a Middle East/African summit there," Alaa laughed afterward. "He's cool. He's a character. That's part of his persona, and that's fine."

On January 6, Petrie, Buckwalter, and Brad Greenberg — the club's director of player personnel— met with Adelman and assistants John Wetzel and Jack Schalow after practice to make their final roster decision. It was a stormy four-hour affair. The following day, the Blazers announced they were going to keep Strothers and place Young on waivers. The personnel side — Greenberg and Buckwalter — had a vested interest in Strothers, felt he showed promise, and didn't want to let him go. The coaches wanted to keep the 29-year-old Young, who was not playing on a regular basis, but was still of value.

Young had been the backup to Porter the previous two seasons and had turned in solid, if unspectacular, play. Young was a good position defender, a player prone to few errors, and he could hit the 3. Since the first six games, when he was one for 13 from the field, he was now 15 for 28, and had committed only four turnovers in 75 minutes. Robert Pack had moved in front of him early in the season, but Pack's game had plateaued. He was turning the ball over more, and his minutes were dropping. As for a fifth guard, Adelman would go to Young in a pinch, but he wouldn't use an untested rookie such as Strothers.

Petrie was somewhere in the middle on the Strothers/ Young controversy, and eventually became convinced it made sense to keep Strothers. Adelman was a hard sell. Danny Ainge was struggling, and Adelman had pretty much decided he needed to get Ainge going by playing him more at the point. Still, in the event of an injury to one of the first three guards, Rick wasn't comfortable using Pack for big minutes. Ennis Whatley, 29, and boasting experience with a half-dozen NBA clubs, was running and ready to return to practice, and the Blazer coaches liked him and wanted to give him a chance. But he was with them for such a short time before he hurt his ankle they weren't sure how much he could help them.

Young was a nice safeguard. He was also a popular member of the team who fit in and wouldn't complain no matter how limited his role might be. And now he was gone.

Adelman was furious. He could hardly contain himself while talking to a reporter before practice. "I feel really badly for Danny," he said. "He has made a valuable contribution to our success the past three years, more than a lot of people realize. That's one of the bad things about this business, that a person of the quality of Danny Young has to be let go."

Some of the veteran players didn't agree with the decision. "I think it's a mistake," said Ainge, who later was admonished by Greenberg for the way he phrased his criticism. "I understand why Portland wants to keep Lamont . . . but Danny Young is a quiet guy who, because of his personality, is left out a lot. He hasn't gotten much of a chance to play this year. There has been a tendency to evaluate people on what they can't do, instead of what they can."

Added Porter: "I hope I don't go down now (with an injury). Pack is going to be a good player, but to put him out there for long minutes on an elite team that has a chance to go to the Finals . . . I don't know how he'd handle the pressure. And I'm sure Danny Ainge would be the first to tell you it'd be hard for him to play the point 30 minutes a night."

"There were some risks in doing it," Petrie said after the season. "And emotions did run high in making the decision. Let's face it, you're like family, especially when you're winning like we're winning. Danny had been here and had friends on the team. It's tough to see someone like that go. There's a closeness there, a sense of loss."

After the season, Adelman reflected on the decision this way: "Danny was a victim of circumstances. We had too many players, and Danny had not shot well and I could see the reasoning why you'd want to go with younger players like Pack and Strothers. It was like a Catch 22. I liked Danny, he was a positive influence, and he still could have helped us later in the year. I wanted to keep him, but it wasn't worth fighting about at the time. I fought for as long as I could, but I saw the reasoning."

Greenberg looked back at the situation after the season, and said he didn't consider there to be any serious conflict between he and Bucky and the coaches over the Young/Strothers debate.

"The biggest reason we came to the decision we came to," Greenberg said, "was because we saw potential in Lamont and, at that point in the season, Pack was playing the backup point guard minutes behind Terry. It didn't concern me. The year before Danny hadn't played very much in the playoffs.

"I don't think there were any hard feelings over the decision. It was discussed, everybody had a chance to voice his opinion, and we came to an agreement. The only hard feelings were the ones I read about in the paper. I didn't see it as a big issue at all. It became a big issue — partly because of what came out in the paper — but we were talking about a player who was shooting in the mid to high 30s and was not playing compared with someone who was going to get better and was only a rookie.

"It became a big thing, but I couldn't understand it. I guess it was loyalty to a player who had been around. Danny is a really good guy and was good team people. But at that time we had a rookie playing ahead of him at the point, and we had another point guard (Whatley) on the injured list we weren't sure about. It wasn't that hard a decision."

Adelman considered it one of the hardest decisions he'd made as a head coach. It was clear that the Blazer coaches had some hard feelings against Buckwalter and Greenberg. A conflict between a player personnel department and coaching staff isn't unusual in the NBA, because the personnel guys are always looking toward the future, and the coaches are always playing for now.

Most of the players understood Greenberg and Buckwalter were doing their jobs, knew they were just trying to make the team's talent base better, and were friendly with them. But at least one kept his distance.

"I know Brad, but I don't know Brad," Duckworth said. "How do you become a friend with a guy who is going out recruiting people to take your place? Nothing against Brad, but I don't want to be nobody's friend like that."

The rift in the front office went beyond the Young decision. The coaches didn't have a lot of respect for Buckwalter, whom they didn't dislike, but regarded as lazy in many of the ways he went about his job. Bucky had been with the Blazers since 1979 and had served in nearly every capacity, from scout to assistant coach to his current position as vice president/basketball operations. He had at one time negotiated contracts, and was one of the first NBA people to look overseas for talent, an endeavor that produced Drazen Petrovic for the Blazers.

Bucky is an unusual study, from his friendly grin and always-deep tan and flashy array of jewelry, to his interests in music and drama and art and travel, to the two movies he played bit parts in ("Pillars of the Sky," a Western, and "McQ," a John Wayne detective thriller), to his days with the Utah Stars of the ABA and his wooing of 17-year-old Moses Malone with the first lucrative underage pro basketball contract. The label Renaissance Man isn't altogether inappropriate. At 57, the La Grande, Oregon, native was beginning the final stages of his career, and his duties were primarily to work with Petrie on trade possibilities and to evaluate college talent with Greenberg and scout Keith Drum.

The Sporting News named Buckwalter as its NBA Executive of the Year following the 1990-91 season, but the coaches privately guffawed at the award. Bucky had good instincts when evaluating talent, and espoused the quick, athletic-type prospects for their "upside" over the more cerebral types with perhaps less potential. He had done some good things for the organization during his career. But he wasn't willing to dig as hard as some of the younger, more aggressive peers that were working for other clubs in the league. There were times when Buckwalter's whereabouts during "scouting trips" were known only to him. His contributions to the club's computer scouting database were minimal.

There were times when Greenberg got on Adelman's nerves. A thorough scout and a hard worker, Greenberg was in his second season as director of player personnel. He had a good handle on college talent — his area of specialization — and had made some good recommendations on players, including Cliff Robinson, who had turned out to be a plum at the No. 36 pick in the 1989 draft. But he was aggressive in pushing for some of the players he had a hand in bringing to the team, and made some recommendations that Adelman had a hard time accepting. He liked being around the players and hanging around the dressing room, which sometimes annoyed Adelman. Rick liked people who gave him a certain space at times before and after games, and Brad never seemed to pick up on that.

On top of that, one of Greenberg's close friends is agent Warren LeGarie — who even represented Greenberg during his initial contract negotiations with the Trail Blazers. LeGarie is the man who represented Petrovic and, in that capacity, alienated Adelman enormously.

During the 1990-91 season, Adelman had acquired Ainge and was using him extensively, leaving Petrovic on the bench. Adelman felt that LeGarie then stepped in and began manipulating Petrovic, resulting in the latter's threat at one time to return to his home in Yugoslavia if he didn't receive more playing time. The player-coach relationship — which had been a solid one — began to disintegrate, and Adelman blamed LeGarie, who was openly critical of Adelman in the press.

That certainly didn't endear Greenberg — who often touted LeGarie players — to Adelman.

It was interesting that the only biographical sketch in the Blazers' media guide not prepared by the team's public-relations department was Greenberg's, written by his wife, Fran, a former *Hoop Magazine* columnist, and one-time director of public relations for the CBA. It was done at Brad's request.

Greenberg, 37, had plenty of drive and ambition. More than anything, Greenberg aspired to higher positions, perhaps to the very top of the basketball side of the Blazer organization. It made for some uneasy feelings from the people working around him.

Compounding the problem for Adelman was his lack of success at landing a contract extension. After filling out the 1988-89 season as successor to Mike Schuler following Schuler's firing, Adelman was given a one-year contract by owner Paul Allen. Midway through the next season, Adelman signed a three-year extension that carried him through the 1992-93 campaign. After taking the Blazers to at least the Western Conference finals in both his full seasons, Adelman wanted the security of another extension and, most important, wanted to avoid going into the final year of his contract as a lame-duck coach.

Adelman's lawyer, brother-in-law Gary Fournier, went to Allen and vice-chairman Bert Kolde prior to the 1991-92 season and was told nothing would be done until after the season. In other words, he had to prove himself one more time before being rewarded with a new contract.

"That's exactly what we were doing," said a member of the Blazers' front office. "It was ridiculous — Rick was going to wind up in a better bargaining position than he was before. That's exactly what happened."

"If you're going to come in and totally restructure this team and build for three or four years, and the coach is sitting there with a one-year contract, it puts a lot of pressure on him," Petrie said. "If you don't win, even when you're rebuilding, your job security can be in jeopardy. I made certain recommendations I felt would be in the best interests of the team. Rick's contract was one of those, and the decision was we would wait until the season was over."

It bothered Adelman for several reasons. One, he felt he had already proved himself as a competent coach, one whom the players had affection and a great deal of respect for. Two, he was making an average of about $300,000 a year, while higher-profile names such as Larry Brown, Chuck Daly and Pat Riley were commanding salaries in the seven-figure range. Third, the Blazer personnel people were pushing players who might be able to help in the future over those who might be able to help today. And to the coaches, there was pressure to win today, or there might be no tomorrow.

"I don't resent anybody having an opinion on what they think should be best for the team," Adelman said later. "I resent something somebody is doing to try to self-promote, because of a decision they made a year ago (in the draft). The coach is the guy who ultimately has to deal with the people on the team. I do think they wanted to keep younger people. I don't blame them for that. We're a veteran team. We were caught in a situation where you're trying to win a championship, and you're trying to bring along younger players. You'd like to do both, but sometimes that's not easy to do.

"Danny Young was a known quantity and the other people weren't. Ennis Whatley was still on the injured list, and I didn't know if he was going to hold up. There were a lot of ifs there. Geoff and I had talked that through and had gone around and around on it. That was one instance where we had some differences of opinion. It was a very tough call for me. I finally said, 'Yeah, let's do it,' but I had an uneasy feeling about it."

"These kind of things happen in a lot of organizations," Schalow said. "Personnel people look at potential, the coaches look at what the player can do for your team right now. You think, 'We can't worry about three years from now. We have to take advantage of where we are right now. Let's win a championship right now and take care of the future later.' When you're so close, really . . . but once everything was aired, the guy who did a great job was Geoff. You don't feel he's on one side or another. We always felt he was looking out for us."

"I have to balance both sides, or try to," Petrie said. "Everybody has a say to some extent. The more people you have in the decision-making process, the less chance everybody is going to agree all the time."

With Young gone and, by the weekend, in the Los Angeles' Clippers fold, the Blazers mopped up on Orlando 104-89 at home to go 21-11. The game's most interesting twist came in the second quarter when Adelman called Alaa Abdelnaby's number from the bench. Abdelnaby began peeling his warmups off as he headed for the scorer's table when he realized he'd forgotten something — his uniform top.

At least it wasn't his shorts.

Abdelnaby raced to the dressing room to retrieve his top and returned moments later with an embarrassed smile as the crowd, finally clued into what had happened, tittered at the scene. By that time, Adelman had already called upon Wayne Cooper to report. Abdelnaby spent the rest of the night on the bench.

Alaa said when he came back from early shooting before the game he noticed his game top had a "cut under the armpit." He said he beckoned Roger Sabrowski, the team's equipment manager.

"I yelled to Roger, 'Do you have another jersey, or can you do something with this one?' " Alaa said. "I gave it to him and threw a t-shirt on to stay warm. Then somebody yells, '18 minutes (until tipoff), we got to get out on the floor,' so I put a sweat top on and went out to the floor. Then when I went to go into the game, I had my t-shirt on instead of my jersey."

Sabrowski tells a different story.

"That didn't happen," he said. "There was no jersey given to me. I would have remembered that. If there was a cut on it or something, I never saw it and he never told me. It's never been fixed.

"Alaa had his t-shirt on for (early) shooting, then came back into the dressing room. Then he got ready to go back out and got to talking and forgot he didn't have his jersey. I ran in to get it with him (during the game) and it was hanging right there in his locker."

After Abdelnaby returned to the bench, his teammates ribbed him pretty good, and Alaa laughed along with them. That annoyed Adelman. It was one of the rare instances where he let a player's actions get under his skin in a public forum. A little contrition would have gone a long way in Adelman's mind.

"I couldn't understand it," Adelman said. "Here's a chance for a young guy to play, and he doesn't have his uniform on. It should have been more embarrassing for him. I would have reacted different had it happened to me. I didn't think it was something he should have joked around about."

"What could I do?" Alaa said. "I laughed about it. That's the only way you can look at it."

The Blazers hit the road for a four-game trip that began at Detroit. "I'm looking forward to this trip," Ainge said. "Very seldom do you look forward to a challenging trip like this, but I am. I think we're ready for it. A month ago, I couldn't have said that. We'd have been in serious trouble going into a trip like this. We have a lot of improvement to make in certain areas, but generally, we've been playing real well."

The Blazers bombed in an 86-81 loss to the Pistons. They had another ridiculously inept second quarter, sinking four of 20 shots from the floor to fall behind 46-31 at the half. Somehow the

Pistons managed to win on a night when their two authentic offensive weapons, Isiah Thomas, and Joe Dumars, combined for seven-for-30 shooting.

The Blazers charged back, and when Drexler buried a 3-pointer, it was 82-79 Detroit with 36.2 seconds to go. Then, with Adelman screaming "Don't foul!" to his players, Clyde had brainlock, fouling Dumars with nine seconds on the shot clock, and 21.7 seconds on the game clock. "My fault," Adelman said afterward. "It was miscommunication." He was merely trying to take the rap. It had clearly been Drexler's blunder. It was only Portland's fourth foul of the period, but it meant the Pistons could run out the clock. Dumars then made a pair of foul shots when the Blazers had to foul and it was over.

The bench rose up and keyed a 115-93 win at Charlotte the following night, with Ainge playing the lead role with a season-high 23 points. It was a long time coming for Ainge, who came into the game shooting .398 from the field. "Danny got it going tonight," Adelman said. "He did a good job taking it to the basket, and he played a really complete game. He's been struggling; I hope this will get him going."

Ainge had come to Portland amid an avalanche of hoopla in the summer prior to the 1990-91 season. A native of Eugene, just 100 miles south of Portland, and arguably the finest all-around high school athlete in the state's history — he was all-state in football, basketball, and baseball two years in a row — Ainge carried with him nine years of NBA experience, including 7 1/2 years in Boston that had produced two championship rings. That impressed the Blazer braintrust, which felt his drive and leadership and knowledge of what it takes to win would be a positive influence on his teammates.

The Blazers pulled off a sweet deal with Sacramento, landing Ainge for little-used guard Byron Irvin, two draft choices, and cash. And Ainge was ecstatic to be back in his home state, playing for the team he rooted for so fervently as a kid.

Ainge was the toast of the town through the first half of the 1990-91 season, bombing in 3s with incredible frequency, backing up Drexler and filling in for Porter at the point on occasion, and making the Blazer front office look like a billion bucks. But his shooting fell off late in the regular season, and Adelman appeared to lose some confidence in him. Ainge's minutes dropped in the playoffs, and he wound up averaging eight points and 17 minutes in 16 postseason games.

Ainge went through his contract dispute and was not a happy camper to open the 1991-92 season, and his shooting didn't make a lot of people happy, either, through the first 33 games. Ainge, a starter through much of his career, had adjusted well to the bench in his first season, but now seemed to be struggling with a drop in minutes. Adelman insisted Ainge's playing time had lessened because his performance had dipped, but Ainge wondered if it might be the other way around, that he wasn't playing as well because he wasn't on the court as often to find his groove.

"One of the hard things for me is playing behind Clyde," Ainge said. "No matter how well I play, I'm still out of the game. I can play great for seven minutes, and Rick has to get Clyde back into the game. I understand that. I don't take it personally. I'd get Clyde back in, too, if I were Rick. But sometimes I thought maybe he should have taken out Jerome or taken out Buck, and used Jerome at power forward a little more."

The previous week after a practice session at Lewis & Clark, Adelman sat down with Ainge for a private talk. They talked about Ainge's role and how Adelman planned to expand on it. The coach told the player he hadn't lost confidence in him and was counting on him to come up big the rest of the season and in the playoffs.

"It was healthy to know what he was thinking," Ainge said. "Yeah, I do think he had lost confidence in me at the end of (the previous) season. I really believe that was unjustified. But I appreciated the talk, and I think it helped. I think I was trying to do too much. I have a tendency to worry too much about things I have no control over."

All along, Ainge remained a big supporter of Adelman. "I really believe Rick does an incredible job," he said after the season had ended and he was on his way to Phoenix. "Rick's biggest strength as a coach is in dealing with the players and in communicating with them in a way that is honest, yet he doesn't make you promises he can't keep. At the same time, he tells you the things that are your weaknesses. He does a good job of dealing with personalities, keeping guys motivated, keeping guys happy."

And if Ainge was a little more vocal than the average Blazer about his feelings, he also did a little more to try to get the best out of his teammates than the average Blazer, too. Tips from Ainge and Walter Davis helped Williams post a career-high in free-throw percentage during the 1991-92 season. Ainge worked with Robinson, a notoriously poor foul shooter, and helped him make a remarkable 31 of 32 attempts midway through the season. He was one of the more vocal cheerleaders off the bench, often imploring his teammates to play hard and reminding them of their assignments. He was good for the young players on the team, such as Abdelnaby and Pack, who willingly accepted his advice. The intangibles Ainge provided through his leadership and intuitive play on the court were invaluable.

Strothers made his NBA debut in the Charlotte game, playing the final four minutes as his college coach, C.J. Woollum, looked on. The first time he got the ball, Strothers drove the lane for what appeared was going to be a wide-open dunk attempt, but he panicked, and the ball slipped out of his hands. He did swish a jump shot, though, to get his first pro points. If Strothers seemed a bit wide-eyed, it wasn't surprising. Until this season, the Suffolk, Virginia, native had never seen an NBA game in person. "I'm a country boy," he said, smiling. "The closest NBA city is Washington, and that's three hours away."

The Blazers followed with their best road performance of the season, a 121-114 win over Cleveland. The Cavaliers had emerged as an outstanding team in the East, entering the game with a 24-9 record, a 15-1 mark at home and an 11-game win streak. No. 12 would have meant a franchise record, and the Cavs and their fans wanted it badly.

Nuh uh, said the Blazers. Clyde was the man, leading the way with 34 points, knocking down 11 of 18 from the field and 12 of 13 from the line. And Portland's half-court offense was on, drumming up a 56-26 advantage in points in the paint. "Our biggest win of the year by far," Adelman chortled afterward. "Beating a team on the road playing as well as they have been … it was really something. Even if we'd lost, I'd have been happy with the way we played. It reminded me of the way we played so often last year."

Portland ended its trip 3-1 by downing the New York Knicks 96-91 in Madison Square Garden. The Knicks, another one of the East's powers, led through much of the early going, but the Blazers used a 25-6 surge late in the game to take charge. Porter came up big with 18 of his 22 points in the second half, and contributed the biggest play of the game. With Portland ahead 88-83 and little more than a minute to play, Porter had the ball in a semi-break situation against two New York defenders. He slowed up as if to set up the offense, and the two Knicks relaxed for a minute. Then Porter knifed to the basket for a layup that sealed the Knicks' doom.

"I was going to play time off the clock," said Porter, "but then I saw an opening and took off. I think I caught them off guard."

The victory improved the Blazers' record to 24-12, leaving them percentage points behind Golden State in the tight division race. Indeed, as the teams headed toward the All-Star break, the heat was on in more ways than one.

7

"Chambers was Holding Me Like He Was My Woman, and He's Not My Type."

1/16/92 NBA Pacific Division Standings								
	W	L	Pct.	GB		W	L	Pct.	GB
Golden State	22	10	.688	-	LA Clippers	19	19	.500	6
Portland	24	12	.667	-	Seattle	18	18	.500	6
Phoenix	24	13	.649	½	Sacramento	10	26	.278	14
LA Lakers	22	14	.611	2					

Trade winds were swirling again. One Philadelphia report had the 76ers prepared to send Charles Barkley to the Blazers for Kevin Duckworth, Jerome Kersey and two draft choices. TV versions had Portland considering a deal that would give up Duckworth, Kersey, and Danny Ainge for Barkley — one reporting the deal was imminent. *USA Today* said the Blazers had made an offer for Minnesota point guard Pooh Richardson.

The Blazers had won nine of their last 11, and 11 of their last 14, and were finally putting some bloom to their roses. *Sports Illustrated's* Hank Hersch was in town to do a piece on them. The players were showing the old confidence that had made them the best team in the NBA through much of the previous season. And now, all these reports had them busting up the nucleus of the team. It didn't make sense. It wasn't going to help the psyche of the players any to hear such rumors, and management wanted to quash any kind of trade talk.

"None of that is true," Geoff Petrie said. "We are making calls all around the league — not just to Philadelphia — as a course of normal business . . . But as far as Barkley is concerned, nothing is happening, and we have not made an offer for Pooh Richardson."

The truth was, the Blazers were intrigued by the possibilities of landing Barkley, but it was just too difficult. First of all, they were over the salary cap and could not aggregate salaries unless they could get under it. That could have been done with the trade of a player for a draft choice or the reworking of a player's contract, with added reimbursement to come later in his career. But while Petrie admired Barkley's skills and thought there was a good chance he could fit in with the Blazers, he was concerned that Barkley's propensity for finding trouble might be a negative influence.

The players heard the rumors, too, and were able to joke about it. "At least I'll still be with Jerome," Duckworth said. "Maybe we can get an apartment together in Philadelphia."

Kersey admitted the rumors worried him, but just a little. "It's not like you can totally put it out of your mind, but you can't let it be a total distraction. I don't really think there's anything to it." He was right.

Portland mopped up on Charlotte for the second time in a week, this time thrashing the Hornets 120-104 in the coliseum, with a 65-42 backboard pounding pretty much telling the story. The Hornets were without injured front-line players J.R. Reid and Mike Gminski, and it was strictly men against boys.

"They manhandled us inside," Charlotte coach Allan Bristow said. "We're not strong enough to handle them. They're big and physical and have great guards."

Clyde Drexler had another of his seemingly endless string of great nights with 25 points — 14 in the first quarter — to go with six rebounds and 11 assists. But the man Bristow wanted to talk about afterward was Buck Williams, who collected 14 points and a season-high 15 rebounds and did a defensive number on touted Charlotte rookie Larry Johnson for the second straight time. Johnson wound up with 12 points and nine rebounds.

"Buck is the reason they're a great team," Bristow said. "In my view, he's their most valuable player. It all starts with him. He comes out and rebounds, plays great defense, draws the toughest assignments . . . he sets the tone. I'd say he is Dennis Rodman, plus much more. He does the intangible things and he's probably the best defensive player in the league night in and night out."

Drexler was Portland's most valuable player beyond a shadow of a doubt, but Bristow had a point, particularly about Williams' defense. He wasn't a great "help" defender within the team context, but he was terrific at taking on a player one-on-one and making him earn everything he got. And his assignments were rugged every night out — Larry Johnson, Karl Malone, Charles Barkley, Horace Grant, A.C. Green, Shawn Kemp, Terry Cummings, Danny Manning, Wayman Tisdale, Tom Chambers, and on and on.

Buck brought a toughness with him that the Blazers had previously lacked, when he came to Portland prior to the 1989-90 season from New Jersey. After eight years, he had grown tired of toiling for one of the league's consistently weak franchises. The Blazers gave up oft-injured Sam Bowie — the same Sam Bowie they had chosen instead of Michael Jordan in that ill-fated 1984 draft — and a first-round pick for Williams and considered it one of the best trades in franchise history. Buck's rebounding, defense and determination were integral parts of the Blazers' winning formula, and his work ethic rubbed off on his younger teammates.

Williams was one of those players willing to sacrifice personal glory — read, points — to help his team win, and selection to the All-Defensive Team two years running was a fitting tribute.

The Blazers headed for Phoenix for an important date with the Suns, but football was on the mind of Cliff Robinson. The Buffalo native grew up idolizing his heroes on the Bills — he was actually a fine quarterback before giving up the sport for basketball—and was thrilled his team was in the Super Bowl against Washington. The defending champion Redskins were solid seven-point favorites, but during practice in Phoenix, Cliff was taking on any and all comers with even-up bets. Kersey and Ainge got in on the action, along with Geoff Petrie at $100 a pop. Even Bill Schonely shook hands on a $50 wager, no small change for a man of Schonely's reputed conservative financial approach.

"Everybody is taking Washington, but they forget the Bills went to the Super Bowl last year," said Robinson, who picked Buffalo to be the winner by a 27-21 count.

"The guy is blinded by his loyalty to the Bills," kidded Ainge. "Cliff obviously doesn't know much about football. He has about as much credibility as Jimmy the Greek."

Final tally: Washington 37, Buffalo 24. Give Cliff credit: He paid up promptly and made only a few excuses for his beloved Bills.

Rick Adelman wanted to win the Phoenix game, and not only because it was against a key Pacific Division rival that had handed the Blazers their heads in Portland in the second game of the year. The coach with the best record in each conference through a certain date of the season got to coach in the All-Star Game, and that date was coming up in a week. Portland had the best record in the NBA through the previous season, and Adelman very much enjoyed his experience coaching the West team.

It had been a chance to get to know players such as Magic Johnson, James Worthy, Karl Malone, Chris Mullin, and John Stockton on a personal level, a rare opportunity for a person as low-key and unpretentious as Adelman. He was also able to bring his entire family to Charlotte for the game, along with his assistants, Jack Schalow and John Wetzel. Coincidentally, trainers are selected on a rotating basis, and it happened to be Mike Shimensky's year. Drexler, Duckworth, and Terry Porter were chosen as players, and Ainge flew back to take part in the 3-point shooting contest, so it was one big, happy Blazer family there to enjoy All-Star Weekend.

It was particularly fun for Adelman to have Schalow, Wetzel, and Shimensky along. Adelman had been an extremely loyal assistant to both Jack Ramsay and Mike Schuler before taking over the head-coaching reins and believed it was always important to support the head man. In many ways, Wetzel and Schalow were the same type of assistants as Adelman had been, and if there were times when they didn't agree with their boss — those times weren't often — it didn't go outside the coaches' office. They genuinely liked and respected Adelman, and the chemistry between the three was about as good as it can get within a coaching staff. Wetzel, who had served one season as head coach of the Phoenix Suns, had aspirations to be a head coach again, but he believed in Adelman, and in no way was after Adelman's job.

Shimensky was true-blue loyal to Adelman, too, and was guarded and uptight about outsiders invading the private circle of the Blazer "family." But he also had a fun sense of humor and was well-liked by the media covering the team. A good rapport with the trainer was important, because Shimensky was the intermediary on much information regarding practice and travel schedules.

Adelman thought it would be fun to be All-Star coach again, but he hadn't made it a crusade like Golden State's Don Nelson, who had never participated in an All-Star Game in 30 years as a player and coach. With two weeks to go before the January 26 cutoff date, Nelson began to chart the schedules of Portland and Phoenix, trying to figure out which team had the best chance to hit that date with the best record.

NBC came up a winner in the Phoenix-Portland game, even if the Blazers didn't. Chambers, Dan Majerle, and Jeff Hornacek came through with tremendous performances, as the Suns took care of the Blazers 132-128 in an overtime thriller.

The Blazers played hard and played well, and normally under those conditions they win. The Suns had just a little bit more, though, pulling a half-game ahead of Portland and within a half-game of Golden State in the tight division race. "What a great game," said Phoenix coach Cotton Fitzsimmons, positively busting the buttons on his sports coat as he entertained the media following the game. "It was tough for either team to lose. I don't think anybody watching on TV got cheated. I don't think anybody in this building got cheated."

Fitzsimmons was on the Blazers' hit list. Earlier in the season, he had been quoted as saying: "We aren't like Portland, who can just go out and overwhelm you with athletic ability. We're a bunch of Hornaceks. We have to overachieve to win."

Cotton held great admiration for the Blazers, and it was entirely possible he meant what he said only as a compliment. The implication in the comment, though, was the Blazers were overwhelmingly talented and only by the benefit of outstanding coaching were the Suns able to keep astride. And several of the black players on the Blazers thought there were racial undertones.

"He's just blowing smoke," Adelman said at the time. "I don't know what he's talking about. That's a way of saying if they win, it's because of hard work; if we win, it's because we have so much talent. That's not true. They have so many skilled players —Kevin Johnson, Tom Chambers, Andrew Lang, Dan Majerle— and great shooters like Hornacek and Chambers. (Cotton) is always saying things like that, and I don't know why, because we work as hard as any team in the league."

Portland led 106-95 with eight minutes remaining before the Suns, with Chambers, Hornacek, and Majerle absolutely on fire, came storming back to score on 19 of their last 24 possessions and force overtime. Phoenix led 130-128 in the closing seconds of the extra session when Drexler drove the middle with Majerle draped around him. Referee Dan Crawford called Clyde for traveling, and the game was over. Adelman blew a gasket over the call, and a livid Drexler sought out Crawford with a piece of his mind after the final buzzer, but the Phoenix win was in the books.

"(Majerle) had my arm tucked behind my back," said Clyde, who finished with 39 points, 11 rebounds, and five assists. "But there was no call, so obviously it was no foul."

"Of course he'd think that," Cotton said afterward. "I'm sure Clyde never fouled anybody in the game. Did he have any fouls in the game? (Clyde had four). I know he wasn't called for any in the first half. I thought we did a nice job of defending him on that last play. He tried to spin, he had nowhere to go, and he traveled."

But Cotton, who was retiring at season's end, had a stream of kind words for Drexler's play. "I always say this about Michael Jordan when we play Chicago. I kept looking for Clyde to take off his cape. That was Superman out there. He was absolutely poetry in motion. He was on the other side, but I found myself watching in awe."

Cotton is one of the best at filling a reporter's notebook, and his accommodating, friendly manner makes him a popular man with the media. But he has a sarcastic side that makes you never quite sure whether he's being genuine or not. And when he repeated his "praise" of the Blazers after the game —"they're great athletes and they really take it to you"—some of the players took offense.

"You get tired of hearing about what an athletic team we are," Williams said. "You can read into it what you want, but I think Cotton is making a statement about how smart he thinks our team is."

"It's like he's saying, 'They're dumb athletes,' " Kersey said. "It's like we can't play the thinking-man's game. That's the impression I get."

The "dumb" label would catch on at midseason, and would haunt the Blazers to the end of the playoffs. It was overblown, but there was some truth to it, too. There was an example late in the fourth quarter of the Phoenix game. With Portland holding a precarious lead, Duckworth was fouled by Chambers. Duck took offense at the foul and pushed Chambers, drawing a technical that resulted in a costly free throw at the other end.

Duck, though, did get off one of the best quips of the year.

"Chambers was holding me like he was my woman," Duck said, "and he's not my type."

The Portland-Phoenix series was showing signs of replacing the Portland-Lakers series as the biggest rivalry in the Western Conference. The teams were looking forward to the next meeting three weeks down the line in Portland. "I wish it were tomorrow," Williams said.

Next up, though, were the Lakers — or what was left of them. Magic Johnson's retirement had left a gaping hole that couldn't be filled, and Vlade Divac had missed much of the season with a back injury. Missing for this game, too, was James Worthy, who scored 27 points in 27 minutes the night before in Seattle, but woke up in the morning with a sore knee.

It left the Lakers in way over their heads, and the Blazers made the hurtin' worse with a 131-92 thrashing in the coliseum, presenting owner Paul Allen with the perfect gift on his 39th birthday.

It was the worst honest loss in Laker history. The only more one-sided defeat came in Portland, too, in the final game of the 1989-90 regular season. The Lakers had already wrapped up the best record in the Western Conference and Coach Pat Riley chose to rest most of his regulars in a meaningless 130-88 rout.

Portland forced the team with the fewest turnovers in the league into 20 giveaways, ran up 47 fastbreak points, and shot a season-high .590 from the floor. Nobody had to play more than 30 minutes in what amounted to as easy a night as the Blazers could hope to have.

Byron Scott said he was disgusted by the way the Lakers handled themselves at the game-day shootaround.

"Guys were laughing and goofing off and shooting the ball when Mike (Dunleavy) was talking," Scott said. "Maybe it takes something like this to get our attention. We can't afford to be nonchalant. If the coaches tell us the things we need to do to win and we're not listening, it's our fault, not theirs."

Even the best-laid plans wouldn't have carried the Lakers to victory on this night, and Scott realized it. "The Trail Blazers— the way they played tonight— that's the best team we've faced. They're more athletic and run better than any team I've seen."

Adelman learned before the game that he hadn't been in the race to serve as coach of the West All-Stars after all. An article in the January 20 edition of the *NBA News* — a weekly newsletter sent to the media from the league's public-relations office— said Chicago's Phil Jackson had clinched the East coaching berth. It also mentioned the West position was undecided, but that it wouldn't be Adelman, since a no-repeat rule was in effect for the first time this year.

That was news to just about everybody—to Adelman, to Nelson, and to members of the media in the Bay Area and in Portland. A call to the league office revealed the rule was instituted in previous years, and a grandfather clause set off its implementation until this year.

Ironically, Nelson served on the coaches committee that instituted the rule. "But I was on the general managers committee, too, and I might not have been around when it was voted on," he said.

Brian McIntyre, the NBA's director of public relations, called the Blazers' John Lashway to clarify the situation and apologize for any misunderstandings. Lashway relayed the word to Adelman.

"I had no idea that would happen," Adelman said after the season. "The whole criteria for picking the coaches is ridiculous, anyway."

Adelman thinks there are two appropriate ways for selecting all-star coaches. One would be to throw out the no-repeat rule and just give it to the coaches with the best records. Preferable in his mind would be a rotation on a seniority basis.

"The guys who have been coaching in the league and have never coached in the all-star game deserve the chance," he said. "I mean, give everybody a chance. It's such a great experience."

A visit to Seattle allowed the Blazers to spoil new Sonic coach George Karl's debut with a 113-109 win, which improved their record to 27-13 with the 14th win in their last 18 games. The Sonics pushed the tempo, and the Blazers benefited with a wealth of transition points. Kersey was the chief beneficiary, staging his own personal dunk-a-thon with a half-dozen slams.

Kersey remains one of the NBA's most spectacular dunkers, and it plays a part in him serving as one of the Blazers' most popular players with the fans. Once runner-up to Michael Jordan in the NBA slam-dunk contest, Kersey still likes to turn on the fans with the right stuff.

"You can feel those vibes when you dunk the ball . . . feel a really warm feeling in the building. You know everybody is anticipating it, and you try to make it fun for the fans."

But at 30, dunking has gotten a little old for the Mercy Man. There is a need to limit the strain on the body than necessary.

"It's still fun," he said, "but not like it used to be. When you've done every dunk you can do, you might start laying a few up. I laid a few up this year. I'll still go in and dunk it, but it's not the thrill it used to be anymore."

Thousands of Blazer fans made the trip north and turned the library-like atmosphere of Seattle Center Coliseum into a rock concert. Tickets are generally easier to get for Portland games in Seattle than they are in Memorial Coliseum, where season ticket-holders own almost all of the seats, and the few tickets reserved for single-game status are gobbled up quickly.

Sonic crowds are typically among the least vocal in the NBA, and Jim Moore, the beat writer for the *Seattle P-I*, grumped about the change in atmosphere as he wrote his story after the game. "Why do all these Portland people have to come up and spoil our peace and quiet?" he said with a wink.

The Seattle game was the 18th straight game the Blazers had made more field goals than the opposition. Remarkably, over the last 14 games, the Blazers had been outshot and outscored 12 times from the foul line. They were shooting only .735, 24th of the NBA's 27 teams, and it was causing more pressure than necessary at game's end. It cost them at times — they missed six free throws in the fourth quarter of the loss at Phoenix the previous week — though strong rebounding and defense were making up for it.

Earlier in the day, it was announced Drexler would be a starter in the All-Star Game for the first time. Drexler, a five-time All-Star going into the season, received more than three-quarters of a million votes, second only to Karl Malone on the West team. He would team with Magic Johnson in the West backcourt.

Weeks earlier, Drexler told *The Oregonian* it didn't really make any difference whether he was chosen as a starter for the game. He felt he'd been slighted in a couple of the previous All-Star votes and that obviously had hurt his pride. "After what has happened in the past," he had said, "I couldn't really care less, to be honest."

At that time, Drexler agreed with many of his teammates in the debate whether Johnson should or should not be included in the All-Star Game. The best quote on the matter came from Kersey, who asked bluntly: "It's hard to understand why, if he is retired, he should play in the game. Now are you going to say Dr. J can play, too?"

Clyde privately agreed at first, and he also had reservations about the chances of Johnson transmitting the AIDS virus on the court. "If doctors could assure us we're safe," he said, "that would be my biggest concern."

But Magic Johnson transcended the normal boundaries of rational thought. This was a living legend, a man highly regarded in all circles, the epitome of class and grace, and the way the game should be played. He would still be the best point guard in the league were it not for his HIV-positive status. And gradually, most people — including Drexler — came around to the belief that if an exception should be made, Magic should be the one.

"It's a great honor to be on the court with him — as long as he's healthy enough to play," Clyde said before the Seattle game, retaining a cautious approach to the issue.

The next night in the coliseum, Atlanta had more field goals than the Blazers — 45 to 43 — but lost the game 125-117 in one of the league's high-velocity games of the season. Portland tied franchise records with seven 3s in the first half and nine in a game, and the Hawks set their own club mark with 10 from beyond the stripe. The Blazers won the game by coming through in the clutch with the final seven points of the game in the last 50 seconds . . . all from the foul line.

It was a nice win against a hot Hawk team that shot 15 of 19 from the field in the third quarter and got superlative performances from Dominique Wilkins (34 points, seven rebounds, eight assists) and Kevin Willis (27 points, 17 rebounds). The Blazers had to play their hind ends off to win and inch ahead of Golden State for the division lead.

"I have to give our team a lot of credit," said Drexler, who had another sterling game with 29 points and eight assists. "We played extremely well after a big road win last night against a team that played as well as they can play. It was a lot of fun out there . . . it was one of those nights where you just feel like playing basketball."

Portland ventured to Oakland in a virtual tie with Golden State for the Pacific lead and flew home with an exhilarating 124-116 overtime triumph to celebrate. Sixth-man Sarunas Marciulionis was hurt, but Mario Elie — destined to one day become a Blazer — filled in with a career-high 23 points and some solid defense on Drexler before fouling out.

Clyde still came through with 39 points, 13 rebounds, nine assists, and four steals in 50 minutes, reaching the 14,000-point mark for his nine-year NBA career. But the Warriors should have won the game and would have, had Vincent Askew converted a cinch layup after an offensive rebound in the closing seconds of regulation. He missed, and the Blazers took off in overtime for their biggest win of the year to date.

Strothers didn't make the trip. He strained the rotator cuff in his right shoulder in the previous day's practice, and, after examination when the Blazers returned to Portland, was returned to the injured list. Remarkably, this happened when the deadline for making a decision on Ennis Whatley — who had been on the injured list all season after chipping a bone in his foot during the preseason but had been practicing full-bore for a month — was just about up. So Whatley was activated, and Strothers, who had seen action in only four games, was sidelined again.

Strothers said he hurt the shoulder when Kersey came down on his arm during a scrimmage session. None of the media attending the workout noticed any collision. "It was painful," the rookie said, "and then when I got home it was worse. I couldn't raise my arm."

Golden State had flown Strothers out for a pre-draft visit and he had gotten to know Don Nelson, and his son, Donn, an assistant coach. Strothers said he hated to miss the trip. "It pissed me off because I wanted to see Nellie and Donn," he said. "They were nice guys."

The Blazers kept on rolling with a 113-108 win at home over New Jersey, their 11th in a row in the coliseum and their 17th in the last 21 games to improve to 30-13. It was Giveaway Night, with 48 turnovers — 25 by the Nets — and the Blazers almost blew a 12-point lead in the fourth quarter. Drazen Petrovic, released from his incarceration behind Ainge on the Blazer bench and now a blossoming star in New Jersey, missed a wide-open 3 in the closing seconds that would have forced a tie.

"I couldn't believe I was that wide open," a disappointed Petrovic said. "If I'd known, I'd have hit the shot."

He didn't, and the Blazers lucked one out. Now they were feeling pretty darn good about themselves as they headed into February.

8

"Just Because I Play Basketball Doesn't Mean You Have to Hound My Brain."

2/1/92 NBA Pacific Division Standings								
	W	**L**	**Pct.**	**GB**		**W**	**L**	**Pct.**	**GB**
Portland	30	13	.698	-	Seattle	22	23	.489	9
Golden State	27	13	.675	$1\frac{1}{2}$	LA Clippers	20	24	.455	$10\frac{1}{2}$
Phoenix	29	16	.644	2	Sacramento	14	30	.318	$16\frac{1}{2}$
LA Lakers	27	16	.628	3					

Had it been a horse race, Portland would have won by 15 lengths. Had it been softball, the 10-run rule would have been enacted. It was that bad as the Sacramento Kings were sacrificial lambs in a 147-107 slaughter in the coliseum, the sixth straight win, and 18th in 22 games for the streaking Blazers.

The Pacific Division was by far the toughest in the NBA, with six playoff contenders and only Sacramento scaling the bottom with the league's patsies. The Kings were the NBA's worst rebounding team and the Blazers hammered them 53-34 on the boards. Portland bolted to a 42-point first quarter, then did itself better with 43 points in the second quarter for an 85-60 halftime lead— a point shy of the franchise record for points in a half.

Nine Blazers hit double figures, and Alaa Abdelnaby was a basket away with eight points. Ennis Whatley, playing nine minutes in his debut in a Portland uniform, was the only Blazer who failed to score. "Sweet without the sugar," said Kevin Duckworth, who hit seven of 11 shots and tallied 18 points. Terry Porter was eight for eight in the first half. Cliff Robinson was zero for six in the half, but made six of eight in the second half to score 18 points. It looked as if he'd score about 30, until Rick Adelman took him out of the game with more than four minutes to play.

"I probably could have," said Robinson. "We had a lot of guys going good. (The Kings) seemed slow in reacting on defense. They're still a few players away from being a quality team."

Before practice the following day, Danny Ainge and Clyde Drexler found themselves next to each other, shooting 3-pointers. Earlier in the season, when Ainge's 3-point percentage was down around 26 percent and Drexler's was at an all-time high 37 percent, Ainge had proffered a $100 bet he'd surpass Drexler by the end of the regular season, and Clyde had accepted.

Clyde was still comfortably ahead of Ainge and took the occasion to rib his teammate. "You got to quit shooting those 3s," he said.

"You want to make it $200?" Ainge asked. That was fine with the Blazers' captain.

They exchanged a few more barbs, and Clyde asked finally, "Do you want to go more?"

"No," said Ainge, "because then I'll start rooting for you to miss."

The Blazers were on to their final games before the All-Star break, a two-game stop in San Antonio and Dallas, and Jerome Kersey was hurting. He was playing every night and his production was still good, but he knew the right ankle wasn't right. He was still spending a lot of time every day getting treatment from trainer Mike Shimensky, but it just wasn't coming around the way they'd hoped.

"Ice, the Myomatic, whirlpool . . . I think I tested them all," Kersey said. "Nothing really worked. I tried not taping, changing shoes, wearing high-tops, wearing lows . . . anything to make the ankle feel more comfortable."

Some days it was OK. Other days it was almost unbearable. Kersey was still missing practice as often as not. He hated it.

"I reached the point where I was really frustrated with everything I was doing on the court," he said. "It wasn't enjoyable, playing with the soreness and the pain. Nobody wants to go through that. As tough as I think I am, it got to the point where I just wanted to stop and take whatever time it took to let the thing completely heal."

Kersey talked with Shimensky about it, and they considered having him stay home from the Texas trip. "The thing is, Jerome," Shimensky said, "you're going to have five days through the All-Star break. That will help."

Kersey agreed and made the trip to play the Spurs and Mavericks, hoping the rest after that would go a long way toward healing the ankle. It didn't.

"It helped," Kersey said after the season, "but once the pounding started, it came back."

Still, it was worth it, Kersey thought. "I think I was still able to help the team," he said. "I guess I decided that me playing 80 to 85 percent was better than me not out there at all."

Portland's stand at the Alamo was a futile one in a 95-88 loss to the Spurs. Drexler barely missed out on what would have been the ugliest triple-double in NBA history. Clyde had 23 points, eight rebounds, and nine assists, but was an unconscionable 10 for 32 from the field. Porter was an even more embarrassing five for 23, and Ainge three for 10 off the bench, as the three guards combined to make 18 of 65 shots, including two for 15 from 3-point territory.

Under those circumstances, it's a wonder the Blazers fell by only seven and were in the game right to the end. Portland led 80-71 with less than eight minutes to go and was still ahead by three with 1:48 to go. The Blazers had only one field goal over the final four minutes, though, in a game that ended with Drexler drawing a pair of technicals and automatic ejection.

Even the most objective observer would agree it was a strange call referee Jim Capers made to turn the tide the Spurs' way. Clyde had spotted up for a 3-pointer from the corner that would have tied the score with three seconds remaining. Clyde appeared to try to draw the foul from defender Sean Elliott, and Capers called an offensive foul, evidently for kicking his left leg out and tripping Elliott on the shot.

Clyde's technicals come in bunches — the previous season he had 11 that included an NBA-high five two-T games — and he got a pair quicker than a flood flashing as he jumped on Capers with a verbal barrage.

"Unbelievable," Drexler said afterward. "They said I kicked a guy. That's doubly tough when you're shooting a jump shot. I thought he was calling a foul on Elliott." Clyde said he was sorry to lose his temper, but "I couldn't let that one go. When you go to the basket 15 or 20 times in a row, and no one goes to the line, you've got to say something."

Rick Adelman was fuming afterward. The Capers call infuriated him. "I have no idea what he called. I think it was an offensive foul on a fadeaway jumper, but you'd have to ask the official."

Later, Drexler acknowledged his temper occasionally gets the better of him. But he wasn't ready to concede it's something he needs to control.

"I've always been a guy who believes in principles," he said. "If I think I'm being wronged, I'm going to speak up. I'm not going to be quiet and let somebody wrong me. I could be wrong sometimes, too, but I'll stick up for myself. Sometimes it gets me in trouble, but I'll bet if you look at the replay of that call, I was absolutely correct. I'm not going to let somebody run over me. That's just not my personality. I'm a nice guy, but don't try to run me over."

The Blazers felt David Robinson was getting away with murder, and indeed he killed the visitors with a game that included 23 points, 14 rebounds, and a season-high 11 blocked shots. He got only one foul, which Adelman regarded as a mystery.

Dallas had lost 18 of its last 19 games and was well on the way to its worst season since the franchise's first season, but the Blazers were fortunate to escape with a 103-98 win. Portland made only five of 22 shots in the fourth quarter to fritter away most of a 21-point lead. The Blazers shot only .376 from the floor but won by making their last 10 foul shots over the final 1:07.

"We might have gotten a little complacent," Kersey said in the night's biggest understatement. Clyde led the way with 32 points and, while his teammates were scattering to enjoy a five-day All-Star break in various vacation spots, he was heading for Orlando for his starting assignment in the All-Star Game.

Clyde was happy to be playing in an All-Star Game again and was tickled he would be able to bring along his wife, Gaynell, and their two small children, Austin and Elise. They made the trip to Texas, visiting with relatives, and then flew with Clyde to Orlando, where Mickey and Minnie Mouse would be their hosts for too short a stay.

The starting assignment was no big thrill. Drexler is a prideful man, and he felt for too long that his talents were under-appreciated, at least on a national scale. He had been an all-star five previous times, including the last four in a row, and had quietly watched as other guards teamed with Magic Johnson in the starting backcourt for the West.

"After eight years in the league, I felt I was deserving of a starting spot three or four of those years and it didn't happen," he said. "I'm never a guy to have ill feelings about anything, but it kind of took the credibility away from it for me. Whether you start or come in off the bench, it doesn't matter to me. Stuff like that doesn't matter to me. It should, but it doesn't."

It does, of course. Clyde normally steers away from controversy the same way he tries to avoid a six-car pileup. Occasionally a reporter — especially one he trusts — will get under his guard and will draw out some true feelings. Later he often thinks about what he has said and tries to draw back. On other occasions, he'll respond to a question with something that sounds good, then seem to forget he said it. Later, when asked about his comment, he'll think about it and either try to qualify it or wriggle away from it. It's amusing because such things are so human and, superstar or not, Clyde is human.

Drexler is better than most at resisting the star treatment. He enjoys his status as Oregon's most popular personality, but doesn't abuse it. He genuinely enjoys his contact with fans, and is one of the best of the Blazers about signing autographs. Most of the players understandably have grown tired of having their privacy invaded with aggressive fans and autograph seekers. Most comply with children, but have grown increasingly resistant to autograph hounds, particularly those in the business.

"I'm willing to do them, but I don't enjoy autographs," said Wayne Cooper. "I hate to hurt a kid, but the last few years I've been turned off by a lot of people, especially with the cards. A lot of the adults force the kids to ask. It got to the point where I didn't want to sign. I told a lot of kids I'd sign a piece of paper but not a card, and they didn't want that. And some people are so rude. I hate to be interrupted in the middle of a meal, but they just don't care. They want what they want, and you wind up feeling like a piece of meat."

"Just because I play basketball doesn't mean you have to hound my brain," said Kersey. "Guys yell at you as you walk down the street, and if I don't holler back, I'm a jerk. That's idiotic. There's no sensitivity from a lot of people. It used to be I'd enjoy the opportunity to give someone my autograph. I'd say 50 percent of autograph seekers nowadays, they don't care what you're doing, they want their autograph, now. They have no respect for you, even if you're with your family, a girlfriend, your friends, whatever."

Like many of his teammates, Kersey has no problem signing in an isolated situation. But if there is a crowd, he will either adopt the "sign-on-the-move" technique or politely turn down the requests altogether.

"You do one, two, three, four, five, and the crowd keeps getting bigger," he said. "People expect you to hold up what you're doing and just keep standing there signing autographs. If you stop, you're an asshole. You can feel people watching you. They're egging on their kids who don't want to come over to you. It's the parents who really want them. If there are one or two people and I can do it, bam, I'll do it. But if I can tell there is going to be a lineup . . . I would rather not start and be fair to everyone."

Kersey said men are worse than women. "A woman will ask sincerely for your autograph," he said. "Guys want to shake your hand and talk to you and show their buddies they know you — the macho deal."

"The last two years is the first time I've ever refused to sign an autograph," said Buck Williams. "Sometimes if I'm out in the community with my family, I've refused. I feel horrible doing it, and sometimes I'll say hi and shake their hand, but I'm out with my family and I just can't sign. I love our fans, but it just gets to be too much."

"I don't like doing it," Duckworth said. "I can understand the fame and glory, but I always believed to meet a person, or take a picture with him, is more important than signing a piece of paper. Collecting cards is great, but what do you need to get it signed for? Now I tell people I'm on vacation, or I'm really trying to get away from that. Some people get mad. Last year, one guy called me a fat slob. The thing I hate most is when a parent makes his kid come down and ask you. The kid will say, 'Who is he?' Or they give you a sad story about their father being paralyzed from the neck down and he would love to have your autograph.

"The hardest thing in the world is to turn down kids, but if you sign one, you got to sign them all. I can understand why Kareem just stopped signing, period, because people start becoming an ass about the whole situation."

All the Blazer players love their fans, but the adulation and crush on the players' time reaches epidemic proportions. Go to the supermarket and sign autographs. Go to a restaurant and sign autographs. Go to a movie and sign autographs. You get the idea. Anonymity is an impossibility.

Almost all of the Blazers spend a lot of time in charity work. Kersey and Porter are among the best, and have given an extraordinary amount of time, energy, and money to the Boys and Girls Clubs of America. Ainge has chosen one charity to devote his time to—the Children's Miracle Network, of which Doernbecher Hospital is the Portland chapter.

"I wanted to pick one charity to really spend time and be a volunteer with," he said. "I like to speak at banquets to the kids who have benefited from the program. I have four healthy kids of my own, and to have the opportunity to help kids who are less fortunate is a pleasure."

Ainge views autographs in a less-kind light.

"I love little kids and want to make them happy," he said, "but I don't feel autographs are an obligation for who I am. Normally I don't mind signing, and I probably do it 60 or 70 percent of the time. But it bothers me that people have the attitude I owe it to them. I don't feel I owe it to them. I enjoy doing it for kids. I do it for charities. The situations I avoid are when there are 200 people waiting for you. I say 'not tonight,' and I don't feel bad about it. And I don't have any patience with the collectors, who have six different cards they want you to sign.

"The insensitivity some people have about me making a big salary and I should drop my whole life, I have a hard time with that. And with people being rude and shoving . . . I love the fans, but autographs isn't being part of being good to fans. I learned a long time ago you can't please everybody, so don't even try."

The Blazers have several days during each season where players get together and sign balls and posters for charitable causes. It's in each player's contract, and most don't mind. During the 1991-92 season, Ainge chose not to take part on several occasions, and was fined $500 each time. He said it had nothing to do with the causes and everything to do with his contract situation.

"I was just going to play basketball," he said. "I never held out of practices or games, because that affects Rick and my teammates, who had nothing to do with it. But one thing I felt I could do was say, 'Forget it, I'm not doing anything you guys want me to do outside of basketball.' "

The shame of it, of course, is that the losers in that situation are the recipients of the balls or posters the players are signing. Such were the deep-rooted ill feelings of Ainge toward Geoff Petrie in the negotiation of the contract that never came off.

Drexler has many of the same feelings as his teammates but has always handled the attention that is lavished upon him with class and style. After the annual Blazer Boosters banquet, only one player stayed more than five minutes afterward to sign autographs — Clyde Drexler. A half-hour after the banquet ended, Clyde was still signing, and he signed until every last person was satisfied.

"It's an honor to have people feel that way about you," he said. "I think they can tell I'm a nice guy. It gets to be too much at times, but that's the nature of the business. I'm not going to complain about it."

Clyde arrived in Orlando with a bit of trepidation. Don Nelson was the West coach. Clyde was not a member of the Nelson Fan Club because, as far as he could tell, Nelson was not a member of his.

Two years earlier, Nelson made remarks to *San Francisco Chronicle* columnist Lowell Cohn that found their way into print. It happened not long after Mike Schuler — a long-time friend and former assistant under Nelson — had been fired as Portland's head coach. Schuler's poor relationship with Clyde did not help Schuler's standing, and Nelson seemed to be sticking up for his pal when Cohn asked him who he considered to be the league's most overrated player.

"Clyde Drexler," Nelson said. "He chips away at what an organization is trying to do. He's the worst of all kinds, because he comes off as polite. He's religious, devoted to family. Yet in the context of a team, he's destructive."

Those comments seemed in line with those quoted from an anonymous source by talk-show host Roy Firestone. "It's not that Clyde is not a nice guy. He is a nice guy. He's one of those guys who carries a switchblade in his back pocket. He's late all the time. He doesn't work hard enough in practice . . . He's always complaining to the front office — all those things that can hurt a team a thousand ways, especially if he's your star. . . . He always seemed to be one of those guys who thought it was more important to be cool than anything else. What kind of 'star' is that?"

"It sounds like a coach who has been fired and is blaming other people for his failure," Clyde told Firestone, insinuating the remarks were made by Schuler. He was irked at Nelson's salvo as well. It was not the first time Nelson had made disparaging remarks about a Blazer player. Years earlier, when Danny Ainge was playing for Boston, and Nelson was coaching at Milwaukee, Nelson accused Ainge of "undercutting players" and charged him with three incidents of deliberately intending to injure Bucks players. The league fined Nelson $1,000 for his remarks, but Ainge felt what he said was for tactical reasons, and that they went a long way toward developing his reputation as a dirty player.

"He said those things after I scored 25 points in the first half of a playoff game," Ainge said. "I don't think he believed what he said, but it affected me. We got swept that series and I remember in the game after Nelson said that, I got three fouls in the first five minutes. I thought it affected the officials, too. It bothered me the whole summer and a little while after that, too."

Drexler believed Nelson had an ulterior motive this time, too—to help Schuler get another head-coaching job. The summer after the Cohn piece was printed, Nelson sent a letter of apology to Drexler, which remained on file with Clyde's attorney, Gary Vandeweghe, the uncle of friend and former teammate Kiki Vandeweghe. But Nelson had never apologized in a public forum, and because of that, Drexler did not consider the matter closed.

"I've never understood how somebody can make comments like that without even knowing you," said Drexler, straying from his normal role as Mr. Politically Correct. "I don't know Don Nelson. What he said was wrong, any way you look at it. It took every piece of restraint in my body not to go after him when I first saw him (after the article appeared). I think he should have been fined by the league when he made that statement. When you talk about my character like that . . . he insulted my whole family. That's something he has to account for.

"I'm not out to start a mass character assassination on Don Nelson, but I have to admit, there is a lot of uneasiness on my part playing for him. I'd feel uncomfortable playing for anybody who made comments like that about me."

When Drexler's comments were relayed to Nelson by an *Oregonian* reporter on Friday of All-Star Weekend, the Golden

State coach's mood darkened but his response was even and softspoken.

"I've said all along I made a foolish mistake a couple of years ago when I said those things," he said. "I've apologized publicly many times about it. If that's what he wants, let me say, 'I'm sorry, Clyde. I was foolish.' It will have no effect on our relationship. He's been the bigger man by accepting my apology and befriending me and making me feel better about a foolish statement. There, is that groveling enough?"

Nelson sought out Clyde at the first West practice in Orlando and they talked. "We straightened out our differences," Clyde said. "He told me what he was thinking at the time, and he apologized and I accepted it."

The All-Stars were staying at the Dolphin, a resort hotel located right on the Disney Grounds close to all the special attractions. On Saturday after practice, Clyde and Gaynell took their kids to the Magic Kingdom. Austin, not yet two, enjoyed seeing the sights and partaking in the smallest of the kids' rides. Elise, seven months, wasn't sure what to make of it all.

Clyde had maintained a cautious public approach to playing with Magic Johnson. "Since he has been cleared to play, the doctors must consider it safe," he said. "I have no qualms as long as it's safe for everyone involved."

Bob Cook, team doctor for the Blazers for many years, was in the minority opinion that Johnson should not participate.

"I fully agree the likelihood of anybody contracting AIDS in the game is remote," Cook said. "But undeniably there is a possibility, however remote. That's going to make some people uncomfortable to be on the court with him. I think it would be to his, and to everyone else's, best interests if he were to simply thank everybody, acknowledge his gratitude, and take himself out of the game."

Magic wasn't about to do that, of course. Since the November 7 announcement that shocked the world, he had pined for the moment he could return to the spotlight he so cherished, if only for a day. He would be out there again with the best players in the world, smiling and passing, and directing, and leading the guys like only he can do. "The pre-game stuff, hearing the crowd again, guarding Isiah (Thomas), throwing that first pass . . . I'll suck it all up and bottle it and put a cap on it and never let it go," he said at an emotional news conference on Saturday.

Even Magic, though, couldn't have dreamed up better drama than Sunday's game provided. He collected 25 points and nine assists in 29 unforgettable minutes, and capped the day with an off-balance 3-point field goal that ripped twine in the game's closing seconds. "It's like I'm in a dream right now, and I don't ever want to wake up," Johnson said after being handed the game's most-valuable-player trophy. "If this is going to be it, I wanted to go out this way."

If not for Magic, Clyde would have been MVP hands down. As it was, he earned two of the 11 ballots, including that of Jack McCallum, the respected NBA writer for *Sports Illustrated*. The Glide was superlative, contributing 22 points, nine rebounds, six assists, and two blocked shots as the West rolled to a stunning 153-113 win over an East team led by Michael Jordan, Patrick Ewing, and Charles Barkley.

With two minutes to go, Clyde was a good bet to claim the MVP. Then Magic buried three straight 3s, milking impromptu one-on-one sets with Thomas and Michael Jordan for all they were worth. "I've been working on a script for this all weekend," Johnson said afterward. "I was at my typewriter, and I couldn't come up with an ending. Well, that final shot was it. That was my period."

It seemed so appropriate for Clyde to shine, only to be overshadowed by an even greater presence. For years he had been compared unfavorably to Jordan — how else can one compare?— among the game's great two guards.

But Clyde handled the whole thing beautifully. On Magic's final basket, Jordan applied some defensive pressure on him, as Clyde tried to get him the ball, and he almost turned it over. But Clyde made sure to get it to Magic, then watched as his West teammate put that MVP trophy on ice.

Drexler made 10 of 15 shots from the field, made a pair of 3s and several skywalking dunks, dished out a number of spectacular passes, and turned in some nice defensive work on Jordan as the West breezed to the second most one-sided triumph in All-Star history. Afterward, he earned praise from all sides.

"If there is anyone in this game who comes close to Michael in terms of talent, it's Clyde Drexler," said Chicago coach Phil Jackson, who coached the East. "Basketball aficionados think his game is absolutely terrific, and he was terrific today. There are two spots left on the Olympic team, and I'm definitely lobbying for this guy to be on the team."

"Clyde plays in a small market," Jordan said, "but you could see what he did out there today."

Nelson made sure to use Drexler down the stretch with Johnson.

"I thought it was between those two for MVP, and I didn't want to influence that," Nelson said. "I wanted to have them both on the floor at the end. Clyde had an amazing game. Not just his offense, but he was very good defensively, and he was our leading rebounder."

A Bay Area writer asked Nelson if he has changed his opinion of Drexler.

"I told him that in several huddles today," Nelson said. "I was definitely wrong about the guy."

Johnson threw in an endorsement for Clyde's performance, too.

"A lot of guys on our team could have won the MVP," Magic said. "Clyde, for one, really put on a show."

Later, as Johnson entered the West dressing room, he locked eyes with Clyde and nodded. "You were wonderful," he mouthed.

"For you, babe," Clyde responded.

"It didn't bother me at all," Clyde said when asked if he should have been MVP. "My sentiments were with Magic. I just enjoyed being on the same court with him. I'm really glad he won. There is no better way to honor a guy who has been a legend in our league. It was truly a Magic-al moment."

The only thing that went wrong all weekend came with Drexler's forgetting to bring his Blazer warmup to Orlando. He and David Robinson were the only players who didn't have theirs, and they warmed up with Orlando Magic jackets through pregame drills. The two were kidded about it by their West teammates, and Clyde wore that familiar, sheepish grin.

9

"Does This Mean if You're Overweight and Out of Shape, You Get First Priority?"

2/10/92 NBA Pacific Division									
	W	**L**	**Pct.**	**GB**		**W**	**L**	**Pct.**	**GB**
Portland	32	14	.696	-	Seattle	24	24	.500	9
Phoenix	32	16	.667	1	LA Clippers	22	25	.468	$10^1/_2$
Golden State	29	15	.659	2	Sacramento	16	31	.340	$16^1/_2$
LA Lakers	28	18	.609	4					

Back in Portland, Clyde Drexler got a huge ovation when he was introduced prior to the Blazers' next game, a date with Denver. Clyde couldn't suppress a somewhat embarrassed smile, and Rick Adelman took the occasion to kid him. "After that, you better go out and put it to them," he told his captain.

A weary Drexler scored a game-high 28 points, and the Blazers needed all the energy he could muster in a come-from-behind 121-112 win over the woeful Nuggets. The Blazers committed 23 turnovers, and Denver, 17-30 at the time, led 57-45 late in the first half before Terry Porter came alive to get Portland within five at the break. Portland dominated the boards 27-14 in the second half and took care of things down the stretch, but it was no first-rate performance by any means.

"We played kind of crummy," Drexler said. "But it's good to win one when you don't play that well."

"To lose that one would have been devastating," Jerome Kersey said. "Especially since tomorrow we're playing the team right behind us in the standings."

The reference was to the Phoenix Suns, and the Blazers made the trip to Fiesta land a happy one with a 107-97 victory that snipped the Suns' 19-game home win streak. It was a huge win, since Phoenix had beaten Portland in the first two meetings, and since the Suns, on a roll, had advanced to within a game and a half of the Blazers in the division race.

Drexler had a busy night. Out of a game-long set of discussions with referee Ronnie Garretson — Darell's son — came a technical and plenty of dirty looks from both sides. Clyde also found time to come within an assist of a triple-double with 24 points, 11 rebounds, and nine assists.

Adelman loves to talk about rebounding and defense, and they were the keys to this win as Portland improved to 34-14. Kevin Johnson, who hit 10 of 16 shots and had 21 points and 11 assists, was the only Phoenix starter who was on. The Blazers blasted to a 25-10 lead, and the Suns spent the entire game in a catch-up mode.

One of Drexler's main desires in assuming the captain's role was the opportunity to plead the Blazers' case with officials. He used it in the second quarter after tossing up an airball on a 3-point attempt. Clyde felt he got fouled on the shot, and was doubly mad when he was whistled for a foul for throwing an elbow seconds later. Garretson, Mark Wunderlich, and Clyde's old friend from San Antonio, Dan Crawford, all got an earful, and Clyde got a technical. But the Suns felt as a result he got the benefit of the doubt the rest of the way.

"Clyde's no dummy," said Jeff Hornacek. "After he cussed out the ref and got the technical, they didn't dare call another foul on him."

It's the star treatment that players of the magnitude of Michael Jordan, Larry Bird, Magic Johnson, and Karl Malone get. Clyde finally seemed to be joining that select company, in the minds of coaches, players, fans, and, yes, referees.

Phoenix fans are noisy, at least when the Blazers come to town, and they rained plenty of abuse down on the visitors during the game. Some of that was directed at assistant coach John Wetzel, who had spent one season as the Suns' head coach in the aftermath of the drug scandal that set the franchise back several years.

One fan of particularly poor taste is allowed to walk by the bench every game and direct a few invectives as security conveniently turns its head. The target as the game ended this time was Wetzel, and Jack Schalow took offense.

"What are you being such a smart ass for?" Schalow asked the fan. "Why don't you get the hell out of here?"

They continued to argue as Schalow walked toward the dressing room. The two reached midcourt —"they were going at it like two little banty roosters," Wetzel remembers — when Harvey Shank, the Suns' vice president/marketing, jumped into the middle of it, siding with the Phoenix fan.

Shank, who occupies a front-row seat behind the scorer's bench, is a notorious referee-baiter who has been known to get on players and coaches. Shank had a few words with Schalow, who was acting like he was going to go over the scorer's table after Shank, but Wetzel got there first.

"Fuck you, Harvey," he said, and Wetzel and Schalow walked away into the dressing room.

The assistants' loyalty doesn't extend just to Adelman. The two have an enormous amount of affection and respect for each other. "Our staff has never had a major argument," Schalow said. Schalow's coming to his comrade's defense was not all that surprising except for the fact that Schalow is a congenial and mild-mannered person.

"The whole thing really bothered me, because I have a lot of respect for John," Schalow said. "He didn't deserve that. I like John a lot. He has a great sense of humor, and he's an excellent coach. I have learned a lot from both him and Rick about dealing with players. In college, I was one of those coaches who wanted the player to do it right every time. That's not realistic, and that's not the way it's done anymore.

"I enjoy being around John. He's a very caring person. When somebody new comes to our team, he's the first one to ask the guy to lunch."

Schalow is as genuinely nice a guy as one could meet. A farm boy off his father's ranch in Velva, North Dakota, he had gone on to be an army paratrooper and, after discharge, a fine basketball guard at the University of Pacific in Stockton, California. He was a bit of a coaching vagabond, putting in stints with Bucky Buckwalter at Seattle University, with Hubie Brown at Duke, and with Dale Brown at Louisiana State. He had also been a head coach at Seattle University and in the CBA before joining the Blazers as a scout in Jack Ramsay's last year as coach.

Schalow was good with the players. "Part of your job as an assistant coach is to make the players feel wanted and appreciated," he said. Jack was great at that, leading the NBA in butt pops after timeouts and smoothing any ruffles in the players' feathers when necessary.

To Schalow, basketball was on a par with horseback-riding, which put basketball in heady company. He owned a cutting horse and a roping horse and spent many hours during the season and in the summers with the horses, both in competitions and just for fun. "A lot of times I'll go out there for a trail ride and think about things before a game," he said. "It's relaxing and kind of clears your mind." Goodness knows, coaches can use as much of that as they can get.

The next game was in Sacramento, and it started 23 minutes late because referees Hugh Evans, Wally Rooney, and Mike Callahan got caught in a lightning-caused traffic jam on the way to Arco Arena. Their decisions were a big reason why the Blazers escaped with a lucky 107-106 win.

Clyde's availability was in question until almost game time because of a sprained big toe on his left foot. He opted to play, and made only seven of 26 shots, but it was his three-point play with one second to go that rescued the Blazers.

Spud Webb gave Sacramento a 106-104 lead with 14 seconds remaining, and Adelman, rather than calling timeout, waved Porter upcourt with the ball. Porter found Danny Ainge open on the wing, but he missed a 3-pointer with 10 seconds on the clock. Kersey tipped the rebound to Porter, who found Drexler under the basket. Clyde went up hard, and was fouled as he put in the layup. He converted the foul shot, and the Blazers' shaky win was in the books.

"Very, very sore" was the way Drexler's foot felt afterward. That described the way the Kings felt about the loss. They didn't like the final call that put Clyde at the line and they weren't pleased, either, with a technical foul on interim coach Rex Hughes — who had taken over for the deposed Dick Motta — with 35 seconds left and Sacramento ahead by two. "I cost us the game, I admit," Hughes said later.

The LA Clippers were coming to Portland with a decidedly different look. Gone was Coach Mike Schuler, who had worn out his welcome and been fired a week and a half earlier. In was Larry Brown, the coaching nomad who had chosen the Clippers as the latest point to put down his bags.

Brown was less than a month removed from the head coaching position in San Antonio, where he won back-to-back Midwest Division titles and had been expected to contend for an NBA title this season with an emerging David Robinson in the middle. But Brown continually parried with owner Red McCombs over financial support and control of player development. Brown, an outstanding coach who had experienced great success in every job he'd taken in college and the pros, had lost the support of some of his key players, including Robinson. Brown wanted to win so badly, he often let it get the best of him. At times, he was the perfect blend of coach and person. At other times, he was tough to live with.

The Spurs were not winning as often as they'd hoped, and, on January 20 McCombs told Brown he had decided to let him go. Brown sent the Spurs through a spirited workout session that afternoon —"the best practice I've ever been associated with," Brown said — and by evening McCombs had evidently reconsidered and said he wanted Brown to stay.

What happened the following day is murky. McCombs said Brown asked to be relieved of his duties. Brown said he was fired.

"Red said he wanted to make a change," Brown said. "He hired me to win a championship in San Antonio. He felt I wasn't doing the job he'd hired me to do, and I understand that."

Robinson had addressed the Brown issue at the All-Star game, and he didn't mince words. "I love Larry as a person," he said. "He's one of the nicest guys you'd ever want to meet. As a coach, he was very, very difficult. He and I didn't operate very well together at all. He just seemed disenchanted in San Antonio, and he didn't get the support of the management or the players. I don't see how that's really going to change in Los Angeles."

Robinson's words seemed to surprise Brown. "I didn't have any problems with the players," he said. "I taught them as much as I could. I felt good about what David accomplished under me."

But he always had wanted more from Robinson, a complex person with a variety of interests. Brown felt— and stated publicly — that if Robinson would ever put his mind to basketball and do everything he could to make himself a better player, he'd be the greatest center ever. David didn't want to make that kind of a commitment.

McCombs, though, was the main reason Brown left. Brown considered him cheap. McCombs scrutinized every player move Brown wanted to do for monetary reasons. Brown felt if he really wanted to win, he ought to give him the financial support to get it done. The Spurs flew commercial even when more than half the NBA clubs were flying on their own, or leased, private jets. Only when Robinson made it a public crusade did McCombs get it done.

Later, when the Spurs let point guard Rod Strickland go and Portland was able to sign him as an unrestricted free agent after the season, Brown knew the reason... and it had little to do with Strickland's checkered personal life.

"Money," he said. "That's Red McCombs. I thought he'd be perfect for Tark (new San Antonio coach Jerry Tarkanian), and Tark wanted him. You just can't release a point guard like Rod. But would Red have paid Rod? No. I think it was unfortunate for Tark, but fortunate for Portland."

Brown was excited to be in LA and to be reunited with Danny Manning, who starred on Brown's Kansas team that won the 1988 NCAA championship. The money — $750,000 per year over five seasons — didn't hurt, either. The Clippers had given him two wins, including a big one over Phoenix, in his first two games, but he downplayed any talk of coming away with a victory in Portland, against whom the Clips had given new meaning to the word "pushover." The Blazers had beaten them in 30 of the previous 31 visits to the coliseum and had won 27 of the last 29 overall.

So, even with Drexler on the bench resting his sprained toe, the Clippers' 107-106 win was a foray into fantasy. James Edwards' fadeaway 12-footer from the baseline with 5.7 seconds to play gave the Clippers their only lead of the game. The Blazers couldn't even get a shot off at the other end, and they walked off the floor with a sick feeling in their stomachs.

"I'm still surprised," said Kevin Duckworth afterward. "The buzzer sounded, I looked up at the scoreboard and I thought, 'Did we really lose?'"

Defense buried the Blazers. LA scored on 10 of its final 11 possessions.

That's what bothered Adelman the most. "All we needed was a stop on one possession down the stretch, and we'd have won," he said. "We couldn't get it done."

If anything, the Blazers' performance gave wind to the Drexler-for-MVP campaign. Without him, at least against the Clippers, they were the pits.

Lamont Strothers, who had been out since Ennis Whatley was activated on January 27, was back practicing and said his shoulder felt "great." A decision between keeping one of the two seemed imminent. "We'll probably give Strothers three or four more days to get into shape," Geoff Petrie said. "We want to get a look at Whatley in the next couple of games. Then we'll go from there."

Drexler played— did he ever — and the Blazers got big-time performances from reserves Ainge, Cliff Robinson, Alaa Abdelnaby, and Robert Pack in a 129-116 romp past Phoenix in the coliseum. Kevin Johnson was virtually unstoppable, sinking 17 of 24 shots from the floor en route to a 40-point game, but he finally wore down in the fourth quarter, perhaps a result of fatigue after a 46-minute showing in a 98-96 loss at Seattle the night before.

Clyde, who hadn't practiced since injuring the toe, didn't decide to play until the late-morning, game-day shootaround. "It felt pretty good, so I decided to try it," he said. All Clyde did was lead the Blazers with 28 points, eight rebounds, and five assists in 33 minutes.

"Clyde never ceases to amaze me," Adelman said. "He can be out three or four days and just pick up where he left off. Just having him on the floor was a steadying influence to our team. Having him out there makes me a much better coach."

KJ buried nine of 11 shots in a scintillating third quarter and had 36 points going into the fourth quarter. Porter had a nice offensive game, too, going for 24 points on nine of 13 from the field and six of six from the line. Not bad for two point guards not good enough to make the 1992 All-Star Game.

Robinson came through with 17 points on seven-of-12 shooting and went the entire fourth quarter at center in place of Duckworth. That didn't sit well with Duckworth, who quickly showered and left the Blazers dressing room even before Adelman and the players came out to meet members of the media.

Adelman, always supportive publicly of his players and, in particular, of Duckworth, admitted Duck's pouting and quick exit was something he didn't like to see.

"That bothers me," he said. "I feel strongly the reason we win a lot of games is all the players contain themselves emotionally within a team framework. It's not always going to be your night. If you win the game, that's the only thing that counts. If you're unhappy about anything else, that comes the next day. Frustration and negative feelings about things is something Kevin needs to work on."

Duck was feeling picked on because he was playing considerably fewer minutes than any of the four starters. Part of that was Adelman's feeling that he needed to find more minutes for Robinson, who was more mobile and versatile and whom Adelman considered a better defender. And part of it was due to the fact that Duck was struggling. He was shooting only .433 from the field, .707 from the line, and was averaging only 10.7 points and 5.9 rebounds. Over the previous three seasons, he had shot a collective 48 percent from the floor and 76 percent from the line, averaged 16.7 points and 6.9 rebounds, and had been selected twice to the All-Star Game.

"I hate to say I'm frustrated, because when I get frustrated, it affects my game big-time," he said. That's exactly what was happening. He had become unsure of himself when he got the ball. And he wasn't getting the ball as regularly as he had in the past.

"I don't want to take the shot, that's the bad part of it," he said. "I'm really not looking to take it. I'm head-faking and looking to throw the ball to someone else."

Duckworth was particularly sensitive to fans' criticism. He felt like a fall guy, even when he wasn't getting the ball as often. "When I don't score, everyone says Kevin didn't play his game," he said. "I'm damned if I do, damned if I don't."

Adelman liked Duckworth very much personally, and had a lot of respect for him as a player. "Kevin has struggled a little more this year than in the past," the coach said. "It creates a perception — and a false one — that I have lost confidence in him. It's not the fact I don't want to play Duck, but we're better with Cliff in certain situations. I try to talk to Kevin and explain. I would feel the same way he does. I don't have any problems with a guy being down and disappointed, as long as he plays hard."

Duck was playing hard, "as hard as I've seen him play for awhile," Drexler said. "He wants to play all the time, just like everybody on this team. But you have to be mature about it. If the team is doing well, you have to be happy the team is doing well."

Duckworth wasn't on the receiving end of as many Porter passes off the pick and roll. Sometimes he was open and simply did not get the ball. But Porter felt Duck was not getting down court quickly enough to get into the right position.

"I didn't lose confidence in the pick and roll at all," Porter said after the season. "It was a matter of him not getting down the floor. He got frustrated. He'd get taken out. He thought everybody was easing him out and moving Cliff in."

Ainge didn't consider Duckworth's attitude a cancer.

"I didn't see it as a problem at all," Ainge said. "Everybody knows Duck by now. I don't believe anybody really cared what he was worried about. It was nothing new."

The words sound cold, and that's misleading, because Ainge has a warm spot in his heart for Duckworth. Ainge, impish by nature, is one of the NBA's all-star needlers. "The best I ever played with were Kevin McHale and Larry Bird," he said. "I'm pretty good myself."

When he came to the Blazers, Ainge found protocol was to leave Duckworth alone, especially when it came to matters of weight.

"I teased him about his weight and everybody said, 'Hey, he's sensitive, don't ever tease Duck about his weight,' " Ainge said. "I still did on occasion, just because, hey, are you like hiding it? One day we got into a little punching match, me and Duck. He punched me in the chest and I punched him back and I said, 'Is this a little secret or what? You don't want anybody to know?' "

There was another incident during the 1991-92 season. Some of the players ride the stationary bike in the coliseum training room after a game, with a player's seniority in the league getting priority. Ainge found rookie Robert Pack on the bike, kicked him off and began to ride. Soon thereafter, Bryan Casper, the team's physical therapist, entered the room.

"That's Duck's," Casper said. Ainge kept riding.

Duckworth came in. "That's my machine," he said.

"I thought we do this by seniority," Ainge said. "I have a lot more seniority than you, so when I'm done, you can have it."

"Get off the bike," Duck said.

"Yeah, you have to get off," Casper reiterated. His orders,

Casper said later, were that Duckworth "was to have seniority over everyone."

"Does this mean if you're overweight and out of shape, you get first priority?" said Ainge, laughing. Ainge wasn't intending to be malicious, but he saw no reason to defer to Duckworth and didn't intend to get off the bike unless they threw him off. Other players saw what was happening and wondered what Duck would do. But the big guy let it pass.

Things like that happen between teammates during a long, pressure-packed season. Sometimes there are hard feelings. In this case, it didn't mean the two weren't friends.

"I understand Duck a lot more than I did when I first came to the team," Ainge said. "I really like him and appreciate him as a person."

The admiration is mutual.

"Before I met Danny, I wanted to tear his head off," Duck said. "But he became a great friend. He has a sense of humor, he's carefree, he's a terrific guy to play with."

Ainge felt Duckworth's early success in Portland may have worked against him in the long run.

"Kevin is a good player," he said, "but sometimes players get to believe they're a little better than they actually are. Making the All-Star team and being the first one (on the team) to get the huge contract, that might not have been the best thing for him. There are only a handful of centers in the league better than him, and it makes it seem like he's a more valuable player to our team than he is. But he is not better than Jerome or Buck or Cliff. He's really the sixth-best player on our team. There are times when Duck is a better player than Cliff, but Cliff is more versatile."

Ainge, like everyone else, wished it didn't matter so much to Kevin.

"The bottom line is, we have seven very good players, and it doesn't matter who is going to be on the court. Sometimes it's going to be you, and sometimes it isn't."

But Duck was really down in the dumps over the situation. He was trying to fight through it.

"I don't feel I'm out of shape," he said. "I feel great. But I'm working out extra because I want people who are important to me to be happy with me. I want everyone to be pleased. I want to be happy. I want to feel confident about myself. I want to lose weight. That's my main goal right now. I believe if I can get this thing conquered, I'll be all right."

The Blazers went ballistic for a 123-116 win over the Clippers in the LA Sports Arena, burying a club-record 12 3s. Portland out-rebounded the Clippers 49-30, and outscored them 9-2 over the final 45 seconds to overcome the suddenly confident Clippers.

Porter went six of 10 from 3-point range to score a season-high 30 points and Drexler, sinking three 3s himself, scored 31. The backcourt pair combined for 42 points in an awesome second-half display. The Clippers shot .725 from the floor in the second half and still wound up losers in one of the best-played games of the season.

"When you get in a groove like this, the feeling is you're not going to miss, no matter what type of shot you take," Porter said. "When the ball leaves your hand, you know it's good."

"I thought we played great," Larry Brown said. "They just played super. I don't think many teams would have beaten Portland on a night like this."

The Blazers were something less than super the next time out, in a date with the Seattle Sonics in the Kingdome. The past few years the Sonics, one of the cheapest teams in the NBA, had scheduled a home game with Portland in the cavernous home of the Seahawks and Mariners. Thousands of Blazer fans gladly drove the three hours north to cheer for their team. What it amounted to was the Sonics giving up homecourt advantage to make a buck.

The Sonics went into this one without injured regulars Ricky Pierce and Derrick McKey, and Blazer fans who made the trek north — roughly half the NBA season-high crowd of 38,610 — expected nothing short of an easy victory. The Blazers sent them down Interstate 5 unhappy after losing 113-104.

Eddie Johnson bombed in 29 points off the bench and the Blazers couldn't buy a basket. The final .417 field-goal percentage was misleading since it was lathered up with several easy baskets after the issue had been decided.

Drexler scored 21 of his 25 points in the second half but was only seven of 18. Porter, who had tied his club record with six 3s against the Clippers, was zero for four from beyond the stripe, and four of 13 overall.

"It was one of those games where we just didn't have it," Adelman said. The Blazers, especially Kersey, who purported to guard Johnson most of the time, looked tired. "I was a step slow tonight," Kersey said. "We just didn't play with that zest we've been playing with."

The loss dropped the Blazers to 37-16, percentage points behind Golden State in the still-torrid Pacific Division race. The important issue, though, was to finish with the best record in the Western Conference, thereby assuring homecourt advantage in the playoffs, all the way to the Finals. Chicago was 44-10 and too far out in front to even think about. Portland's next opponent, Utah, came into Memorial Coliseum 37-18 with a chance to get even with the Blazers with a win.

The Blazers gutted out a very important 110-107 win. Karl Malone and John Stockton were truly Olympian down the stretch, but the Blazers were unflappable, making free throws and holding off every Jazz charge.

Malone and Stockton combined for 29 of Utah's 40 fourth-quarter points, and it was all the Blazers could do to win. Portland's bread and butter was the give-and-go, with Drexler posting down low, receiving a pass, and then finding a cutting Williams or Robinson for a layup. Malone, not one of the better defenders in the league at the four spot, was victimized time and time again. "They must have been eight for eight on that play," Utah coach Jerry Sloan said. Said Williams: "Clyde put the basketball right where I want it. He threads the ball in there between defenders all the time. I don't know how he does it, but I'm confident the ball is going to arrive."

Ainge came off the bench for 14 of his 16 points in the second half, hitting four of his last five shots from the field and six of six from the line. The Blazers shot an excellent .537 from the field and .889 from the line. It was a good thing.

The Blazers were off on a three-game road trip that was to end with the long-awaited matchup against the Bulls on March 1 at Chicago Stadium. First stop was the Meadowlands, where they would meet up with old teammate Drazen Petrovic, now bombing in baskets from long range for the New Jersey Nets.

Petrovic had come to Portland amid much hoopla for the 1989-90 season. The 6-5 star from Yugoslavia had been an Olympic-team hero for his native country and was hailed as the European Pete Maravich after his play with Real Madrid in Spain. A third-round draft choice by Portland in 1986 — and actually the fifth player the Blazers took that year after Walter Berry, Arvydas Sabonis, Pano Fasoulas, and Juden Smith — Petro had always wanted to prove himself against the best. Bucky Buckwalter and Brad Greenberg worked on him and, with the help of a lucrative contract and agent Warren LeGarie, got him to Portland.

Petro lived out his dream during his first season in Portland. He had a spot in the rotation behind Drexler at the two-guard and made a solid contribution to the Blazers' drive to the NBA Finals, averaging 7.6 points and 13 minutes a game. That was a good start, and Petro hoped for a more expanded role the following season.

Adelman enjoyed Petrovic as a person, but wasn't enamored of him as a complete player. Like most Europeans, Petro had never worked much on defense and was not very effective at that end of the court. When the Blazers had a chance to get Ainge after the 1988-89 season, Adelman was all for it, and suddenly Petro was relegated to the fifth-guard role. He saw only 133 minutes of action in 18 games before he went to New Jersey in the three-way deal that brought Walter Davis to Portland.

One person who was sorry to see Petro go was Drexler.

"He's going to be an All-Star in two or three years," Clyde told Williams. Clyde said later he wasn't sure obtaining Ainge and letting Petro go was the right move.

"I still think Petro would have been a great player for us," Clyde said. "I have a lot of respect for his game. It's probably the only mistake our organization has made in the last four years in terms of personnel moves. I understand why we did it, but he is a very good player. I played against him every day in practice. I knew."

Davis never made an impact with the Blazers, and Petro seemed a blossoming star in New Jersey, where he was averaging nearly 20 points per game, shooting .518 and leading the NBA with a .450 3-point percentage. And now he was going to get another shot at his old club, less than a month after missing the 3 in Portland that would have forced an overtime. "If I get that 3 again," he said on the eve of the rematch, "I'll try to make it."

The Nets went into the game without injured frontline starters Sam Bowie and Derrick Coleman, and it seemed a lost cause. It was — for the Blazers, who were outrebounded by a shocking 64-38 margin in a 98-96 defeat. "It's probably as poorly as we've played all year," Adelman said. No exaggeration there. Terry Mills, replacing Coleman, grabbed a career-high 19 rebounds, 10 off the offensive glass. Chris Dudley, stepping in for Bowie, had 17. Small forward Chris Morris added 10 and played the dunkmeister role, his last five baskets coming on slams.

And still the Blazers very nearly saved face with a miracle rally. They trailed 91-79 with 2:54 to go when Adelman went to a trap with a unit featuring Drexler, Porter, Pack, Kersey and Robinson. The Nets completely unraveled, turning the ball over three times in a row, and when Clyde swished a 3, New Jersey's lead was 97-96 with 43.6 seconds remaining.

Portland forced a wild Morris shot and the Blazers blew back, with Drexler going to the well for a driving layup that was clearly goaltended by Mills with five seconds left. There was no call from the referees, though, and the Nets rebounded and secured the win with a free throw before the final horn.

Lead referee Joey Crawford said there was no goaltending call because "I thought it was short, and (referee) Derrick Stafford thought it was, too. It has to have a chance to go in (to be goaltending). It didn't, in my opinion."

Unfortunately for the Blazers, replays showed it very much had a chance to go in. It was one of the few mistakes made by Crawford, a man with a wealth of integrity who is regarded by most as one of the best officials in the game.

Adelman wasn't placing any blame on the referees. "That play wasn't what lost the game," he said. "We lost the game way before that."

The Blazers were clearly one of the better teams in the league. They were laying enough eggs, though, to cast a few doubts about their ability to sustain the consistency necessary to claim an NBA title. The disturbing trend would come back to haunt them in the Finals in a few short months.

Drexler was steaming after the game, and on the post-game flight to Washington, D.C., he initiated a bull session with all the players. He kept it light, but he hammered home some points he felt needed to be made about the effort and hard work it would take to become the team they felt they should be.

"It was time to open the lines of communication," Drexler said. "It was amusing in a way, but it was very constructive."

"Clyde better have a great game, all the trash he was talking on the plane," Ainge said later. "It was kind of in fun, but it made everybody a little more aware of what we have to do. I don't think anybody wants to take abuse for two more hours after the next game."

For a half, the Blazers didn't get the message. Portland trailed Washington, at 18-38 one of the NBA's weak sisters, 50-48 at the half and, on Ugly Blazer promotion night in Capital Centre, there couldn't have been a more appropriate theme. Then the Blazers, with Drexler leading the way, clicked into gear for a 117-96 victory to improve their record to 39-17.

Clyde went berserk in one of those amazing bursts of his, scoring 17 points on five of six from the field and seven of seven from the line in the third quarter. By that time, the Blazers had the game under control.

Drexler ended the month with one of his best all-around games of the season, finishing 11 of 18 from the field — including four of five from 3-point range — and 10 of 11 from the line for 36 points to go with six rebounds, seven assists, and two steals, all in just 35 minutes.

And now it was time for Chicago and the big, bad Bulls, the showdown that NBC was hyping as a preview of the Finals matchup. The talk around Portland for weeks had been about the game. It was all kind of annoying to Drexler.

"I can't wait until the game is over," he said. "There's been such a buildup. The talk is it's going to be the championship matchup. It could very well be, but who knows? It's an important game, but it's just another big game on the schedule."

The Blazers were soon to find out it was going to be a little more than that.

10

"You Guys Are the Dumbest Team in the World."

	W	L	Pct.	GB		W	L	Pct.	GB
Portland	39	17	.696	-	LA Lakers	30	26	.536	9
Golden State	38	17	.691	$\frac{1}{2}$	LA Clippers	28	28	.500	11
Phoenix	36	22	.621	4	Sacramento	20	37	.351	$19\frac{1}{2}$
Seattle	31	26	.544	$8\frac{1}{2}$					

3/1/92 NBA Pacific Division Standings

If disappointment and embarrassment are the foundation for motivation and improvement, the Trail Blazers built a very solid base on March 1 at Chicago.

Perhaps never had this core group of players been as humiliated as they were that day at Chicago, right there in front of a national television audience on NBC. The Bulls spanked Portland 111-91 and on top of that, joined the growing legion of people questioning the Blazers' collective intelligence.

Labels and stereotypes are dangerous things, as the Trail Blazers would find out. Once someone is branded a racist, a homosexual, or a communist, for example, everything he does is evaluated within that context, and it becomes almost impossible to deny. It's the same thing when you're called stupid.

"They run the open court so well," Michael Jordan said of the Trail Blazers. "We try to get them in a halfcourt game and make them utilize their minds as much as possible. Look at their team. They have more athletic ability than we do. But to win, you have to play together as a team, and you have to play smart.

"I'm not saying they're not smart. With our experience of playing together and going through a system here these last three or four years, it gives us a big advantage over them. They've played well together for a period of time, too, so I can't take that away from them or their coach. But I like to give the edge to us because we've been together so long."

But Michael, the Blazers have actually been together just as long, if not longer, than the Bulls.

"Well," Jordan said, "that's just their problem."

Added Scottie Pippen: "They get a lot of easy baskets out of their transition game but we never let them get it going. You want to force them to make decisions. They're a very athletic team, but when you play against a good smart team like us you have to be a smart team, too."

The Blazer players burned when they returned home to read those comments and hear, too, that Chicago coach Phil Jackson had said during the NBC telecast that his team's strategy against Portland was just to stay close down to the end and wait for the Blazers to "self-destruct."

Much later, of course, a Blazer player would look back at the statements and try to change history. Clyde Drexler would say that questions about his team's intellect were "racist," and others simply kissed them off as something created by "the media."

The fact, though, was that it was largely other players and coaches in the league — most of them black, in fact — who continued to raise the question.

For the most part it was unfair. The Blazers, because of their frenetic style of play, were prone to more mistakes than some of the other, more deliberate teams in the league. At the same time, they weren't blessed with outstanding spot-up shooters or talented one-on-one players. Thus, Portland's halfcourt game was predicated on execution from all five players — making it more delicate and prone to breakdown.

But intelligence in all of professional sports is much more closely tied to talent than IQ. Chicago looks very smart when the ball is in Jordan's hands, and he is able to erase two teammates' offensive errors by just taking the ball to the basket and getting off a good shot. The Lakers always looked smart when the ball was in Magic Johnson's hands — he is a marvelous player capable of making something happen even when his four teammates are out to lunch. The San Francisco 49ers always looked like a brilliant team when Joe Montana was at the controls.

Certainly, all of those superstars are inherently smart. But their talent helped make them that way. There are plenty of 5-foot-10 point guards running around college basketball making

Head coach Rick Adelman and assistants Jack Schalow (left) and John Wetzel (right) in the heat of the battle.

Danny Ainge, Clyde Drexler, and Terry Porter argue their point in the Blazers' stirring come-from-behind victory in Game 4 of the NBA Finals.

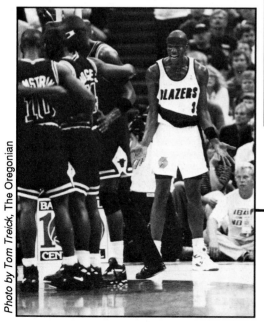

"Not me!!" Cliff Robinson reacts with disbelief to an official's call in Game 4 of the NBA Championships.

Coach Adelman reviews the game video of the Blazers' playoff victory over the Lakers.

Kevin Duckworth's strong play against Utah's 7'4" Mark Eaton led the Blazers back to the NBA Finals.

Adelman and Drexler discuss the Blazers' next trip downcourt.

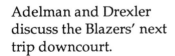

BLAZERMANIACS!

Photo by Michael Lloyd, The Oregonian

Photo by Brian Drake

Photo by Brent Wojahn, The Oregonian

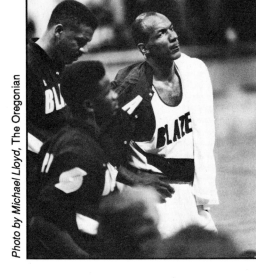

Robert Pack, Wayne Cooper, and Clyde Drexler show the disappointment of letting Game 3 of the NBA Finals slip away to the Bulls.

Jerome Kersey delivers over the Mailman, as Ainge looks on.

Clyde drives past Michael in the marquee matchup of the 1992 NBA Finals.

Ainge and Charles Barkley have taken their aggressive play to Phoenix for a Western Conference showdown with the Blazers in 1993.

Portland's depth off the bench, led by Ainge, Robinson, and Pack, was one of the keys to the team's success.

The early-season emergence of rookie free agent Pack led to the Blazers' "agonizing" decision to release veteran Walter Davis.

Buck Williams and Larry Bird, two of the fiercest competitors in the NBA, take a quick breather at the free throw lane.

Alaa Abdelnaby, who was often in the coaches' doghouse for his laid-back demeanor, takes his game to Milwaukee for the 1992-93 season.

Buck keeps Air Jordan from taking off toward the hoop.

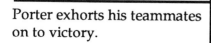

Porter exhorts his teammates on to victory.

Photo by Tom Treick, The Oregonian

Duckworth protests his technical foul in the first game of the Utah series.

Kersey rises over Scottie Pippen to score in the Blazers' Game 4 victory over the Bulls.

Photo by Michael Lloyd, The Oregonian

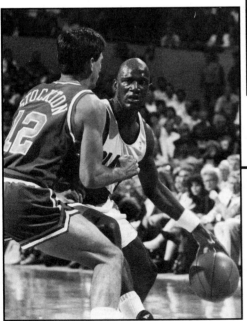

Photo by Tom Treick, The Oregonian

Eyeball to eyeball, two of the NBA's best point guards battle during the Western Conference Finals.

intelligent plays. But they don't make it in the NBA because they aren't tall enough, quick enough, or good enough.

It's like that celebrated "triple-post" offense of Tex Winter's that the Bulls run. It's been hailed as a key tool in the building of the Chicago dynasty when, in fact, it's nothing much different than many other teams in the NBA have used for years. Certainly it never did much for Winter before he landed with the Bulls. The big accomplishment in Chicago was getting Jordan to settle down and run *any* offense — sharing the ball and the responsibility with his teammates. The simple fact is, with Jordan as the last resort and safety valve, the wishbone or the T-formation would work for the Bulls.

But the Blazers would begin to wear that "dumb" label like a scarlet letter the rest of the season.

"Dumb?" Danny Ainge would say when the season ended. "The dumb tag is thrown out because of the style of play. Everywhere I've gone this summer, that's all I've heard. 'You guys were the dumbest team in the world.' I don't agree with it. Hey, we were the second-best team in the world."

Off the bench against the Bulls, Alaa Abdelnaby had 13 points and five rebounds in 23 minutes, but it proved a game that would haunt him. He wrenched a knee and missed the next four games. By the time he returned, Mark Bryant had taken his spot as a backup on the front line. "Clyde came over to me before the game and said, 'Hey, we need you big fella, don't get hurt,' " Alaa said later. "Then I go down. Guess it was fate."

———————————

At season's end, some players would look back at the Chicago disaster as a turning point of the season. The time of playing in cruise control was over. It was time to crap or get off the pot.

Portland came home to get a season-high 30 points from Terry Porter in a 105-101 win over the Lakers. But it wasn't easy. The Blazers were outrebounded 37-32 and had 18 turnovers against a Los Angeles team that lost for the 10th time in its last 11 games.

"It's a good win, a win we had to have," Adelman said. "If we'd taken care of the ball and the boards we'd have been in better shape, but I feel a lot better tonight than I did Sunday."

Indeed, the memory of that Sunday massacre in Chicago would hang around for a while. The Blazers went to Denver and dismissed the Nuggets 129-100, getting stellar play from Ainge, Bryant, and Cliff Robinson off the bench.

Bryant, who went through a stretch of 10 straight games in February where he didn't get off the bench, went 6 for 7 from the floor and finished with a season-high 18 points to go with seven rebounds.

"I can't say enough about Mark," Adelman said. "As much as he sat, he stayed in shape and waited his turn. He looks now like the Mark Bryant we saw during the preseason."

For Bryant, life in the NBA has been one long search. First it was a search to find his niche. When he came into the league in 1988 he was almost immediately installed as a starter by Coach Mike Schuler — a position he was wholly unprepared for.

After a disastrous start, he found himself in limbo. He languished on the bench for long stretches and when he did play, he struggled. However, in the 1990-91 season, he had begun to show signs of finding out what he needed to do in order to be a contributor. His medium-range jump shot began to go down and he showed an eagerness to accept the tough defensive assignment.

But he went down that season with a broken foot, just as he was playing the best basketball of his career. Injuries, in fact, have always been his nemesis.

"It's definitely been tough mentally," Bryant said. "But you can't let up. You have to keep in shape. You never know what's going to happen. I'm going to be ready when the time comes."

Bryant had a terrific preseason and was right in the middle of Adelman's playing rotation at the beginning of the season. But he went zero for six from the field in the season opener and just never seemed to get going. After making only 17 of 54 shots (.315) from the field in the first 13 games, Adelman pulled the string and handed the playing time to Abdelnaby.

"He said I was struggling, and he was going to sit me down," Bryant said. "He said it wasn't just me, the whole team got into a rut. But he felt like he needed to make some changes.

Alaa came in and played well. It's frustrating, but you have to go on.

"You have to stay hungry," Bryant said.

Certainly keeping a low profile comes naturally for Bryant. He avoids the media like a case of the flu and when cornered, seldom has much to say. It's too bad, too. He's a sensitive, strong man who would probably profit from being more outgoing.

Sacramento visited Memorial Coliseum and Wayman Tisdale led the Kings to a 73-61 lead with 6:31 to go in the third quarter. But an exasperated Adelman called for a double-team of Tisdale, leading to a 31-4 Portland run that finally resulted in a 114-106 win.

The Blazers then got their fourth straight win, a 109-97 triumph at home over Seattle, thanks to another huge effort from Drexler, who had finished with 23 points, five rebounds, and eight assists. Bryant came up big again off the pines, with a 17-point, nine-rebound effort.

Back on the road again, Portland marched into Milwaukee and scalded the Bucks with a 126-112 win, winning with hot shooting that resulted in a 30-point lead in the first and third quarters. It was a big win for Porter, who grew up in Milwaukee and always plays in front of a large Stevens Point contingent there.

Porter is an unusual professional athlete. He never was a high school star in Milwaukee and attended Wisconsin-Stevens Point only because it was the lone school that really wanted him. He grew up watching his father work hard and always had the same work ethic.

"There is no way I could have imagined ever having the kind of financial success I have today," Porter said. "But I always felt I would be able to work hard and earn a good living. Professional basketball was the last thing on my mind as a kid. Most of the guys in my neighborhood played football rather than basketball.

"Milwaukee is a blue-collar type of place. Everyone in Wisconsin is a farmer or a factory worker. The people there work hard. My dad did. And Coach (Dick) Bennett at Stevens Point did a great job instilling a work ethic. He always talked about setting goals and working hard to attain them."

But before he landed at Stevens Point, Porter had already worked at several jobs.

"My high school specialized in food service, and a lot of us got jobs at Great America," Porter said, referring to an amusement park that sits on a tollway between Chicago and Milwaukee. "I worked in a fast food place called Blue Ribbon Barbecue. I worked hard, and I enjoyed it. Four or five guys I knew worked there, and we all got up and caught a bus at 7 every day to get there. It was a job, I got extra money, and I liked that.

"I also worked at a golf course for a couple of years in Stevens Point, but I didn't like that as much because I had to get up at 4 in the morning. I worked at a place that sold farm equipment and supplies and I liked that, too. My dad kind of made me work but I always wanted to."

Porter didn't spend his money on a car, like so many students of his era. And there's no doubt major colleges would have had a devil of a time recruiting him — how can you give a kid a free car when he doesn't even have his driver's license?

"I never had my license until I left Point," Porter said. "I learned (to drive) that summer just before I came to Portland. I always had my bike and they used to have a ride board at college, so I could buy someone some gas and get a ride home when I needed it."

An inside player at the NAIA college, the 6-3 Porter had to learn to play guard as a professional and set about learning the trade. He was an adequate ballhandler and clever passer almost immediately. He's always had a little trouble defending smaller point guards and, at first, struggled with his shooting.

"When Rick (Adelman) was an assistant, he spent a lot of time with me in shooting drills," Porter said. "Then Geoff Petrie was the shooting coach for a while, and he helped me a lot. I've improved my shooting — it's like night and day since I came into the league. As a point guard, I have to continue to work on it because it's something that separates me from other point guards."

On this night, though, Porter was just pleased to be able to greet all his friends and former schoolmates with a smile on his face after a win.

"It's always nice to win at home," Porter said. "We hadn't won here since 1987. You always want to win in front of family and friends. You want to have some bragging rights when you go home in the summer time."

"We were really at the top of our game," Adelman said. "I think our guys wanted to make a statement that we're going to have a successful road trip."

The only man who had a rough night was assistant coach John Wetzel, who was late coming out of the locker room prior to the game, and got caught next to the Milwaukee bench when the national anthem started. Wetzel just went ahead and lined up with the Bucks — only to get a lot of razzing from Blazer players, who encouraged him to stay there.

Wetzel took it well, as he always does. One of the few athletes to have his professional sports career shortened because of a military obligation in the Vietnam war, Wetzel served a long tenure as an assistant coach to John MacLeod in Phoenix. After an eight-year apprenticeship, he finally landed the head coaching job with the Suns in 1987-88. But he would get only one year to prove himself — and what a year it was.

A drug scandal broke, tearing his team apart when Walter Davis was given courtroom immunity in exchange for testimony against his own teammates. The Suns swung the big trade halfway through the season that sent Larry Nance to Cleveland and brought Kevin Johnson to the Valley of the Sun, but Wetzel wasn't around to reap the benefits. He was replaced by player personnel director Cotton Fitzsimmons.

Wetzel got a raw deal, and most everyone in the league knew it. "I wasn't a part of the 'master plan,'" is all Wetzel will say about it now. And although he'd love another opportunity to show what he can do as a head coach, he isn't letting bitterness or lust for a better job ruin his life. And he isn't one of those assistants who haunts the press rooms of the league, looking to get his name mentioned in stories and trying to make himself appear to be the genius over the left shoulder of his head coach.

"I'm secure in myself that I'm doing a good job," Wetzel said. "And we have a chance to be successful. I'd be lying if I said that my only motivation is to become a head coach. I'm happy with my life. Over and over I've thought about whether or not I should have taken that job in Phoenix. But I couldn't say no, I don't want your job. I think I could have coached a little better with Tom Chambers and Dan Majerle on the floor.

"But I think about it very rarely now. That part of my life is over. My life has gone on, and I can say that it all happened for the best."

The road trip moved on to Minneapolis, where the Trail Blazers were to meet the Minnesota Timberwolves. The long road swings through the icy parts of the country in the middle of the winter used to be the worst part of life in the NBA. Nightmarish travel schedules always meant early morning flights in crowded airports near holidays, with cancelled flights a common headache. Many times an entire day was wasted in an airport waiting area, trying to find a few winks of sleep or a few hours of relief from a nagging injury.

But that happens no more to the Trail Blazers. Two years ago, owner Paul Allen authorized the use of the team's charter aircraft, nicknamed "Blazer One," for all road trips, and it has done a lot to change the players' lifestyles.

For one thing, most chartering teams now travel out of a town immediately after road games — something usually impossible on commercial airlines. Leaving after the game allows players to sleep late the next day. The players and coaches are pampered to the nth degree on their airplane, which is a palace with wings attached. Gourmet meals, top-drawer service, and smooth flights are the order of the day. Players ride in overstuffed captain's chairs with enough room so that trainer Mike Shimensky can administer to their injury rehabilitation during the ride.

But the charter flights may have an adverse affect on the players over the long haul in some very subtle ways. For one thing, these are men who hardly need further pampering. A Trail Blazer can't pay for a meal or a drink in a Portland restaurant and seems to be treated like a god wherever he goes in the entire state. Furthermore, he's now isolated from the general public even more than normal — a resident of a bubble who is escorted from the hotel to the arena, to the airplane and to the next hotel, without ever having contact with real people.

Those long days spent in airports were many times not all bad. There were wonderful scenes over the years watching the players relate to people — young children and senior citizens, especially — many of whom didn't even know the men played professional basketball. So many of the players — Drexler and Buck Williams come to mind — seemed to enjoy the give-and-take of just chatting it up with strangers who didn't know what they did for a living. But those days are gone.

Sportswriters, very often the only link between players and fans, have been entrusted with the responsibility for telling the public about the players, and they, too, now have much less-frequent contact with the team. Since the team leaves arenas for the airport immediately after games, writers do not travel aboard the charter. Instead, they leave for the next town on the following day, often putting them a day behind the team — checking into a hotel just hours before the team checks out on its way to an arena.

This makes covering a team a more lonely job, but more important, it makes it much more difficult. Stories are harder to come by when the players aren't as accessible, and it becomes more difficult to get a feel for the athletes as people. Where once a writer could amble over to a player in an airport and talk with him for an hour without even touching on basketball, he must now see a player in a locker-room atmosphere prior to a game and compete with other reporters for that player's time.

That, in turn, has probably changed the way teams are covered, both for the better and worse. Because little time is spent with the players, some writers feel freer to be critical and players are protected from their mistakes less often these days by writers. That's good. But gone, too, is the accountability that access brings. Why not give a guy a cheap shot once in a while when you seldom have to see him face-to-face? And gone, too, is the insight into a team or a player that only a person traveling hundreds of hours with a team can deliver.

The losers in the end, of course, are the fans. Players are growing very comfortable being sheltered, and seem — at least in Portland over the past two years — to be getting more and more withdrawn. Many of them change phone numbers two or three times a year, and team management is often at a loss over how to reach a certain player during the offseason. It's too bad. These men, for the most part, are solid people who should be visible and accessible to the community.

More and more, though, the players are becoming irre-sponsible. They're not held to the same standards of behavior as the rest of us. Many of them never return telephone calls, and most are habitually late for appointments or appearances. Drexler, for instance, showed up 28 minutes late for Petrie's wedding in September. One of the best at returning calls, Drexler is one of the worst at showing up on time for anything. But he's far from the only offender.

After being pampered for so long, it was probably only natural that players would develop a sense of irresponsibility. Even the ones who don't have it before they get to Portland soon acquire it. They become products of a very basketball-crazy environment.

11

"Some Nights You Get the Bear, and Some Nights the Bear Gets You."

				3/12/92 NBA Pacific Division Standings					
	W	**L**	**Pct.**	**GB**		**W**	**L**	**Pct.**	**GB**
Portland	45	18	.714	-	LA Lakers	33	29	.532	$11^1/_2$
Golden State	42	19	.689	2	LA Clippers	32	31	.508	13
Phoenix	39	24	.619	6	Sacramento	20	42	.323	$24^1/_2$
Seattle	35	29	.547	$10^1/_2$					

Even with all the arguments for making players more accessible, the Blazers' arrival in Minneapolis pointed out one of the biggest arguments for protecting the players. There, in the middle of the night, sat the usual crew of autograph and sportscard dealers, waiting outside the hotel for the team bus.

They always know where the teams stay and when they'll arrive. And they show up with their cards and pens at the ready, itching to get a signature on a card or ball so they can go out and sell it for a big profit. Players in all sports are getting reluctant to give autographs, and these guys are the big reason. Any Trail Blazer will stop and give a little kid a signature on a slip of paper — they love seeing people's eyes light up with the excitement of what a special moment that can be. But they're real tired of the dealers who want the signatures done 20 times on 20 different cards.

Of course the dealers proved to be peskier than the Timberwolves, who were picked apart 124-113 by the Blazers. Portland was just way too good for the expansion team on this night. The Blazers slapped the Wolves with a 40-point first quarter and coasted home, getting 25 points and 11 assists from Clyde Drexler, and 18 points and 12 assists from Terry Porter. The Blazers had a little trouble in the third quarter with

Minnesota's halfcourt trap — perhaps "make them use their minds" was the strategy — but the Blazers finally adjusted.

"We weren't in the right spots," Rick Adelman said. "And we weren't concentrating. All five guys weren't aware of what we were doing at the same time. We really haven't had that much trouble with the trap all year, and once we straightened things out, we were fine." The Blazers then flew to Atlanta, where Drexler again carried them through a rough night and to a 106-95 win over the Hawks. Clyde scored 33 points, made 13 of 21 from the floor, had five rebounds and five assists.

It was about this time that Drexler was making it clear that someone, somewhere had made a horrible mistake in not including him on the original roster of the "Dream Team"— the U.S. Olympic basketball team. All season long there was speculation about whether or not Drexler would be added to the roster in the spring. But by now, there was little doubt that the Blazer guard was an automatic and a likely first-team all-pro by season's end.

"Clyde was terrific," Adelman said after the turnover-filled game, Portland's seventh straight win. "He's playing at such a high level. I can't believe anybody is playing better in the league this season. He's an MVP candidate and he should be an Olympic team candidate."

Atlanta coach Bob Weiss was impressed, too.

"Drexler was awesome," Weiss said. "(The Blazers) probably made four or five of the best defensive plays I've seen all year. When we had layups, they were blocking them, blocking dunks, and coming from nowhere."

But stress of the road was obvious, too. The rigors of the NBA schedule dictates some sloppy games and short tempers, and this game was a good example. Porter made only two of 12 shots from the floor, Kevin Duckworth was in a funk after getting hit with a technical foul, and Cliff Robinson finished with six turnovers, most of them unforced errors. Robinson, the team's most selfish player, blamed the miscues on his unselfishness.

"I got myself in the mold of wanting to make the extra pass when I had a good shot," said Robinson, who is an outstanding passer when he feels the urge. "I want to be a good all-around player and do everything well, and I tried to do too much at once."

Robinson really did want to be a good all-around player, and there were times when it appeared he might be a more valuable addition to the starting lineup than Jerome Kersey. Adelman would never make such a change as long as Kersey remains healthy and productive, but the time is probably not too far off.

"Cliff has a lot more talent than I have or ever will have," Kersey acknowledged. But Robinson hadn't yet learned how to keep his game under control. "He's naturally a better player when he's on the box posted up," Kersey said. "He's proven he can shoot the ball outside, but he's consistently a better player with his back to the basket. He wants to be a scorer, but he needs the mental discipline to know when to try to score. He just hasn't developed that yet. He has the ability to be a 15-to-20 point scorer in this league."

There has been a competition between the players that has caused only a few sparks to fly.

"There was a spot (in the 1990-91 season, Robinson's second) where Cliff was like, 'I'm coming for your position,'" Kersey said. "I was like, bring it on. There's no animosity. I wasn't exactly fond of Cliff when he first got here, but when I got to know him . . . you have to be around him to really know where he's coming from. And I was finally able to do that this year. I think he respects that I've been around as long as I have, and I still play as hard as I do. It's challenging for me, because Cliff is probably going to be the next small forward here, but I'm not going to just step down and say, 'You can have the position.' I know at some point in my career I'll come off the bench again. I would relish that in a couple of years."

Drexler, relieved at getting the victory in Atlanta, a place where Portland has often struggled, managed a smile.

"You want a pretty game, go watch the ballet," he said. "I thought it was very pretty that we won our third game on this road trip and did it against a team we knew would be very competitive. We met the challenge."

The next and final game of the road trip was the best one, a contest Blazer fans would later wish they had on videotape to save forever. No, not because Portland won. The Blazers frittered away seemingly insurmountable advantages before dropping a 152-148 double-overtime game to the Boston Celtics in the Garden.

What made the game special was not Portland's almost inexplicable propensity for self-destruction, but rather Larry

Bird's journey back into history. For one Sunday afternoon he was able to find the greatness that once marked his every NBA appearance. It would prove to be the last great game for Bird, who retired after the Olympic games. And it was one to cherish.

Bird chalked up 49 points, 14 rebounds, 12 assists, five steals and played 54 minutes. On top of that, he sank an almost impossible 3-pointer at the end of regulation, after the Blazers blew a seven-point lead with 1:52 to play. This from a man who did not practice the previous day, and who was listed as doubtful for the game because of an inflamed right Achilles' tendon and a sore right thigh.

For their part, the Trail Blazers were the perfect foils for Bird, the Jerry Lewises to Bird's Dean Martin. Better straight men you just couldn't find. The *Boston Globe's* Peter May, writing about the game a day later, called them "the NBA's version of Maynard G. Krebs."

Portland made only four of eight foul shots inside the final two minutes and Kersey, never comfortable at the line at crunch time, missed two with the Blazers leading 122-119 and 7.2 seconds to go. Knowing the moment the ball left his hand that the ball was short, Kersey violated the lane and gave the Celtics the ball out of bounds without any time ticking off the clock.

The Blazers wanted to give a foul, but allowed first John Bagley and then Reggie Lewis to touch the ball before Bird got it. Bird pump faked Drexler, who appeared to foul, then seemed to both travel and step across the 3-point line. But referees Bob Delaney and Hugh Evans didn't blink as Bird hammered home the game-tying shot.

"The shot was lucky," Bird would say after the game. "I didn't think it had a chance. I actually got fouled on the play, but as fate would have it, it went in."

Said Drexler: "My first thought was to foul, but I played him straight up. Those were the instructions from the huddle. He leaned into me and bumped me, and I thought that took him over the 3-point line, but I couldn't see where his feet were. He made an incredible 3-point shot. Maybe it was only two and a half, but it was a great shot. Give him three."

Later, teammates would disagree, off the record, with Drexler's version of the instructions in the huddle. Most thought Drexler would wait until Bird got the ball, then immediately foul him. But it didn't happen.

Still, Portland should have won in the first overtime. The Blazers led 134-132 and had the ball with half a minute left after Bird twice missed 3-point attempts. Portland played the clock down before Kersey, of all people, took a shot. He missed, but Buck Williams rebounded and, instead of just dribbling or passing the ball back out to the perimeter — his standard operating procedure — Williams tried to put the ball back in. Robert Parish fouled Williams, and it proved to be the right move when the Blazer power forward couldn't coax either free throw into the basket.

That left Bagley to split Portland's defense and feed Kevin Gamble, wide open on the right side. Gamble knocked down a 20-footer to tie the game at the buzzer. That was it for the Blazers, who were never really in it during the second overtime.

In one incredible afternoon, Portland had managed to enrich its reputation for stupidity while at the same time showing an affinity for choking down the stretch.

Drexler put on quite a show for the losers, getting 41 points and 11 assists. But this was Bird's last hurrah, a game to remember that featured a miracle shot guaranteed to be replayed over and over again. And it wasn't the first time in his career Bird had single-handedly stuck a dagger through the Trail Blazer logo.

Earlier in his career, in a game at Boston, the Celtics trailed by a point and needed a game-winning basket. Coach K.C. Jones drew up a play off a side out of bounds situation, and the ball was batted away by the Trail Blazers. Jones called another timeout but when he got out the chalkboard to diagram another play, Bird— so the story goes — just reached down with his towel and wiped the slate clean.

"Just get the ball to me," he said.

Of course, the Celtics did and Bird responded with a long jump shot from the corner that swished at the buzzer. And it wasn't just the shot. He had fallen back into the front row on his follow-through and was slapping palms with fans before the ball even hit bottom. That was Bird—an overlapping blend of confidence, charisma, and talent, so much so that it was impossible to figure out where one ended and the others began.

Funny thing about the NBA. There's just no way a talented team can ever get into a very prolonged losing streak, because every time there's a chance of falling into a funk, the schedule seems to reach out to lend a helping hand.

Into Portland's Memorial Coliseum on March 17 came the Minnesota Timberwolves, losers of eight straight and itching to make it nine. If there would be any hangover from the Boston debacle, the Wolves would be the perfect Tylenol. Portland raced to a 111-91 win that was easier than the score indicated, and Adelman was able to keep his starters' minutes under 30 apiece.

Duckworth, ever the pouter all season long, found inspiration in his best game in a month when he garnered 15 points and nine rebounds vs. a team with not much to offer in the way of resistance. "That was nice," Duckworth said. "I thanked Clyde after the game for getting me the ball so much. It felt good to get the other team's centers in foul trouble for a change instead of the other way around."

Danny Ainge celebrated his 33rd birthday by scoring 15 points in 22 minutes and forgot until just before the game that it was also St. Patrick's Day. Looking for the luck of the Irish, Ainge sought some green to wear during the game and ended up asking broadcaster Bill Schonely for a dollar to put in his sock.

The dumbfounded Schonely came through — and getting a buck from the tightfisted play-by-play man is tougher than dunking over David Robinson.

The Blazers struggled to their ninth win in 10 games on March 19, when they posted a 98-93 win over the Lakers in the Forum. This time Robinson stepped forward to bail the team out, making eight of 11 shots from the floor and two free throws with 3.5 seconds left. Robinson finished with a team-high 18 points, had three assists, three steals, and four blocked shots.

"Coach Schalow told me before the game I was shooting my shot flat, wasn't getting enough lift in it," Robinson said. "He was right."

Robinson is one of the most intriguing Blazer players. A versatile man capable of playing at all three front line positions, Robinson is an unusual blend of finesse, speed, and rage — with the latter often dominating. He is also capable of making some incredibly bad decisions, on and off the court. Stupid fouls and ill-timed technical fouls? He's your man. Assaulting a female police officer, or getting ticketed for going more than 100 miles per hour in a 55 zone — that's Cliffy.

But he's also a player of tremendous potential, a man gifted as a defender, scorer, and even as a passer, when he feels like it. But Robinson often feels more like satisfying himself first, worrying about his points or overall statistics more than that of his teammates.

There has been concern that Robinson would soon tire of his role as a reserve and demand either a chance to start or be traded. But even after the season, he maintained that he understood the situation in Portland and would wait his turn.

"I'm not going to say I wouldn't want to start," Robinson said. "It's harder coming off the bench than starting because you get only one chance each half. They put you in, and if you don't do it, that's it. As a starter, you always go back in again each half. You have another chance each half. But the guys ahead of me have been around and paid their dues. They deserve the chance to be in there.

"Jerome waited for a long time before he started. Buck's paid his dues. I can't go to Rick and say it's time for me to start."

Robinson seemed to appreciate his team's chemistry and it's always been to his credit that he is very interested in winning, be it a scrimmage or a regular game.

"As long as my playing time goes up, and I get to play at the end of games, I'm satisfied," he said. "My time has gone up each year I've been here."

Robinson believes he has matured since his early days with the team, when he used to have shouting matches with coaches and teammates.

"I'm able to flow along with the team now and not stir things up," he said. "But I'm competitive, and I tend to get high strung. I think I know more now what the right time is to let that out. But everybody loses it once in a while."

Robinson slid from a first-round pick all the way into the second round of the draft when the Trail Blazers picked him in June of 1989. And it was no accident. Most teams just didn't want to have anything to do with him. But Portland has become a team willing to take on the Walter Berrys, Ronnie Murphys, and Cliff Robinsons of the world— placing a big onus on coaches and veteran players to keep the rebels in line.

It's often perplexing to insiders to see that Robinson has become such a hero to some of the fans in Memorial Coliseum, when evidence of his antisocial behavior has been so obvious. So many fans wearing Robinson headbands and t-shirts certainly seems to prove that the era of the anti-hero isn't dead. And it graphically illustrates what a lot of players have known — and taken advantage of — for a long time: If you can play ball, there are people willing to forget about everything else.

It didn't come as any surprise when the Trail Blazers journeyed into Salt Lake City and dropped a big stink bomb in the Delta Center, a 95-77 loss to the Jazz. It was the 19th time in the previous 21 games Portland has lost at Salt Lake City.

An old nemesis — poor shooting from the field — emerged once again as a problem. The Blazers made only 35.2 percent of their shots and coughed up 20 turnovers. Utah's 35-year-old mountain man, Mark Eaton, blocked eight shots, even though he played only 26 minutes.

It was a problem that has haunted the Blazers for years against the Jazz. When they don't get good ball movement and good player movement, Eaton lays in the middle of the defense and cuts off the lanes to the basket. Adelman screams for illegal defense calls, and the Blazers get annihilated.

"They defended us well," Adelman said after the game. "But I don't think either team played that well offensively. Against Eaton, you have to move and find the openings, and we didn't do that. Even when we got good shots, we didn't hit them. A lot of the time I was surprised we were as close as we were."

Drexler, who made only 10 of 24 shots against Jeff Malone and had a team-high six turnovers, also totaled 26 points and 10 rebounds. "It got to the point where I was just happy to see us get a shot up," Drexler said. "If the ref lets him hang on you, it makes it kind of tough."

The Blazers didn't stay down long, thanks again to the schedule. The perfect prescription for a case of the blues, the Dallas Mavericks, made a house call, and Portland responded with a 109-83 drubbing of the hapless Mavericks, who lost for the 14th straight game. Injuries cost Dallas the services of Fat Lever,

Brad Davis, and Terry Davis; Roy Tarpley was history because of his substance-abuse problems and James Donaldson had been traded to New York.

"It's just an impossible task to expect them to win games with the players they have now," Adelman said. "Four of their top eight players aren't playing."

Richie Adubato, the nice-guy coach of the Mavericks who watched his team shoot only 31 percent in the first half, was wearing down a little, and looked every bit a man ready for a vacation.

"Our cold shooting killed us," he said. "But their defense is so good. You have to shoot it quick against them and you have to move the ball."

Portland then showed signs that some things were beginning to come together. The Blazers traveled to Sacramento and hammered the Kings 128-106 in a solid wire-to-wire performance very atypical of their usual games at either of the Arco Arenas. The Kings have played host to some of Portland's most nightmarish games — including a one-point win earlier in the season and two losses the previous year.

But not this time, as the Blazers cruised to their 50th win of the season.

"We talked about our problems here before the game," Ainge said. "But we'd talked about it before, and it never worked very well. This has been a tough place for us to play. I know everyone around the league thinks this is a place where we should win, but it hasn't been easy."

Arco II is an intimate building that houses some of the best fans in the league. In spite of getting stuck with a franchise that just never seems to find a way to win, the denizens of the community continue to support the Kings in a first-class manner.

For sports-minded Portlanders, visits to places such as Sacramento and Milwaukee are painful. These are cities similar to Portland in many ways, yet they have sports facilities far and away better than anything Oregonians dare ever dream about.

Blazer owner Paul Allen put his Oregon Arena plan out on the table during this season and it was being kicked around all summer by wary and naive Portlanders, who looked the gift horse in the mouth so long that they were nearly bitten.

Allen proposed building a 20,000-seat arena, a state-of-the-art building adjacent to antiquated Memorial Coliseum that also included offices and entertainment venues. The city and county government, along with many citizens, responded by balking at the $37 million in user fees and non-tax generated funds Allen asked the locals to kick in for their share. Allen's share was about five times that figure, of course, and he doesn't even live in Oregon.

Yet in cost-conscious times, everyone worried about getting stuck with a bill they couldn't pay. "Why doesn't he pay for his own arena?" so many people wondered. "Why should we give this rich guy any help?"

The answer, of course, is you don't have to. You could just roll over, go back to sleep, and eventually lose the team to another area—be it at a location in the Portland suburbs or another state. The fact is, profits from Memorial Coliseum bankrolled Portland's municipal white elephants—Civic Stadium and the Performing Arts Center—for years.

Allen's building could become a money-maker for the Blazer owner, and it should be. That's why he's building it. But the sad side of the story is, the city fathers should long ago have seen a need for a new sports complex and gotten the government involved. That way, it would have been the city making the profit instead of Allen.

What? It may not make a profit?

Well, that's possible, too, and the city should have the foresight to deal with that. After all, there are certain amenities associated with living in major metropolitan areas. Cities are known to build auditoriums, museums, zoos and stadiums, to enrich the quality of life of the people who live in that city. Although other metropolitan areas have long ago recognized the value — both aesthetically and economically — of bringing professional sports into a city, the men who have been the caretakers of Portland's future have been blind to it.

So instead of building a domed stadium years ago and courting the National Football League and major-league baseball, they've sat back and thought of reasons why such a thing would never be possible, anyway. The most prevailing of the excuses, of course, is that there's just too darn much to do in the beautiful state other than watch sports. Sure, and there's nothing to do in San Diego, Los Angeles, and New York.

Instead of building a comfortable new home for their basketball team—the city's pride and joy—they chose to build a convention center that most of Portland's residents will probably never see the inside of. It's a facility that looked 20 years old two years after its construction, and it's absolutely guaranteed to lose money.

Portland is a city, anyway, struggling hard with its own identity. There is no fisherman's wharf in Portland. No Space Needle. No Disneyland. No aquarium. There's no major tourist attraction or gathering place to serve as the city's calling card. Portland is known throughout the country for two things—its dreary weather, and its basketball team. And the city has had a hell of a tough time figuring out what to do about either one.

But hey, if it's Sunday afternoon, and you've got nothing to do in Portland, you can always bundle up the kids and go down to the Convention Center. Perhaps you may even get lucky and see some out-of-state guy wearing a big "Hi, I'm ——" badge solicit a prostitute.

The Blazers returned home to dispatch the Houston Rockets, but again they caught a lucky break. Houston center Hakeem Olajuwon had been suspended by team management for either suffering from or faking a hamstring injury. Without Olajuwon, the Rockets were left to the outside shooting skills of inconsistent guards Sleepy Floyd, Vernon Maxwell, and Kenny Smith.

The Blazer strategy against the Houston guards is always the same — they back off the trio and make them prove they can hit 3-pointers. Usually, one man gets hot, but the other two are cold and the majority rules. One thing is sure, none of them are known for taking good shots.

For a half, the Rockets stayed right in the game. It was 52-52 at the half but Houston came out and hit only 12 of 36 from the floor over the last two quarters, and Portland coasted to a 115-95 win.

"We struggled some in the first half," Adelman said. "But it was a really good second half by the guys at both ends of the court. We played pretty well the last few minutes of the first half, and I had an idea we were going to come out pretty good in the third quarter. This was a good win for us at this point of the season."

Coaches often talk about "good" wins. As if a "bad" win is possible.

But the month ended with a "bad" loss. New York visited Memorial Coliseum and used the shooting of Patrick Ewing, spectacular rebounding and good control of the tempo to hand Portland a convincing 107-96 defeat.

It was a terrific win for the surging Knicks, culminating a three-game sweep of a Western Conference road trip. Ewing scored 17 of his 33 points in the fourth quarter, and the Knicks got seemingly every important rebound. In the fourth period, New York claimed 16 of the available 22 caroms.

"They were really the aggressors," Buck Williams said. "They came up with a lot of rebounds and loose balls through work. They out-hustled us."

That isn't something that happens often, but it was true on this night. New York, too, executed well on offense, and scored on 10 of its last 11 possessions. Ewing was at his best, hitting shots from everywhere en route to a 15-for-22 night.

"We had defenders all in his face, and you'd hope he'd miss in that situation," Williams said. "But he was knocking them down."

Said Drexler: "Patrick was hitting everything from everywhere. When that happens, it's usually trouble. "

Drexler had a rare off-night, hitting only eight of 24 shots and missing his final eight shots. Duckworth, who normally fares well against the top centers, didn't get the ball much and went pout city again.

"We didn't occupy Ewing enough," Adelman said. "You have to make him play somebody, make him work on defense. We did that a little early with Duck, but not much after that."

As so often happens when he's in the midst of a rough night, Drexler got into it with the officials. Then on the way off the court, he bumped referee Bob Delaney — by accident. Delaney wasn't so sure, and reported the incident to the league. However, witnesses to the collision said that Drexler never saw the official, as the player plodded off the court with his head down, and that the contact was incidental.

The league bought it, and Drexler escaped a fine.

Things didn't get any better on the final day of March when the Trail Blazers went to Phoenix and got routed 128-111 by the Suns. Jeff Hornacek and Kevin Johnson combined for 61 points, and Johnson dished out 20 assists to lead Phoenix, which presented Coach Cotton Fitzsimmons with his 800th career victory.

"That's the way it goes in this league," Fitzsimmons said. "Some nights you get the bear, and some nights the bear gets you."

The defeat sliced Portland's Pacific Division lead to just a game and a half over Golden State and three games over the Suns. And with only nine games remaining in the regular season, it was time to get serious.

The Blazers had finished the month just about the same way they'd opened it — with a difficult loss.

12

"We'll See You Ho's in the Playoffs."

4/1/92 NBA Pacific Division Standings									
	W	L	Pct.	GB		W	L	Pct.	GB
Portland	51	22	.699	-	LA Clippers	40	32	.556	10½
Golden State	49	23	.681	1½	LA Lakers	39	32	.549	11
Phoenix	48	25	.658	3	Sacramento	24	49	.329	27
Seattle	41	32	.562	10					

The final month of the regular season opened with a home game against the Utah Jazz, and it opened with a big question mark — involving Clyde Drexler's right knee.

The All-Star guard was getting pain and swelling after almost every game, and the situation was beginning to worry the Blazers. But there was little chance of getting Drexler any rest down the stretch of the season, because the team found itself in a dogfight for the Western Conference's top seed.

And Drexler has always been one of those players who will play hurt.

"When he started getting fluid on it and they had to start draining it . . . that's when I got really concerned," Rick Adelman said later. "When it was swollen up and he couldn't practice, I knew it was something to worry about. We never made any mention of it, but it affected him the rest of the way. He practiced maybe one or two days. He just couldn't go. It bothered him more sometimes than others, and I could tell when he just wasn't right."

Even in the early days, Clyde showed he was what the players call a "gamer." Those early days for Drexler, though, were trying times. He arrived in Portland in 1983 with his Phi Slamma Jamma fraternity pin and little else from the University of Houston. It was not a place where basketball's basics were hammered home. The coaching staff at the time thought he was short on the game's fundamentals and wasn't anxious to give him any lengthy playing time. Besides, All-Star Jim Paxson was at the off guard and Drexler seemed better suited to playing that position than small forward.

But during training camp of Drexler's second season, Paxson was a contract holdout. While he was gone, Drexler stepped in and took over the spot — eventually forcing a problem for Coach Jack Ramsay. When Paxson got himself in shape, he returned to the starting lineup and Drexler became a terrific sixth man off Portland's bench. Ramsay later even experimented a little with Paxson at point guard. But it was soon apparent that Drexler was going to be the Blazers' starting off guard for a long time to come.

Ramsay and Drexler had an interesting relationship. Both men speak with great respect for each other these days, but at the time they worked together there were problems. Drexler, impatient to take his place as a superstar, felt held back by Ramsay. The coach, on the other hand, was frustrated with Drexler's unwillingness to accept instruction and his disinterest in playing defense. Communication became a problem, as it often does in such situations.

Ramsay departed after the 1985-86 season, and if he'd lasted much longer, Drexler may have been traded. Ramsay, a patient and resilient man who is one of the best coaches in the history of the league, was that frustrated with him.

Ramsay was replaced by Mike Schuler, whose nervous demeanor was an almost instant clash with Drexler's laid-back approach to the game. Schuler, like so many other coaches in professional sports, seemed to dwell more often on what his players couldn't do, rather than what they could. He grew impatient with Drexler's occasional daydreaming and casual approach to practice, and didn't know how to handle it.

By the time Schuler got the gate, there was plenty of animosity between the two.

Adelman, though, had been an assistant coach under both Ramsay and Schuler and had seen from a ringside seat what didn't work with Drexler and many other players. He'd tried to advise Schuler on how to handle his players, but the latter didn't listen. Adelman, who spent eight seasons in the NBA as a player, knew the reality of the league. For players who play hard over the full 82-game load of the season, practice can be a nuisance.

Conditioning for bench players and walk-through situations for
starters is about the only purpose they serve. Drexler, who plays
hurt and plays hard, needed to be cut some slack — in practice
and in games.

Perhaps Adelman's biggest asset as a coach is his ability to
allow players to be themselves. Unlike so many coaches who are
looking for robots, Adelman enjoys the individuality that each of
his men brings to the mix. He lets them approach the game in
their own way with performance being the ultimate measure of
their contributions.

In fact, instead of worrying about the things Drexler couldn't
do — shoot well from the outside and go to his left off the dribble,
among other things — Adelman and his staff went to work trying
to plan ways to better take advantage of the things Drexler could
do. And the rest is history. Drexler has been allowed to blossom
under Adelman, becoming one of the best players in basketball.
He's a leader and a captain, neither of which would have been
possible under his previous coaches.

Drexler had first injured his knee in the loss to the Knicks
and then felt pain in the game at Phoenix. He had made only 12
of his 41 shots in those games. But he came out on April 2 against
Utah in Memorial Coliseum and hit 13 of 16 shots, scored 33
points, and led his team past the Jazz 118-86. Portland held Karl
Malone to 10 points, and John Stockton to just three assists — 10
below his average.

"There was no doubt in my mind Clyde would play,"
Adelman said at game's end. "It was his call, but he told me he
was OK at shootaround. And he was tremendous tonight."

Said Drexler: "You have to go for it. The doctor cleared me
to play, and I wanted to go out there and push it to the limit.
Sometimes when you're not 100 percent, your concentration is
better."

Adelman resorted to one of his favorite tricks to get his
team ready for this game. When his team serves up a clinker of a
defensive performance, he loves to have Dan Burke, his videotape coordinator, put together a tape of some of the team's most
embarrassing plays. They weren't too hard to find in the loss at
Phoenix, and Adelman served up a 75-minute showing for his
players prior to practice the day before the game. They saw Kevin
Johnson do more driving than Richard Petty does on a Sunday
afternoon.

"We talked a lot about that," Adelman said. "I think watching the tape opened a lot of eyes. We didn't help Terry Porter at all defensively against Phoenix. We were much more focused tonight. That's what makes us good. When we play defense and rebound, we're able to run on offense."

Next up for Portland were the two most important games of the regular season, a back-to-back, home-and-home series against Golden State, which had crept to within two games of the Blazers in the Pacific Division standings. Going into the series, Adelman made a conscious decision to tighten the screws on his team.

"I talked with John (Wetzel) and Jack (Schalow), and we agreed that we had to make our move now and establish ourselves, to let everyone know we were the team to beat and establish a tone for the playoffs," Adelman said later. "I told the team that our playoffs began with those two games. We had to make a statement."

And things were different in Blazerdom. Adelman closed his practices so he could get more vocal with his players (he doesn't like ripping them in front of the media) and his demands went up appreciably.

"It was important for me to challenge them," Adelman said. "We were going to pay attention to detail and realize it was time for us to put it on the line. From that point, we really came out and defended well and our mental toughness was not going to let us lose. We have an experienced team, and it was time for them to quit making the same mistakes.

"As a coach, you try to read the team. You try to figure out when to let things go and when to tighten up. Sometimes you need to let it go, other times you can't let it go. But about this time, it was time to turn it up."

Wetzel marvels at Adelman's ability to read his players.

"He has a great sense of what the team needs," Wetzel said. "He seems to know when they need to be patted on the back, and when he needs to jerk the reins a little bit. He sensed it was time to get their attention.

"The other thing we did about this time was simplify what we were doing. We threw out a lot of stuff and really concentrated on executing what we had left. We were more concerned about doing things right. We spent a lot of time in practice fine-tuning our halfcourt offense."

The first of the two Golden State games was at Oakland, and it turned out to be a backbreaker for the Warriors. The Blazers hung tough in the face of a brilliant Golden State shooting performance early in the game, then pounded out a 130-122 win behind Drexler's 34 points and Terry Porter's 31.

"To this point, definitely our biggest win of the season," said Jerome Kersey, who totaled 23 points and eight rebounds. "We came in and beat a hot team right on our heels in their own building. I think that says a lot for our team."

Kersey and his teammates had a little extra incentive against the Warriors. "You don't want to lose to those guys because they talk junk," he said. "Not Mullin, but guys like Askew, and Elie, and Hardaway, and Billy Owens. They'd make a shot and then a comment like, 'We punked you, chump.' I remember Cliff dunked one down the middle on them, and it was like, 'Yeah, we dunked that MF on you.' We kicked their butts and it was like, 'Hey, this is for you.' "

Adelman, as is his custom, categorized it as a "great win."

"They came out so strong and shot so well, but we stayed with it," he said. "I'm really pleased with the way the guys responded."

Drexler finished with nine rebounds and 11 assists. The Warriors lost Sarunas Marciulionis to a sprained ankle early in the second quarter and had execution problems down the stretch.

"Tuesday's game is still very important," Drexler said, looking forward to the second half of the series. "But this takes a little of the pressure off. It's not as pivotal as it would have been if we'd have lost here."

But injured Marciulionis and Tim Hardaway didn't make the trip to Portland, and the Blazers, in spite of an early letdown, carved out a 110-101 win to slice their magic number in the division race down to two. Kevin Duckworth had his second straight strong performance, getting 12 points and nine rebounds, and Porter had 26 points.

"Terry and Duck were the two stars tonight," Drexler said. "When we run our offense right, they both get open shots."

For Duckworth, things were suddenly looking up. A couple of weeks earlier, Drexler and Buck Williams cooked up a plan to get Duckworth and Adelman together, to sit them down and make sure they were on the same wavelength down the stretch of the season. The meeting was held at Porter's house on April 1

—which happened to be not only April Fool's Day, but appropriately enough, Duckworth's 28th birthday.

The players weren't sure how Duckworth would feel about such a meeting, so Drexler volunteered to get him to Porter's. "Clyde tricked me," Duckworth said later. "He picked me up and said we were just going for a drive, and then he took me there. I was pissed at first. I didn't want to go. I just want to play ball. That's all I want to do. I'm here to play ball, not to be nobody's friend."

"I just wanted to get him there," Drexler said. "And once I did, I think it was very productive."

"I think Duck had gotten frustrated," Porter said. "He'd get taken out, and Cliff would play some of his minutes. He kind of thought that everybody was easing him out and moving Cliff in. The three of us — Buck, Clyde, and me — thought we needed to do something about closing the gap. We knew that come playoff time, we'd need Duck. In order for us to win a championship, Duck is going to have to be a key factor for us."

Adelman said Drexler and Porter approached him about the pow-wow. "They felt we needed to be on the same page, talk things through," Adelman said. "It was really not just Duck, but the other guys, too. I'm never afraid to hear what they have to say. We're all in this thing together. I never really looked at Duck as a problem. We had had a number of meetings before that one.

"Kevin needs to stay in a positive state of mind. We had talked about that right along. I talked to him about only worrying about the things he had control of. The playing time was my decision. I was going to play the people who had the best chance to win, in my opinion. I wanted him to be a factor for us. It was performance I was looking for. I never questioned his work ethic. But I also believe that any player on our team needs to be in the best shape to be the best quality player he can be."

Drexler said Duckworth's attitude left no negative impact on the team. "He always wanted to do well," Clyde said. "If you have a bad game and the team wins, you have to forget about it and concentrate on the next one. I think Duck does that."

Clyde wouldn't name names, but he said at least one player exhibited more selfish demeanor than Duckworth.

"We'd be up by 40, and he'd go in there for four or five minutes at the end of a game and screw up once or twice," Drexler said, "and he'd come into the locker room kicking chairs after the game."

Adelman admitted that he was bothered by some of Duckworth's post-game quotes throughout the season — grumbles about playing time and not getting the ball. But coach and player talked it through. Buck, Clyde, and Terry listened and added a few comments, and Duck said he felt better.

"The great thing that came out of it was the other guys had an opportunity to hear what I was thinking," he said. "Me and Rick had talked before and I basically repeated myself to him. The only thing that disappointed me was when Rick said he had been disappointed in the shape I came into camp in. He could have said something about that way back then."

The Blazers all felt it had a major impact on the team's success the rest of the season. "I think it turned our season around," Drexler said.

Duckworth had actually begun his resurgence a week earlier, going six for nine and scoring 14 points and grabbing eight rebounds in a win over Dallas. In five games over the next eight days, he made 24 of 35 shots from the floor. But if Duck thought the meeting had done some good, well, it had done some good.

"We're in the place we want to be, with them chasing us," Duckworth said after the second straight win over the Warriors. "I'm happy I gave myself a chance to score and happy we won both these games against them. We got down and upset, but we didn't get taken out of our game."

With the division race all but locked up, Adelman was finally able to give Drexler a well-deserved night off. Wayne Cooper, bothered by the flu, could not play, and Robert Pack suffered a dislocated shoulder in the first half. That left the Blazers shorthanded, and the Los Angeles Clippers took full advantage, fighting off a late Portland rally to hold on for a 106-100 win at the Sports Arena.

Porter stepped up in a big way in Drexler's absence, getting 19 second-half points and 30 total, but Robinson fouled out with

8:07 to go, and the other Blazer big men were also hampered by foul problems. This one wasn't meant to be.

Drexler suited up for the next game, a home date against Seattle. Again, the schedule had pitched in to help the Blazers. The Sonics were shorthanded due to injuries to Benoit Benjamin and Derrick McKey, then lost Shawn Kemp to early foul trouble. That led to a 46-33 rebound edge for Portland, and that was the fuel for a 113-106 win. The Blazers had a 32-11 advantage in second-chance points.

Drexler, obviously less than 100 percent but eager to help his team wrap up the pennant, scored 17 points.

"Clyde wasn't himself," Adelman said. "He felt we needed him to play. He played pretty well, but he was just a little out of sync. He hasn't been able to practice for about two weeks because of the knee. He needs rest and when we do clinch this thing, he's going to get it."

And Portland did wrap up its second straight Pacific crown in its next outing, a 123-97 win over San Antonio on NBC — without Drexler, who just couldn't make it to the post. But David Robinson didn't play either because of surgery to a ligament in his left hand, and that more than evened things out.

Porter, rounding into playoff form, had 28 points, 10 assists, and seven rebounds. Duckworth, like a frisky colt with David Robinson on the sidelines, contributed 23 points and 12 rebounds. Duckworth hit 10 of 16 shots in 32 minutes and received a loud standing ovation when he finally left the court.

"That didn't feel good," Duckworth deadpanned after the game. "That felt terrific. If I could have kissed everybody up in those stands, I would have."

Ah, true love was blossoming again. The division crown was clinched, and Drexler would get the rest he needed the remainder of the way. Porter and Duckworth were rolling, and Kersey was as close to healthy as he would get.

"I couldn't be prouder of this team," Adelman said after the game. "The guys deserve tremendous credit. They stayed with it all year long. It says a lot about the guys in that locker room."

There was concern about Drexler, though. He missed the San Antonio game because his knee just wouldn't allow him on the court.

"I couldn't have played today, even if it were a playoff game," Drexler said. "It's not comfortable when I try to run. I don't know when I'll be back. I'm going to take it on a day-to-day basis and do what Dr. (Bob) Cook tells me to do."

Cook prescribed rest as the most effective remedy.

"We've excluded serious things like cartilage and ligament damage," Cook said. "It's an inflamed knee that accumulates a little fluid with activity. The solution is inactivity. I feel real pleased with the way everything has checked out. We haven't come up with anything ominous. I think it will recover with proper rest."

With the title clinched and the injured licking their wounds, Portland flew to Houston for the final road trip of the regular season. On Blazer One, Porter, Williams, and Drexler argued good-naturedly over who was the best golfer (of the three, it's Porter, hands down). Ainge, as he did throughout the season, spent time doing homework. He was nine credits short of his degree in communications at Brigham Young University and had made a commitment to his college coaches he would get his diploma some day. So he was taking extension courses in communications, sports psychology, and teaching of the living prophets. In June, he would get his degree. "Education is great," he said. "I hope to continue taking courses and learning about life."

While everyone was devouring the good food always provided on Blazer One and topping it off with helpings of cake and ice cream, Duckworth was eating fruit and salad and taking the skin off his broiled chicken. Despite his reputation as a glutton who ate up most of the profits when he was working as a kid at Burger King, Duckworth hadn't eaten red meat for about five years. Doctors had determined him to have what he called a "chemical imbalance," and medication was helping him control his weight.

"I don't have an eating problem," he said. "I don't eat all day and night. Sometimes I eat three meals a day, and I might eat a candy bar sometimes, but I eat good food and I don't have a problem."

It would have annoyed anybody in Duckworth's situation, then, when callers to a local radio talk show said they had seen him eat two hot dogs on the Portland bench during a December 29 game against Miami. The culprit was actually Miami's Willie Burton, who was on the injured list and in street clothes at the time. How people could confuse Burton, a stick-like 6-8 and 210, with Duckworth was pretty amazing. "You'd have to be pretty stupid to order something to eat when you're trying to do your job," Duckworth said at the time.

During a typical flight aboard Blazer One, most of the Blazers chatted amicably, argued good-naturedly, watched movies on the VCR, or snoozed. There was a special camaraderie among the players. For the most part, they genuinely enjoyed each other, and they liked the coaches, too.

"The chemistry of our team is great," Duckworth said. "The guys have been together for awhile, and we can talk to each other about things. I think the way we feel about each other helps us do well on the court. If our backs are to the wall, seven out of 10 times we're going to come out on top."

"We all got along so well," Abdelnaby said after the season. "You have a wide diversity of age and personality, but we all related to each other, all liked each other. You could go out on a given night on the road with any different combination of guys. We'd beat on each other at practice, but loved each other the rest of the time."

The younger players were kidded but not ostracized.

"I was surprised how well these guys got along," Pack said. "You hear about bickering and animosity on pro teams, which you even get in college. But we had guys who could hang out together . . . there was a real togetherness feeling on the court. That's what helped me feel comfortable and relaxed as a rookie. Almost every guy on the team helped me in different ways, and I have to say Clyde the most. He sat me down early and told me things that could help me both on and off the court. To have a guy of his stature do that . . . was really something."

Neither was Ainge isolated by the fact he was the team's only white player. He was simply one of the guys.

Being the only white player "didn't bother me a bit," Ainge said. "There were all sorts of jokes, and I enjoyed that. I didn't feel like an outcast. Most of the time I'd go my own way off the court, but on the court whether you're black or white is insignificant."

"You know, when you're doing your job and you're with your family (the team), there is no color," Duckworth said after the season. "We knew Danny was Mormon. I drilled Danny about everything I didn't know, why there were no black Mormons and that kind of thing. When you're with all black guys, you don't learn about other cultures. Danny was great. It was like Danny Ainge, the brother."

And during the Finals, when Spike Lee sent along some Malcolm X hats and t-shirts to the Blazers to help promote his new movie, the players made sure Ainge got one. "Danny was part of the team, too," Duck said.

"We called him token, in a light-hearted sense," said Abdelnaby. "I called him 'Ritz' for cracker, and he called me 'Mandingo.' I've played with a lot of white people, and I don't know too many other people who could have handled it as well as Danny. That's probably the thing I most respect him for. There was never an inkling of anything from him of racism, of being uncomfortable . . . I don't think I could have handled it as well as Danny. We would talk black-white relationships. Part of the reason Danny and I got along so well is he was naive to what was going on as a black person. He never even saw the color."

Abdelnaby was of Egyptian heritage, but carried himself much like the team's blacks. "No question, he's more black than white," Ainge laughed. "I used to joke with him that I wasn't the only white guy on the team, that it was me and Alaa. He hated that."

"You're a product of your environment," Abdelnaby said. "We were poor and I grew up with Hispanics and blacks (in Harrison, New Jersey). I guess I'm sort of a chameleon. Get me around a Duke environment, I get preppy on you. Around blacks I fit in pretty naturally, too. I used to get resentment from both sides. Blacks would say, 'Man, you ain't no brother.' I'd say, 'Right, I'm neither. I'm Egyptian.' "

Ainge received good press in part because he was a native Oregonian, but he said he never felt resentment from teammates because of it.

"I was very concerned with that when I first got to Portland," Ainge admitted. "But I didn't sense any of that after I was here for awhile. The guys all realized it didn't make any difference — they were still the stars of the team."

The Blazers arrived in Houston and went through the motions in a 108-96 loss to the Rockets. Duckworth gave Hakeem Olajuwon a rough night — outscoring him 21-10 — but Otis Thorpe made 11 of 12 shots, and the Rockets had little trouble in the foul-filled game Houston needed in its race with the Lakers for the final Western Conference playoff spot.

Drexler and Kersey watched from the bench in street clothes as the Rockets claimed the season series from the Blazers three games to one.

"That wasn't their real team tonight," Houston coach Rudy Tomjanovich said. "I wouldn't put that much stock in this game. They were missing two great players. It will be a completely different deal if we face them in the playoffs."

At the time, that seemed possible. The top seed meets the bottom seed. But the Rockets wouldn't turn out to be good enough to beat out the Lakers on the final weekend of the regular season. Perhaps the Rockets didn't have the heart to drag the season out 10 days longer just to meet the Blazers.

"I think they have a little bit of a cocky attitude going against us," Houston guard Kenny Smith said. "They believe they can beat us at any time. It's nothing they said, but it's obvious . . . their whole mannerisms . . . they were going big minutes with reserves and they still stuck with us the entire way.

"It was like they were playing with us, which is scary. Maybe they're right. We'll see."

Portland went home for a date with the Los Angeles Lakers, "A weird game," Williams would call it. It was an entertaining contest, one the Lakers needed to win in order to keep their faint playoff hopes alive. Drexler and Kersey again sat the game out, and Duckworth joined them on the sidelines after his second technical foul in the third quarter. The Lakers left town with a 109-101 win. At least no one could accuse the Blazers of taking sides in the battle between Houston and Los Angeles for the final playoff spot.

"We lost to them both," Adelman said. "Now let them decide what happens tomorrow."

What happened, of course, is that on the final day of the regular season, the Lakers managed to eke out an overtime win over the Clippers, and the Rockets lost a home game to Phoenix — allowing the Lakers to sneak into the playoffs.

Late in the game, Vlade Divac was whistled for a flagrant foul on Danny Ainge, prompting an exchange of words. Porter ran in and gave Divac a shove after the incident.

"Those things happen in the heat of battle," Porter said. "Everybody was kind of touchy. You can tell it's getting close to the playoffs."

Laker reserve Jack Haley, a borderline player who rarely plays unless a cheap shot is needed, took offense at Porter's actions.

"If he thought that was a flagrant foul, he's lucky I wasn't in the game," Haley said.

Ainge said he heard Haley encourage his teammates to throw elbows, and the feisty Blazer guard responded with a remark directed at the Laker bench at game's end. "We'll see you ho's in the playoffs," Ainge said.

It seemed out of character for a man of Ainge's religious convictions. Besides, he may not have known what he was saying. When a teammate explained to him that a "ho" is a whore, Ainge blushed and then smiled sheepishly. "Really?" he asked.

"I wasn't angry at all," he said. "I was just having fun."

All in all, though, it was a terrific day for Ainge, who led the Blazers with 27 points on nine-of-15 shooting, and also had a team-high six assists in 41 minutes. And he won his $200 bet with Drexler, sinking four of five from 3-point range to finish the season with a .339 percentage. Drexler, amazingly, ended at .337.

Drexler, meanwhile, said his right knee had improved, and that he had been given clearance to run on it. Practice for the playoffs would begin Tuesday, and he said he was looking forward to being a participant.

"That's what I'm hoping for," he said.

The regular season had ended with another division championship and a solid 57-25 Portland record. It wasn't the spectacular run of the previous season, but it still amounted to the league's second-best record, behind the Chicago Bulls.

And it was just a prelude to what most Blazers felt was the real season —the playoffs.

13

"I Just Gave It the Old College Try, and Down It Went."

	W	**L**	**Pct.**	**GB**		**W**	**L**	**Pct.**	**GB**
Portland	57	25	.695	-	LA Clippers	45	37	.549	12
Golden State	55	27	.671	2	LA Lakers	43	39	.524	14
Phoenix	53	29	.646	4	Sacramento	29	53	.347	28
Seattle	47	35	.573	10					

Final 1992 NBA Pacific Division Standings

The playoffs opened against Portland's almost decade-long nemesis, the Los Angeles Lakers. And even though the beat-up Lakers needed to win an overtime game on the final night of the regular season just to get into post-season play, they were the perfect villains for the Blazers' opening series.

So what, that they're without injured forwards James Worthy and Sam Perkins? And so what if Magic Johnson didn't play this season? This is the team that dominated the 1980s and the team that dealt the Blazers that excruciating Western Conference finals defeat last season. And though it was no big deal to the players, the fans were up for this series. They wanted revenge against the purple and gold.

Danny Ainge was ready for the playoffs, too. He emerged from his team's first playoff practice session wearing a t-shirt with a large picture of the earth on it. An arrow pointed to a little dot in the northwestern portion of North America, where a sign said "Portland." The legend on the t-shirt read, "Us Against the World."

The shirt was a stroke of genius. Ainge was always modeling the latest shirts from a friend's company. The previous year's playoff model became a big seller nationwide. "You can talk the game, but can you play?" it said on the front. On the back, it answered, "Portland. We Can Play."

But this slogan was even better because it seemed to appeal to Trail Blazer fans' most basic instinct—paranoia, an emotion popular with players, too. Not only have Portland players often felt unpublicized and underappreciated, Oregon residents often feel the same way. Heck, most people in the East still pronounce it "Orah-gone" instead of the proper, "Ory-gun."

Ainge knew immediately he had a hit on his hands, or rather on his chest. "It's almost kind of tongue in cheek," he admitted to a reporter. "It's a cliche here."

It was. And Ainge had found just the right way to make money off it and make fun of it at the same time.

Meanwhile, the Blazer front office seemed to be playing it low-key, because there were no embarrassing faux pas as there were last year, when the team's braintrust continually committed public relations suicide with heavy-handed attempts to protect its trademarks from infringement by a tavern owner and several t-shirt makers.

The man who played the point for the front office in all those issues was Marshall Glickman, who has taken over the business side of the team. His father, team president Harry Glickman, is one of the most respected and even revered figures in Oregon's sports history — he was the man who originally put together the deal to bring the Blazers to Portland — but Marshall has created a reputation for himself as an arrogant and obnoxious bully.

It's not an entirely fair label. For those who work with him and under him, Marshall Glickman has proved to be a fair and reasonable man, instrumental in many of the team's innovative profit-making schemes. Inside the team's plush offices, he is considered a rising star.

But someone just has to keep him away from the cameras and notepads, and out of the spotlight. Owner Paul Allen runs from attention and needs a front man, but Marshall Glickman is surely not that man. He just can't seem to pull it off. When late in the summer the Blazers pulled the plug on their arena project while negotiations dragged on, they chose Marshall Glickman to make the announcement.

The result was a negative spin on the Blazers' announcement that was very swift and dramatic. A lot of that came simply because it was Marshall bearing the bad news. Harry could have made the same announcement and had everyone in town on the team's side. But his son is perceived as the rich, arrogant son who was handed the keys to the old man's business before he was ready. It's a bad rap, but Marshall Glickman would be best served to go undercover for a decade or two and hope the animosity disappears.

And while the front office prepared to capitalize on the cable-TV pay-per-view bonanza that playoffs bring to the Portland area, the team prepared, too. In private.

Under Jack Ramsay, Blazer practices were always open — not only to the media, but the general public as well. Ramsay's theory was always that players are more apt to play hard in practice when there are witnesses, that their inherent pride would push them in front of an audience. Ramsay himself was so confident of his own role, too, that he never worried about anyone seeing confrontations with or between players.

Mike Schuler arrived, though, and changed everything. The team's public relations department had to talk him into keeping regular-season practices open, but he didn't like it. The playoff workouts were totally off-limits, with guards at all the entrances to the gym.

Barring media from practices is a ridiculous exercise. It seems to imply that reporters are tied to the teams they cover and would report back to "their" team on what the opponent is doing. That, in itself, is silly. A great many reporters covering teams in the playoffs would just as soon the team they're covering would lose—so that summer vacation starts quicker. None of them is interested in becoming a spy—as if there are any real secrets left in the over-scouted league, anyway.

Adelman doesn't mind the media watching regular-season workouts, but has a problem with fans in the gym. And once the playoffs start, Adelman guards the door with the same fervor Schuler employed. Reporters, for a time, weren't even allowed in the locker room after playoff practices.

Fans probably think that's no big deal, except that the media is increasingly becoming the paying customers' only link to the players. And as the players are closed off from the reporters, they're closed off from the public as well. Oh sure, it's still possible to see pro basketball players up close — but it will usually cost you.

Portland's players command a fee of at least $1,500 an hour for a personal appearance, depending on the player. A fee of

$2,000 an hour is about average, with Drexler getting as much as $10,000-$12,000 an hour. And of course, usually it's customary to guarantee the player at least two hours per appearance.

During that appearance, usually at a department store or a sporting goods store, the player will sign autographs or pose for some pictures. He'll also draw a lot of fans and bring plenty of foot traffic into the store. Each fan gets only a few seconds with his hero, but most go away happy.

The playoffs opened with a rout.

The Lakers stayed with the Trail Blazers for a few brief seconds in the opening game of the best-of-five, first-round series. It was a close game, actually, for about three minutes.

The Blazers came out and set the tone for their playoff run with a first half that showed them at their very best. The half ended with Portland holding a 75-41 lead, which Portland sat on through the second half en route to a 115-102 win. The Blazers scored on 37 of their 47 possessions in the half and dominated the backboards 26-10 while shooting 63 percent from the floor. Los Angeles, totally overwhelmed by the Portland defense, went 11-for-33 from the floor in the first two quarters and had nine turnovers.

The Blazers made 13 of their first 16 shots, led 33-14, and then 35-18 after one quarter. Cliff Robinson scored a career playoff-high 24 points, and even though the Lakers used a 16-0 third-quarter run to whittle the score down to respectability, the Blazers felt very good about this game.

"We were so good in the first half," Rick Adelman said. "Defense set the tone, and we moved the ball so well. We knew they'd make a run in the second half — I'm not sure we expected that strong a run — but I'm really pleased with our effort."

Los Angeles coach Mike Dunleavy, who did a marvelous job of coaching his patchwork team into the playoffs without its best players, saw his worst nightmares come true against Portland.

"Everything we were afraid of happened," he said. "The game was basically over after the first half. They were able to manhandle us. The things they do so well, they did. If they do that, we can't beat them."

The Blazers felt that in their hearts. But, they'd felt it last season, too, and couldn't beat the Lakers. So there was a measure of relief in the solid performance — and mild delirium among the fans, who reacted as if Magic, Kareem and Jerry West had all been vanquished in Game 1.

"We were so sharp in the first half," said Buck Williams, who finished with 21 points and 13 rebounds. "We may have breathed some life into them in the second half, but that'll be good for us. It'll give us something to work on for the next one."

No one made much of the Lakers' big second half. It's one of those things that happens in the NBA.

"Portland had such a huge lead, it was going to flatten out a little," Dunleavy said. "I'm not sure it made any difference. But it was a positive for us."

Clyde Drexler, who had 22 points and 10 assists, called the second half "one of those let's-get-this-over-with halves."

Vlade Divac, the one man Portland feared could cause them problems, was taken completely out of the game by Portland's double- and triple-teams. He finished with five points (on one-for-five shooting), three rebounds, and five turnovers before fouling out.

"We were really active," said Robinson, who is one of the more active defenders in the league. "We wanted to go out and put a lot of pressure on Divac. We wanted to dictate what happened, and that's what happened. We were the dictators."

And it didn't change much in Game 2. Portland's shooting percentage took a big dip, but the Blazers were able to push the Lakers around enough to claim a 55-35 rebound advantage. Portland shot only 43.9 percent from the floor and 63.2 percent from the foul line, but 22 offensive rebounds made up for a lot of those misses.

The Lakers, meanwhile, continued to struggle against the Blazers' underrated defense. LA shot only 38.8 percent from the floor and had nine shots blocked.

"We can win games even when we're not shooting well," Adelman said, "if we defend and dominate the boards. That's all we talked about going into this series."

Indeed, the Blazers were capable of turning this into a wrestling match and did. Only A.C. Green had the muscle and heart to fight back. It was obvious after two games that only a big dropoff in Portland's play would allow the Lakers any chance of winning the series. And as motivated as the Blazers were, that wasn't going to happen.

"We're not going to win a lot of playoff games with our shooting," Williams said after Game 2. "We win by doing the things we did today — getting to the glass, hustling to loose balls, making them earn every point."

And in case anyone hadn't figured it out by now, it should have been obvious in Game 2 — the Blazers entertain with their offense, but they win with their defense.

"Our defense was superb from the very beginning," Adelman said. "And when we took control of the boards, that was really the game. We thought they'd come out playing very hard, but that somewhere down the line, they'd crack. We thought we'd have a spurt that would finally get them."

This time it was Kevin Duckworth leading the way. He pounded out a big edge on Divac for the second game in a row, scoring 19 points, grabbing nine rebounds and playing 39 minutes of one-turnover basketball. Divac, meanwhile, continued to look like a man who wanted to leave work early. He finished with 10 points on four-for-10 shooting, had seven rebounds and four turnovers. This time, Portland changed up on defense and left him one-on-one against Duckworth frequently.

The Lakers limped back to Los Angeles wanting to win just one game, thus avoiding a sweep. The Blazers had no thoughts of a loss, though. "There's no excuse for a letdown now," Adelman said. "Our team has been focused all week. We'll have to play at a higher level on the road. I expect the Lakers to play their best game — and I expect it to be our best game, too."

But what Adelman got in Los Angeles wasn't what he was looking for. In fact, it wasn't what anyone wanted. And who would have dreamed Portland would finally leave Los Angeles without a win?

Full of confidence, the Blazers promptly traveled to Los Angeles and blew their chance to finish off the Lakers in three straight games. And, as it would turn out, they cost themselves a lot of time away from home. The contest was as notable for events before and after the game as it was for the game itself.

Prior to the game, the city of Los Angeles was just beginning to react to the verdict in the Rodney King case. By game's end, their reaction would be officially termed a riot. But early in the evening, before the fans found their way into the Forum, Magic Johnson spent two hours on the floor shooting — a customary workout for the man who would captain America's Dream Team during the oncoming summer.

"I've been working hard, getting ready to see the good people of Portland," Johnson told reporters. "I've been working out two or three times a day, lifting weights, shooting. I feel good."

Johnson said he gave only two teams a shot at beating out Chicago for the NBA title — Portland and Boston. "You can only beat Chicago one way; that's tempo and an inside game. You won't beat Chicago by taking crazy jump shots. You take jump shots, it's over. You try to go inside, and for Portland to do that, they need to get Duckworth rolling. With him, they can do some damage. That's why I say Boston, because of McHale and Parish. Plus, Portland has the bench, so injuries or foul trouble won't be as big a problem."

It was ironic to hear Johnson say it, because he had been critical of the Blazers' on-court mentality in their loss to the Lakers in the previous year's conference finals.

"What I said was Portland had the best talent," Magic said. "Nobody doubted that. But talent doesn't win championships. I didn't say Portland was a dumb team; I said they played dumb at crucial times of the game. If I have that much talent, if I have a guy like Clyde Drexler and I'm ahead with two minutes to go, I don't rush the ball. I slow it up and let Clyde create something for all of us. I'm going to spot you up, Porter; I'm going to spot you up, Duckworth; I'm going to put Danny Ainge over in that corner, and I'm going to give the ball to Clyde like the Bulls do to Michael Jordan.

"Portland didn't know how to win games last year, and (during the regular season) this year, the same thing happened. I remember the Boston game, Chicago at home . . . up four points late in the game and they try to throw the ball upcourt. Why do you do that? You have Terry Porter, you have Clyde — winning close games should be a forte of theirs. What separates the

Chicagos, the Bostons, the way the Lakers used to be, from the rest? In the last couple of minutes, they don't give away games — they make you earn it. If Portland wants to win a world championship, they cannot give away games. They gave us that first one last year, and that was it."

Adelman seemed to be a target in all this every bit as much as the players. But Johnson had kind words for the job the coach had done this season.

"I think he has done his best job this year," Magic said. "He has coached incredible, really. He has prepared them. He has made them attack. Usually, when Portland is up by 20, they let you back. They didn't do that (in the first two games). He has done a marvelous job. I think he has them ready."

By this time, Drexler had become the odds-on favorite to become the 11th NBA player added to the Dream Team roster and Johnson made it clear Drexler was his choice.

"Clyde has had a great season," Johnson said. "He deserved the MVP award at the All-Star Game, too. He was incredible. I'd like to be in there with Clyde because we've known each other for a long time. We're good friends. I'd like to throw it out to him on the wing and watch him dunk over the Russians and Yugoslavians. I think he has a great chance at making it."

Once the game started, the reaction to the verdict hardened. And so did the Lakers. The home club held on for a 121-119 overtime win in a game the Blazers should have won. Los Angeles junked its big lineup — it wasn't rebounding, anyway — and went with a group that substituted Terry Teagle for Eldon Campbell. The added quickness helped the Lakers jump to an edge in the rebound department that lasted until almost the end of the game and gave them a chance to win.

But the best chance to win in regulation belonged to the Blazers, who watched in dismay as Williams' fastbreak layup at the buzzer missed its mark. Drexler showed up in a big way, hitting 14 of 23 from the field and 12 of 13 from the line on the way to 42 points, along with 12 assists.

But the rest of the Blazers had a miserable time at the foul line, hitting just 10 of 20, and didn't defend well. Teagle, starting for the first time all season, scored a team-high 26 points. Drexler had a chance to win the game late in overtime, but missed a free throw and then a jumper after scoring 13 points in the extra period.

This was a night that would be remembered for aggression — in the streets and on the court. "Our defense was not what we wanted," Adelman said. "I thought this was going to be a close game, and you've got to give credit to the aggressor. They were the aggressor, not us."

"We didn't have any luck rebounding the first two games," Dunleavy said. "So I thought we'd try to put our best scoring punch on the floor to start the game. I almost did that in Portland, and I decided before the game if we were going to go down, we were going to do it with my scorers on the floor."

Divac made only eight of 19 shots, but still totaled 18 points, seven rebounds, and five assists. He felt vindicated, to an extent, because Duckworth had made news in Portland, calling him a "wimp."

"When he said that it hurt me," Divac said. "If I am in his position, I would never say that. But we didn't have words tonight. We didn't talk in language, only bodies."

An obviously inebriated Laker owner Jerry Buss wandered through the locker room after the game congratulating his players and slapped hands with Divac. "What's a Duck worth?" he boomed to Divac. "Not as much as Vlade."

Outside, a city began to burn. The crowd was able to escape to the suburbs, quick to put the clouds of smoke from burning buildings in their rearview mirrors. But the whole thing didn't end on that Wednesday night, April 29. It would go on for days. And so would this playoff series.

The Blazers were supposed to play the Lakers in Game 4 Friday night, but it became obvious by Thursday that there would be no game in the Forum that night. The league, desperate for a game on NBC Saturday, tried to persuade the Lakers to play that day, but the team refused. Instead, the contest was moved to Las Vegas' Thomas and Mack Center Sunday afternoon.

Meanwhile, the Blazers were holed up in Marina del Rey, a well-to-do coastal community several miles from the eye of the storm in south-central LA. It was a surreal situation amid the beauty of the ocean and the palm trees and the luxury of the Blazers' first-class hotel, the Ritz-Carlton. For just 10 minutes away, fires burned and looters worked the streets, and people were being injured and even killed in the mayhem.

"We're sort of secluded here," Williams said. "We don't get a true feel for the violence." For that, they were relieved.

All of Los Angeles County, which included Marina del Rey, had been shut down with an evening curfew. By 6 p.m. on Thursday and Friday, nearly every business, restaurant, and store was closed. Grocery stores were jammed during the day with shoppers loading up as if preparing for a nuclear disaster. Lines at service stations were reminiscent of the 1981 gas shortage.

The Blazers were pretty much left to stay in their hotel after practice at the Forum both days. The streets were all but deserted. Even during the day, the atmosphere was uneasy. Mark Bryant took a stroll with some teammates down the street. Nothing was said to them by pedestrians they passed. Nothing had to be. "There's a tension in the air," Bryant said. "People looking at you — I definitely felt uneasy. I just tried smiling and going about my way." The 6-9, 235-pound Bryant wears an intimidating look, though, even when he's not trying. Given the circumstances, people's reactions were not surprising.

Wayne Cooper noticed it, too, on the bus ride to the hotel after Game 3. "I was frightened a little for the first time," the veteran center said. "It was scary on the bus ride from practice, too. You could look over at cars and see couples holding hands while they were driving. I think everyone is paranoid right now."

On Thursday, as the Blazers practiced in the Forum, smoke was visible from at least two fires set only blocks away to the east. As they neared the end of their workout, security officers converged to warn them that incidents were being reported in neighboring blocks. They bused back to the hotel without incident, but it did little to quell their concerns.

It all had a familiar feel to Ennis Whatley. He had been a young child in Birmingham, Alabama, when the demonstrations for racial equality swept through that southern city. "I saw the riots then," he said, "and I did not understand what was happening. I do now."

Two years earlier, Whatley had played on a team playing for the championship of The Philippines when a coup attempt was made on President Cory Aquino's regime. "I heard bombs and gunshots," Whatley recalled. "I went out on the streets for a minute last night and saw nobody out there, and it was like deja vu."

Now the Blazers were spending most of their time in their hotel rooms, watching the news reports on television. "You get emotionally involved in it," Duckworth said. None of the players agreed with the King verdict, but none condoned the heinous rioting, either.

Everyone was happy to get out of Los Angeles.

"Considering all that has happened in LA, it's a bonus to get out here and concentrate on the game," Drexler said.

"It's exciting to play here," added Kersey, once the Blazers had arrived in Las Vegas. "It's a real nice facility — one of the best college facilities in the country — and not a bad place to play a playoff game. It's very important to wrap this up Sunday. We definitely don't want to go back and play Monday because that would make the next series tougher."

Said Adelman: "We have to get the game in somewhere. Both teams have been sitting around a long time. We've been sitting in a hotel room much longer than we thought we were going to be. This is fine with me. We're ready to play."

By the time Game 4 finally got under way, it may have already been decided. The Lakers have always considered Las Vegas their territory, since their games have long been aired in that market. But the Blazers won over a good portion of the crowd in pre-game warmups, when Drexler soared for some spectacular dunks.

Just a few weeks shy of his 30th birthday, Drexler seldom dunked much in warmups. In fact, he's never been as good a dunker in shows as he is in games. His best dunks have always meant two points, rather than 10.0 in a contest. But on this afternoon, he caught the fever from teammates Robinson, Alaa Abdelnaby, and Robert Pack. College players can't dunk during warmups, and once the Las Vegas faithful caught on to the Blazers' little exhibition, they really got into it.

When Drexler closed the show out with a 360-degree backhanded slam and an off-the-floor, off-the-backboard special—the roof nearly came off the place.

"Just trying to please the people," Drexler would say later. "The fans were calling for it, and it's a good way to loosen up. I bet we won over 500 fans."

Said Adelman: "You don't see Clyde do that very often. I had a feeling he was ready to go when I saw that."

And Drexler's warmup really was preparation for the game. The signature play of the game was his dunk off a Kersey lob that seemed destined to fly off the top of the backboard.

Drexler climbed an invisible ladder, caught the ball with one hand and crammed it through for the kind of dunk you just never see in those lame dunk contests.

"He always says to throw it higher," Kersey said. "He claims he can jump. I saw him coming down on the other side of the court and just sent it up there. You got a guy who can get up there, you don't mind setting him up."

But even Drexler didn't think he could get it.

"My first thought was, 'Oh no, it's over the basket,'" Drexler said. "I didn't know if I could get up there. I just gave it the old college try, and down it went."

The leap came in the midst of a 16-2 Portland run in the second quarter that salted away what turned into a 102-76 rout of the Lakers. Drexler finished with 26 points, 10 rebounds, and seven assists in 40 minutes. But he talked defense after this game.

"When our team defends like we did today, we're a very good team," Drexler said. "When we don't, that's when we have trouble."

But there was no trouble on this day. The Lakers shot only 37 percent from the floor and scored but 33 points in the first half. With seven minutes to play in the game, Los Angeles had 58 points. Dunleavy, who would move on to Milwaukee the following season, shrugged his shoulders and seemed drained from what was an incredibly trying season.

"I don't know if anything had an effect on us other than the Portland Trail Blazers," he said. "They played mentally and physically tough all day long and we weren't able to get untracked. They came up with big baskets every time they needed one. They were definitely the better team."

Ainge had a big game, getting 19 points on six-for-nine shooting in a whopping 34 minutes.

"Today I was probably utilized better than I was in the playoffs at any time last year," Ainge said. "Today I was able to get some open shots when Clyde was double-teamed."

Adelman said his team had finally adjusted to Ainge and his game.

"This is only his second year with us," Adelman said. "Sometimes it takes a while to get used to looking for people, for understanding how you're going to get him open. I think we have a much better understanding of that now. I think the best thing that happened to Danny was when Clyde sat down late in the season, because it gave Danny a chance to get rolling as we came into the playoffs."

And rolling is what the Blazers were.

14

"You Know How You Felt After You Had Your First Kid? This Is It For Me."

The Blazers knew they were dealing with a stick of dynamite in the Phoenix Suns. The trick was to keep them away from a lit match, and that would be difficult.

Phoenix had finished the regular season 53-29, four games behind the Blazers in the Pacific Division race. That set the Suns up for a first-round playoff pairing with the San Antonio Spurs, which was something like a walkover with David Robinson out of commission due to wrist injury. The Suns polished off the Spurs in three games and, with a full week's rest, were riding high going into the series with Portland.

But Kevin Johnson, Phoenix's lightning-like point guard, took exception to the suggestion that the Suns had the easier matchup and more direct route to the conference finals.

"The Lakers were missing a few people, too, weren't they?" he bristled. "The playoffs are no time for excuses. Injuries or whatever, you play with what you have. You win or you lose. You have to win, period. We beat San Antonio in three. That's what we were supposed to do."

Phoenix had won three of the five regular-season meetings with Portland in each of the past two years. In the five games this season, the offense-minded Suns had shot .508 and averaged 114.6 points. Confidence was not going to be a problem.

"We can play with Portland," said Cotton Fitzsimmons, the feisty little Phoenix coach. "I've always said Portland is the best team in the Western Conference—they've proved it with the best record the past three years — and I'm not going to change my tune. They're good. We've always been a notch below them, but we can play with them, and that's encouraging."

The Suns hadn't forgotten the 1990 Western Conference finals, won by Portland in six games in an emotional, hard-fought series that ended with a Blazer win in Phoenix. The Suns desperately wanted to erase those bad memories by beating the Blazers this time. And they felt they had a great chance.

Phoenix's personnel matched up well with any team in the NBA. Johnson and Jeff Hornacek were indisputably one of the best backcourts in the league and had given Portland's touted pair, Clyde Drexler and Terry Porter, all it could handle in the five regular-season meetings. Johnson shot .594 from the field and averaged 25.3 points and 14.0 assists, while Hornacek shot .586 and averaged 25.2 points.

Andrew Lang had replaced Mark West as the starting center and, while he had little offensive game, was a strong rebounder and great shot-blocker. The starting forwards were new—Tim Perry, a 6-9 leaper who had taken the spot vacated by the departed Xavier McDaniel, and 6-6 second-year man Cedric Ceballos, who had moved into Tom Chambers' spot late in the regular season. Ceballos was one of those players who wasn't much of a perimeter shooter but was a slasher and a scorer.

That left a pair of all-stars—the estimable Dan Majerle and Chambers—coming in off the bench. It was a formidable group, and the Blazers were concerned. Rick Adelman pointed to the Suns' versatility and lineup flexibility.

"They're such a good offensive team," he said. "They have good balance and great shooters. Their perimeter guys are outstanding, and their big guys are good scorers."

Porter always had trouble denying KJ penetration — but then, who didn't?— and that meant Terry often needed double-team help. The problem with that was the Suns' array of shooters — Hornacek, Majerle, and Chambers — could move to the open spot and be freed for a jumper. Or Perry and Ceballos could squirm free in the paint for a layup or dunk.

Defense was Rick Adelman's major concern, and he focused on it during the single practice session the Blazers had between the Laker and Sun series. He wasn't exactly sure how they should play it. "We'll mix it up," he confided. "We'll see what's working and go with it for awhile and then change up and see how effective we can be."

Adelman was confident that the Blazers could score fairly easily on Phoenix, too. Drexler and Porter had averaged 46 points between them against the Suns during the regular season, and Adelman felt Danny Ainge could be employed in a three-guard offense a little more often.

The bottom line for Adelman was the Blazers' homecourt advantage. With the exception of the 1990 NBA Finals — where Detroit came into Portland and swept three games in shocking fashion — the Blazers were 16-1 at home the previous two seasons in the playoffs, losing only the first game of the 1991 Laker series.

The Blazers protected their homecourt in Game 1 — but only by the narrowest of margins in a 113-111 win. The Blazers, a mediocre free-throw shooting team during the regular season, won the game at the line, dropping 19 of 24 attempts in the fourth quarter, including 10 of 10 by Porter. Porter started and finished strong, scoring 14 of his game-high 31 points in the first eight minutes.

It was amazing the Blazers were still able to win on a night when they shot just .387 from the field and made only four of 15 field-goal attempts in the fourth quarter. But they wore a path to the line, sinking 38 of 47 to 19 of 24 for the Suns. The Blazers crashed the boards for 25 offensive rebounds. They kept hammering the ball inside — and getting to the line. The officials let the players play, and the result was a physical game that the Blazers got the best of.

"We were very aggressive," Adelman said. "We wanted to keep putting pressure on them, to make them try to play us. They blocked some shots, but we were relentless. More often than not, we really attacked them, and when you do that, you're going to get some free throws."

Terry was the only Blazer who had any kind of touch from the field, making eight of 15. His teammates combined to hit on 28 of 78 (.359). Clyde couldn't buy a basket from the outside, but wound up with 26 points, 10 rebounds, three steals, and two blocked shots.

"We battled," he said. "We did a great job of maintaining our poise."

Phoenix led 102-97 with five minutes remaining, but the Blazers kept attacking. When Jerome Kersey sank a free throw with 1:15 to go, it was 110-110. Perry converted one of two at the other end to make it 111-110 with 51 seconds left, and the Suns had a golden opportunity when Majerle picked Drexler's pocket at the other end. But Kersey dived in on Majerle, and referee Bernie Fryer whistled a jump ball — much to the dismay of the Suns, who screamed bloody murder, demanding a foul. The Blazers controlled the tap and were back in business with 30 seconds to go.

"I thought we had the game won when Majerle stole the ball," Fitzsimmons said. "That's not a jump ball. Kersey jumped on him. If they call that foul, we go down to the other end and make two free throws, have a five-point lead and win the game."

Cotton is no mathematician—the Suns' lead would have been three points—but he made his point, and Majerle agreed with him.

"A bunch of guys just jumped on me," he said. "Nobody really had the ball in their hands."

After Portland won the tap, Chambers committed an embarrassingly ill-advised foul on Porter 35 feet from the basket with 21.1 seconds to play. Porter made both for a 112-111 lead.

Then Terry made the biggest defensive play of the game when he poked the ball away from Johnson. Drexler gobbled up the loose ball and was fouled with 10.3 seconds remaining. Clyde, only six of 10 from the line on this night, ping-ponged the first one in, then missed the second, and the Suns had a chance to tie, or perhaps to win with a 3-pointer.

After a timeout, they inbounded and called time again with 6.1 seconds left. Chambers got the ball, drove and got a good look at a running eight-footer that bounced off the rim and was knocked out of bounds by a Blazer with one-tenth of a second left.

With three-tenths of a second or less remaining in a quarter, NBA rules dictate that a team can score only one way—on a high-feed tip at the basket. The Suns tried to work a play inside, but the Blazers clogged up the middle and Johnson wound up with the inbounds pass out top. It was an inexcusable error — sometimes the poor judgment of NBA players is astounding — and Johnson's shot wouldn't have counted had it gone in.

The fans loved it, waving their red and white pompoms. Hundreds of them had brought signs of support—it had become the calling card of the Blazer crowd in the playoffs the past three seasons—and they were glad their sentiments had not gone for naught.

A mixture of jubilation and relief characterized the mood in the Blazer dressing room afterward. "We missed quite a few layups and had a lot of balls pop out of our hands," Drexler said as the always-heavy crush of TV reporters and cameramen surrounded his cubicle. "But we held together on the defensive end and won the game. You have to win on nights when you don't play well. That's the sign of a good team."

As Buck Williams put it, the Blazers had dodged a bullet. They were three of 13 on layups in the first quarter and missed tips and follow shots with regularity all night. But they turned in 27 second-chance points, were only four short of the club record for free-throw attempts in a playoff game and came up with 15 steals to help force 23 Phoenix turnovers.

"I feel a little lucky," Ainge said. "When you're down five points late in the game to a team like Phoenix, you have to have things happen your way."

In the other dressing room, the despair was unmistakable.

"This is certainly one of those losses that hurts deep in my gut," said KJ, who had 24 points, eight rebounds, and five assists but also committed six turnovers. "If I'm a writer, I'd write it like deja vu—three times. It happened again."

Johnson could have been referring to any of three games during the 1990 Western Conference finals. In the opener, Kevin Duckworth's 10-footer proved the game-winner in a 100-98 Portland win. In Game 2, the Blazers made only six of 23 shots in the first quarter and trailed by 22 points in the first half, 18 at halftime, and by 21 in the third quarter. Then they rallied to win 108-107, one of the most memorable triumphs in Blazer history. And in Game 5, with the series tied 2-2, Phoenix led by five points in the fourth quarter and by one with 47.3 seconds to play before the Blazers scored the final seven points of the game to claim victory.

And here it had happened again. This time, Phoenix could have set the tone for the entire series with a win. The Suns just missed doing that.

"This game hurt more than any game I can remember," KJ said, shaking his head. "Maybe since those last two in Portland." Or last three, for that matter.

Cotton couldn't help but go back to that jump-ball call with 30 seconds to play. TV replays confirmed it should have been a foul on Kersey.

"The officials do the best job they can, I guess," he said, the implication obvious. "Bernie Fryer thought it was a jump. He was wrong. It was a foul on Kersey."

Both teams looked at Game 2 in the coliseum with optimism. The Blazers figured if they played the way they were capable of playing offensively, they'd be in great shape.

Adelman gathered his players for an hour session with the videotape of the opener. What they saw wasn't pretty.

"We didn't move the ball very well," he said. "We tried to attack them after one or two passes and we weren't moving very quickly. Guys were doing things and their defenders were just staring at them. It was not a very good offensive game."

The Suns knew they had to do a better job taking care of the boards and in keeping the Blazers off the line. Other than that, there wasn't much of a need to change things.

"I can stand here and philosophize and say I'm going to make a lot of adjustments," Fitzsimmons told the media. "And when I finish up I'll go out and do brain surgery, too. But see, we are who we are, and they are who they are. We'll tinker a little bit with what we do and they will, too, and that'll be it.

"We need to put pressure on the Blazers. A win last night would have put pressure on them for the first time, and we didn't get it done. We need to win tomorrow and then the pressure moves to them."

Meanwhile came the announcement that the selection committee for the U.S. Olympic team would pick the final two players to the 12-man roster next Monday. For months, Drexler had been asked by the media how he felt about not being included among the first 10, and if he thought he should be added.

When the path had been cleared for pros to compete on the U.S. team the previous summer, Drexler's reaction was the same as many of the game's stars. He didn't think he was interested. Giving up much of his summer to play more basketball after eight straight months of play didn't seem like such a good idea.

But as time wore on, and Magic Johnson helped convince the likes of Michael Jordan and Larry Bird that it was a chance to be a part of history, Drexler became convinced, too, and wanted to be included. In the months after the first 10 players were announced, he admitted he felt slighted by not being on the list and said he would like to be one of the two players added, but that it was beyond his control.

"I'll be glad when they make the announcement," he said before Game 2, "because I won't have to answer questions about it anymore. It would be an honor to play for my country, but I really haven't paid much attention to what they're doing except when people ask me about it. I have other things to worry about right now — like the playoffs."

That was simply Clydespeak. While he was doing all he could to help the Blazers move on, he couldn't help but spend time thinking about the Olympic team. There was an unofficial "Draft Drexler" movement both locally and nationwide, and Clyde's strong play during the season had only added to the momentum. This week his picture adorned the cover of Sports Illustrated. Jack McCallum had opined that Clyde had to be one of the two additions. Most everyone — Clyde included— agreed with him.

Gov. Barbara Roberts sat behind Paul Allen, who was in his customary seat underneath the basket on the Trail Blazers' end for Game 2, and they enjoyed the view in Portland's 126-119 victory. The Blazers had all the best of it in the early going and led 35-16 after one quarter. Fitzsimmons brought Majerle and Chambers off the bench and the Suns went on an 11-0 tear to get to within 45-40. Portland led 56-49 at the half, and KJ was a virtual nonentity, missing his first six shots and scoring two points.

Then KJ went absolutely wild, scoring 18 straight points in one preposterous stretch of the third quarter. He did it on drives and with his jumper, and suddenly Phoenix was in front 82-77. The teams went into the fourth quarter in an 88-88 tie. Cotton gave his quicksilver point guard a rest to start the fourth quarter and Porter and Kersey combined for nine straight points. Cotton hustled KJ back in, but the damage was done. "I tried to give KJ two minutes," he said, "and in that time, Porter opened up on us and it cost us the game."

Cotton sat Perry and Lang in the second half and used a small lineup with Johnson, Hornacek, Majerle, Chambers, and either Ceballos, Ed Nealy or Steve Burtt. "I liked our small lineup better than their small lineup," Cotton said. "I liked it better than our big lineup against their big lineup. We proved that didn't work."

Adelman had a hard time taking Fitzsimmons' statements at face value. Too often, he believed, the veteran coach was playing mind games. "I don't believe their small lineup hurt us," the Blazer coach said. "Kevin Johnson hurt us."

Indeed, Hornacek scored only six points on three-of-10 shooting. Johnson wound up with 33 of his 35 points in the second half, including 16 of 16 from the foul line. He had 22 points in the third quarter, including the 18 in a row.

Cotton had the best line on that, too. "The only way you can stop Kevin is to put a saddle on him and ride him," he said. The Blazers used Porter, Ainge, Ennis Whatley, Robert Pack, and even Drexler on KJ, and no one was able to stay on for the full ride.

Clyde and Terry each scored 27 points, and Clyde, in a typical all-around show, had 13 assists and eight rebounds. Kersey had a terrific game with 25 points and nine rebounds despite sitting out the final 8:26. "I kept trying to figure out a way to get him back in," Adelman said, "but we were playing so good, I just stayed with the group I had."

Kersey hit his first six shots from the field, most of them from the perimeter. He also put together a series of moves to the basket that had Blazermaniacs dancing in the coliseum aisles. He was 10 for 17, and most of his misses were on easy attempts inside. "Jerome easily could have been 14 for 17 tonight," Adelman said. But the coach wasn't complaining. "He was tremendous. Once he gets going and into a positive flow, he can make plays like that."

The 29-year-old small forward hadn't made a lot of them during the regular season. He had averaged only 12.6 points, a low since he had been a starter, and his prominence in the offense seemed to be slowly deteriorating. What was interesting, though, was that his scoring average was significantly higher in the playoffs than in the regular season the previous four years. Since the 1987-88 season, he was averaging 19.6 per game in the playoffs. A portion of that was due to increased playing time, but there was more to it than that.

"I think I'm a little more assertive in the playoffs," he said. "I mean, they're what we're playing for, right? I think it's just the way I am. I'm pretty competitive. A person would like to have me in his corner if he's going down."

The Blazers almost never run plays for Kersey. That's unusual for a small forward in the league. That position is a scoring position. Kersey admits it bothers him.

"I get really frustrated at times because I don't get any plays," he said. "On some nights if I don't get out on a break or don't get baskets off hustle plays, I'm just not going to score. Sometimes I think, 'How about one or two plays to just get me going and I can feel like part of the offense?' Sometimes there is frustration, when we get iced (isolated) on a play for Clyde, or Terry, or Duck. I just kind of let it pass. Rick said before the season he was going to try to get me more plays, and it didn't exactly happen. I'm still waiting."

Kersey laughed. He knows his shortcomings as a player. He is only a streak shooter from the perimeter. When he is on from the outside, his offensive game is virtually unstoppable, because he runs the floor hard and crashes the boards as well as any small forward in the game outside of Charles Barkley. But when his shot is off, his confidence wavers, and he is not much of a threat. But he always hustles. Always.

"I don't see many basketball players out there who are like me," he said. "Some guys would be bothered about not scoring a lot of points and let it affect their game. I'm not going to let that happen. I'm going to help in other ways."

That was the makeup of the team. Kersey and Williams were role players and filled their roles beautifully, leaving the bulk of the scoring to the guys with the shooter's mentality — Clyde, and Terry, and Duck, and Cliff Robinson. It was a big reason why the Blazers were able to be such a successful team.

So the series was shifting to Phoenix with Portland in front 2-0. "We're kicking ourselves, but it's not over," KJ said. "It's different if a team blows you out or you don't perform close to the caliber of your opponent. We've let two opportunities slip away, but what's important is that now we have to take advantage of our homecourt. If we do that, then we'll get another opportunity up here. Sooner or later, we're going to break through."

A loss would pretty much put an end to Phoenix's hopes to advance, and Peter Vecsey, the controversial columnist for *USA Today* who also works for NBC, added a little extra pressure by writing about several of the Phoenix players' unhappiness with

Cotton and quoting the coach in a negative light about Chambers. "I can live with a guy not playing defense," Cotton was quoted as saying, "but Tom doesn't even try to play defense most of the time."

Cotton denied making the comments to Vecsey. "I haven't talked to Peter all week," he said the day the column was published. But Vecsey often wintered in the Phoenix area and had stayed at the home of Cotton and his wife, JoAnn. The relationship, obviously, was more than just coach and writer, and it appeared Vecsey was now making public some long-standing Fitzsimmons feelings.

Later, after the Suns had been ousted from the playoffs, Cotton revealed that was the case. "He won't be staying with us any more," Cotton said of Vecsey.

Chambers, 32, had been one of the game's highest-scoring forwards for years and was a four-time All-Star. The 6-10 gunner had struggled through the worst season of his 11-year career, establishing career lows with a .431 field-goal percentage and 16.3 scoring average. He had missed the final three games of the regular season with an ankle injury, and it was a convenient time for Cotton to move Ceballos into the starting lineup. The Cotton/Chambers relationship, already shaky, took a turn for the worse. Chambers didn't even play in the second game of the San Antonio series. Fitzsimmons brushed it off as a preventative measure for the ankle, but Chambers said he was ready and would liked to have played.

Now, when Fitzsimmons most needed a strong contribution from Chambers, there wasn't a lot of harmony between the two.

"Of course I've been unhappy," Chambers said. "I think I can contribute in a lot more ways than I'm being allowed to. It's frustrating when you're getting along in your career and the playoffs are here, and you're not being used the way you'd like to be."

Chambers was lucky, though, not to be in the shoes of another veteran forward, Kurt Rambis. Rambis, a starter on three NBA championship teams with the Lakers, was riding out the strangest of seasons under Cotton. He had stretches where he sat out 24 and 17 games in a row. Then, suddenly, he was in the rotation, playing in the team's final 28 regular-season games.

Cotton told reporters it was part of his master plan all along, to have Rambis rested and ready for the playoffs.

Rambis was well-rested, all right. Through the Suns' first six playoff games, he hadn't played a second.

"You believed that?" said Rambis in reference to Cotton's explanation. Kurt was by now so disgusted he was rarely talking with the media. "I'm in a position where I can't do a thing about it. I just want to die in peace."

The Suns weren't ready to die, and proved it with a 124-117 win in Game 3 in Veterans' Memorial Coliseum. Hornacek was all over the place, scoring 30 points, and he got major help from Perry and Majerle.

Fitzsimmons had said before the game he wasn't going to "force it" to get Hornacek, who had taken only 19 shots in the first two games, more involved in the offense. "I didn't believe that," Drexler said. "I don't think anybody in Phoenix believed that. Cotton did everything he could to get Hornacek shots except go out there and set picks on me himself."

No, Cotton wasn't out there laying a body on Clyde, but Lang was, along with Perry, and Majerle, and many of their teammates. Horny was on one of those rolls of his, driving for baskets and raining in 3s, and showing why he was selected to the All-Star Game for the first time this season.

"He made some bombs out there," Adelman said. "He made some floaters, some runners through the lane, too. There were some times when we missed assignments, but they did a couple of different things to free him up."

Perry, who had played only 25 minutes and scored eight points in the first two games, was 10 of 14 from the floor, and had 27 points and nine rebounds in this one while Majerle contributed 25 points, nine rebounds and five assists.

This time it was the Suns with a heavy advantage at the line, making 42 of 51 to 27 of 38 for the Blazers.

Portland dug a 30-13 hole, but got hot in the third quarter and actually led 81-80 late in the period. The Suns answered with the final nine points of the quarter, and the Blazers were in a catchup mode the rest of the night.

KJ took only eight shots and scored 16 points, but had 16 assists. "We let Kevin rest a little bit," Fitzsimmons said. "Hornacek handled it some, Danny handled it some, Steve Burtt handled it some. A guy with (Johnson's) particular style can only do so much. He has taken a good beating. Kevin's body is like a prizefighter's after a game. He can hardly move."

Clyde scored 37 points, including his team's final 13 as the Blazers made a futile effort to overtake the hosts. It was an intense game, with several little skirmishes, and the Phoenix fans — one holding a sign that read, "Portland fans have stupid signs" — loved it.

The Phoenix crowd was one of the loudest in the league, certainly louder than Portland's. At one point in the second half, the noise was deafening. "They were making my ears ring," Hornacek said. "There was one time where they were so loud the refs called a foul on Tom and nobody knew it for five or six seconds." Said Majerle: "That's the loudest I've ever heard it, anywhere."

After it was over, KJ reiterated what he had said earlier in the series. "The best team is going to break through on the other team's court. That's what it's going to take to win this thing. If they win, they're not going to win all four on their homecourt. They'll have to win down here."

That's what the Blazers did in Game 4, pulling out a mind-spinning 153-151 win in double overtime on the same day Drexler was named to the Olympic team. It was one of the most momentous days in club history, and the man of the hour — excluding Drexler—was none other than Kevin Duckworth.

Duck, who had hit only two of six shots and had scored six points through the first overtime period, scored eight points in the second overtime session, including four free throws in the final 43.6 seconds, to give the Blazers a 3-1 edge in the best-of-seven series.

"My biggest moment in basketball," said the Blazers' oft-maligned, enigmatic center, who scored two of Portland's first three baskets in the second extra session, then drained the four most important foul shots of the season with the game on the line.

"You know how you felt after you had your first kid? This is it for me. This is the best so far."

Duckworth, a bachelor, hadn't experienced fatherhood, but this game definitely was his baby. He came to the rescue of several of his teammates who had gagged free throws earlier. The Blazers missed seven of their first 10 foul shots in overtime, including a pair by Porter that would have wrapped up a win with 8.4 seconds left in the overtime period.

Afterward, Porter was asked if he were going to send a bouquet to Duckworth's home in gratitude. "Flowers?" Porter laughed. "I'm going to build him a new house."

Porter had been the Blazers' Mr. Clutch at the line many times in recent seasons, but on this night he was only two of six in overtime. "I guess the odds caught up with me," he said lamely.

Game 4 was an incredible display of basketball, despite the missed gift shots. It was three hours, 32 minutes of chest-to-chest combat, and it left the players, coaches, and fans drained. "This one is so satisfying," Adelman said, his shirt and brow dripping with perspiration. "We just refused to quit. They were talking about being due to win one in our building. Well, we felt we were due to win one here, too."

"This is what the NBA is all about," said Drexler, who wasn't far off a quadruple double with 33 points, eight rebounds, 11 assists, and seven turnovers. "That's as good as it gets."

Ainge was sensational off the bench, as Adelman went long minutes with three guards, scoring 25 points on nine-of-14 shooting, including four of six from 3-point range. Porter had 31 points and 14 assists — and only one turnover in 51 long minutes — as the three guards combined for 89 points.

The Blazers knocked down 14 of their first 16 shots from the field and led 42-29 after one quarter. Ainge's 3 closed out the greatest offensive half in club playoff history with 74 points, but they still couldn't shake the Suns, who trailed by only nine at the break.

The race continued in the second half, with the Suns in hot pursuit. Free throws could have won it for Portland in the first overtime, but the Blazers kept missing, and when Porter clunked a pair off the rim with Portland on top 140-138 in the first extra session, it paved the way for KJ to swoop in for a 15-footer with 2.7 seconds left to force a second OT.

Then it was on to Duckworth's heroics. "What a great feeling," he said later. "I remember thinking, 'Shit, the whole stadium be quiet.' I hit those free throws, and I heard the crowd get quiet, totally silent. Knowing you did that . . . my team helped, but I did it. I was there when they needed me. No one can take that away. It was my own individual thing. That's what made it so great. I was on that line by myself."

To quiet one of the rowdiest crowds in the league was indeed an accomplishment. And the Suns' management staff had done its best to heighten the hysteria, flashing a graphic on the reader board from an Adelman quote taken out of context. It read, "The crowd noise doesn't bother us—Rick Adelman." The fans responded angrily with a wild chorus of boos. Adelman coolly acted as if he didn't have a clue as to what was going on.

Duckworth grew up in a religious environment and remains a Christian who is a regular visitor to the pre-game chapel service conducted by Blazer chaplain Al Egg. "I believe what happened that night was meant to happen," Duck said. "I believe that was in the Lord's hands because of the way it happened. I mean, I've never seen Terry miss all those free throws like that, and Clyde miss some down the stretch. It's always said that you give to the Lord and the Lord comes through for you. I've been giving to Him, and things happened for the best."

Participants were quick to search for comparisons between Game 4 and the greatest games in history. Ainge could think of only two of the same magnitude — the seventh game of the 1988 Eastern Conference finals between Boston and Detroit, when Larry Bird stole Isiah Thomas' inbounds pass and fed Dennis Johnson for the series-winning layup, and the game in the 1984 NBA Finals between Boston and the Lakers, when Gerald Henderson's steal and solo layup clinched victory. Adelman said it ranked with the seventh-game win over San Antonio in the 1990 conference semifinals as the most exciting games he'd participated in 17 years as an NBA coach and player. Phoenix president Jerry Colangelo linked it with Boston's triple-overtime win over the Suns in the 1976 Finals — the Garfield Heard game — as the greatest in club history.

Fans back in Portland watched on television in record numbers. Game 4 produced the highest rating ever for a game broadcast by the Blazers with a 48 rating and a 69 share in

Arbitron. At the conclusion of the game, the broadcast received a 56 rating and a 70 share — meaning that 56 percent of all television sets, and 70 percent of those turned on, were tuned into the game. By comparison, the Super Bowl had drawn a 40 rating and a 65 share.

For Drexler, the day included a nice bonus with the news he and college star Christian Laettner of Duke would complete the Olympic team's 12-man roster. The selection committee had met the previous day and had reached a decision. Of course, the committee members wanted to keep it a secret until they could bring out some pomp and circumstance in a press conference the following day.

A representative of the committee called Geoff Petrie, who relayed the news to Clyde about 3 p.m. the day of Game 4. Both were sworn to secrecy, which was ridiculous. Interest was high, of course, especially in Portland, and it was silly to ask them to lie when the media came calling. Club president Harry Glickman admitted he knew whether Clyde had been added but said he couldn't tell. That was more than Petrie would do. He denied he had any knowledge of it all evening when, in fact, he was the messenger for the committee.

Finally, after the game, Clyde took a beat writer aside and admitted, sort of, that he had received the good news. "If it's true, I'm thrilled," Clyde said. "And I'm relieved, too. I've been asked an awful lot about it over the past few weeks. I don't think there's anything better than the opportunity to play for your country."

Adelman was happy, too. "Clyde went out and had such a big year, the committee couldn't leave him off," the coach said.

In a phone interview from New York, Rod Thorn, a member of the 12-man selection committee, agreed with Adelman's sentiments.

"I think when the committee was talking about various players, Drexler really stood out," he said. "Although Clyde has always been a terrific player, he really jumped out at us this year. He is at the peak of his game. If it weren't for Magic Johnson, he was the MVP of the All-Star Game. Things like that happened. It's been like that the whole year. He stepped up into another category within the league as to how people think of him. Everybody always thought he was a great player, but it's beyond that now."

Late that night, as the Blazers' private jet hit the sky for the 2 1/2-hour flight home, Glickman rose for an announcement. "Listen up for a minute," the gravelly-voiced president of the Blazers said. "I'm sure you'll all be happy to know your teammate has been named to the Olympic team." A cheer went up and Clyde smiled widely, accepting Glickman's hand. Everyone came over to congratulate him and some drank a toast in his honor. It was the end to an incredibly exciting day.

The following day came the official announcement and a hastily arranged national teleconference with the nation's media, followed by a meeting with local reporters at the Blazer offices. Clyde admitted he wrestled with his emotions after Petrie gave him the news before Game 4.

"The hardest thing was to control my emotions," he said. "You still have to go out and play, and it was a pivotal game. I had to really focus and concentrate. But I thought it was a good move by Geoff. It was great news and could only enhance my mood."

During the teleconference, Drexler said the Olympic team spot was the biggest achievement of his career and would be even bigger than a championship ring. "Going for the gold medal for your country has to take precedence over an NBA championship at this time," he said. "Of course, an NBA championship is our goal now. The ultimate goal is to win a gold medal for your country."

Nobody could begrudge Clyde such sentiment, though those within the Blazer organization would have rather heard him list his priorities in a different order. And later in the day, when asked about his comments, Clyde tried to reverse field.

"The Olympics is playing for your country instead of just your state," he said. "But winning an NBA championship would be the best thing that ever happened. The next step would be winning a gold medal."

It was another example of Clyde speaking without thinking out his thoughts. The forgiving Portland media didn't make it an issue, and it was forgotten.

The Blazers needed one more win to polish off the Suns, and they didn't want to take any chances by returning to Phoenix for Game 6. A Portland win in Game 5 would make it Cotton's last stand as coach of the Suns, and he wasn't in a mood to hear about it. "Don't even be bringing that up now," he said after the Suns' off-day practice. "I'm not thinking about that at all."

Cotton said he wasn't concerned that the spirit of his players was broken with the loss in Game 4.

"I'm not worried about the mood of the guys," he said. "I think it's pretty good. They feel badly about losing, but what they did was lose to the best team in the West in double overtime. That's nothing to be ashamed of. Resiliency is their middle name. They've always bounced back. I think they will again."

The Blazers figured they had the Suns on the floor, but they had enough respect for their foes to not want to let them up, even for a second "We haven't won anything yet," Drexler said. He meant it. His teammates agreed. Such was the regard the Blazers held for the Suns.

The Suns weren't waving a white flag. "If I was a betting person, I'd bet on Portland to close it out," KJ said. "We've dug ourselves about as deep a hole as you can without being buried. But our team has shown a lot of character. We're looking forward to the challenge."

Cotton didn't want to talk at all about the potential end to the series.

"If I've read things correctly," he rasped, "it takes four games to win a best-of-seven series. I think that's what it says. Nobody's gotten to four yet. Somebody gets to four, we'll declare them the winner. I hope it's going to be us."

The Blazers made sure it wasn't with a 118-106 victory in Game 5. After some rough treatment by Sun fans in Phoenix in Games 3 and 4, Portland's crowd had taken a harder edge for this one. "Phuck Phoenix," read one of the hundreds of signs held in the coliseum.

The Blazers rewarded the fans with one of their best defensive efforts of the playoffs. They turned out 12 blocked shots and 11 steals, and those helped set up a barrage of fast-break opportunities for Drexler, Porter, and Kersey, who combined for 70 points.

"We won 4-1, but 4-1 is misleading in this series," Adelman said. "They played us tough in every game. But our guys played just a little better."

Clyde collected 34 points on 14-of-22 shooting to go with eight rebounds, eight assists, and three blocked shots. Kersey had a terrific game with 16 points, 12 rebounds, a career playoff-high eight assists, and five steals. And Porter continued his sensational play with 20 points and some excellent defensive work on Johnson, who was only four for 13 and finished with 12 points and six assists.

KJ had an outstanding series, averaging 24.4 points and 11.5 assists, but Porter had been at least his equal, averaging 25.8 points and 10.5 assists, shooting .543, sinking seven 3-pointers, and committing only nine turnovers.

Afterward, alone in the Phoenix dressing room, KJ paid tribute to his adversary.

"When you assess Terry Porter's value to the Blazers, don't go by statistics," the Suns' classy leader said. "You have to do it on what he does for that team. It's no secret the Blazers are the best team in the West, and he's a vital reason for that. (John) Stockton gets more assists, and myself and (Tim) Hardaway score more, but that's because of the different makeup of their team. Believe me, he is unquestionably one of the best players in the league. When you're guarding him, you have to be ready on every single play. He's one of the smartest players in the league. He makes you pay every time you do something wrong."

The teams were close in talent. The Blazers were the tighter of the units, though, with each player identifying with his role and adhering closely to it. That slight edge, along with Portland's definite defensive advantage, made the difference. That and the remarkable talents of Drexler and Porter, who was reaching his peak at just the right time.

So it was time to stick the fork in. The Suns were done, and now it was on to another challenge. For the Blazers, it was the Utah Jazz. For Porter, it was Stockton. "No rest," Porter said through a tired grin, "for the weary."

15

"Anybody Should Win Except the Portland Cry Blazers."

Tempo would be a major issue in the Portland-Utah series. "We want to run," said Danny Ainge, "and they're going to want to slow it down."

If that was an oversimplification, at least it was close to the mark. The Blazers were at their best when they were pushing the attack and getting the ball into the open court. The Jazz were better in the halfcourt, with John Stockton and Karl Malone running their two-man game.

"The team that best plays its tempo," Terry Porter said, "will win the series."

A year earlier, in the Western Conference semifinals, the Blazers had taken care of the Jazz in five games in what was a very competitive series. Utah's regulars were the same this season, but the bench was fortified with the addition of forwards Tyrone Corbin and David Benoit. And Jeff Malone, in his second season in the backcourt with Stockton, was much more comfortable in his role with the team and would provide a difficult test for Clyde Drexler.

"This is the best team we've ever had," said Utah president Frank Layden. "There's not even a doubt. We are more athletic and deeper than we have been. And all of our players continue to improve."

Utah had trouble with the LA Clippers in the first round, going the route in a five-game series. But the Jazz had played superbly in winning their conference semifinal series with Seattle 4-1.

One of the interesting aspects of a Portland-Utah series were the individual matchups. There was Jeff Malone against Drexler. Stockton vs. Porter was a contrast in styles, but a delight to watch. And Karl Malone had no tougher customer to go up against than Buck Williams.

Malone respected Williams, but never went out of his way publicly to compliment his foe. And the Buckster wasn't exactly eager to pay tribute to the Mailman, either, opting to lavish the majority of his praise on Stockton. They were both proud warriors. Perhaps they were afraid to give the other even an inkling of an edge.

"Stockton orchestrates everything they do offensively," Williams said before the series began. "He makes the decisions with the ball on all their plays, he gets it to Karl a great deal, he moves the ball in their fast break very efficiently. He is the key player in this whole ordeal."

Like Kevin Johnson, Stockton handled the ball better than 90 percent of the time. Unlike Johnson, who distributed the ball to several of his teammates with regularity, Stockton's target was invariably Karl Malone. Rick Adelman could play Malone straight up with Williams much more effectively than just about any team in the NBA, but Buck would need some good help defensively, too, from Jerome Kersey, and Kevin Duckworth, and Cliff Robinson.

In Ainge's mind, the Blazers were at the top of their game. "Everybody is playing at a high level," he said. "This is the best we've played in the two years I've been with the team."

Adelman was still apprehensive. And he wasn't just blowing smoke.

"A year ago, we beat Utah, and everybody was saying how good we were playing, and then we lost to the Lakers," he said. "But Utah is a very good team with excellent talent. We'll have to raise our level of play to win this series."

Utah-Portland games are typically among the most physical in the NBA. Much of the reason is the Malone-Williams matchup. Williams gives no quarter, and nobody moves a body out of the lane with more power than Malone. An important aspect of the series would be how much the officials would let Malone and Williams get away with.

Williams considers Malone's blacksmith reputation overblown. "Everyone looks at him and sees such a physical speci-
men and thinks it must make for a very physical matchup," Buck
said. "But it doesn't. I've had tougher battles with guys like
Frank Brickowski. Malone's a cakewalk compared to guys like
Maurice Lucas, Lonnie Shelton, and Charles Oakley. His game
has changed. He's a jump shooter now. I'm back off him 15 feet
from the basket and he's shooting a jump shot. I'm like, 'Hey,
make my day.' When he posts up and is aggressive, he makes it
tough on us and can get us in foul trouble. But he didn't do much
of that."

As the teams warmed up before the opener, referee Darell
Garretson called the two power forwards over to meet with him
at midcourt. "He told us he didn't want us to give each other a
kiss like Isiah (Thomas) and Magic used to do," Buck joked
afterward.

In reality, Garretson was trying to prevent any kind of
rough stuff from getting started.

"I knew it was going to be a difficult game to call," Garretson
said later. "Any game with Malone is hard. He's so strong, and
who is to say whether he is getting pushed and held or whether
he is throwing people out of there? I thought it was important to
talk to them and caution them that I wanted the game to be a clean
one, and that I would be watching both of them."

Cynics on press row snickered at Garretson's bravado.
How many officials would take it upon themselves to gather two
of the game's stars and warn them he would be "watching
them?" Williams said he "definitely" saw it as a grandstand
move on Garretson's part. "I've never had a referee call me over
like that before a game," Buck said. "But it didn't bother me at
all."

Nothing much bothered the Blazers in their 113-88 disman-
tling of the bewildered visitors. There were no incidents in the
Malone-Williams matchup, but it was over so quickly, the two
never really had a chance to get into anything.

Just as they had done in the opener of the Laker series, the
Blazers blew their opposition out of the water early. From the
first of a succession of Porter 3s to Robinson's uncontested game-
ending layup, it was strictly no contest. The Blazers put together
a postcard-perfect first half, nailing 24 of their first 30 shots to go
into intermission with a 65-37 lead. The remaining 24 minutes

were fill time as both coaches emptied their benches early with Game 2 of the series already in mind.

"I don't know if we can play any better than that," Adelman said of the Blazers' first-half masterpiece. "We shot it well, we were active, we followed our game plan . . . I don't know if we've had a better half of basketball."

The Blazers shot .761 in the first quarter and .634 in the first half. They cooled off in the second half and wound up at .506 for the game, but they found the open man the entire way, as evidenced by 36 assists leading to 43 baskets. They were opportunists, too, at one time holding a 23-0 edge in second-chance points.

Porter won round one with Stockton going away, opening the game with a pair of 3s, closing out the first half with a 3 and — presto — opening the third quarter with another 3. He finished six of eight from 3-point territory, was eight of 12 overall, and collected a game-high 26 points and eight assists in only 28 minutes.

"Even the ones I missed I thought were good," Porter told a bevy of media afterward. "You have days like that."

Stockton, meanwhile, was never into it. The soon-to-be Olympian hit only one of six shots from the field, and finished with six points and nine assists in 27 minutes.

"Terry came out and dominated us," Stockton said. "I wish I would have guarded him better, but he hit some big shots. He was coming off screens, and I didn't get through the screens very well."

Karl Malone was amazingly quiet, too, going three for six from the floor and collecting 11 points and seven rebounds in 29 minutes.

Prior to the playoffs, *The Oregonian* had put out a special section with a front-page illustration of Kersey dunking on a cowering Malone. It seemed extremely presumptuous at the time. But there on the front page of Sunday's sports section was a photo of Kersey, slamming one through the nets over — yes — a cowering Malone. It was almost as if the artist had a premonition. Actually, the picture should have been of Kersey stepping back to knock down an 18-footer. He was six for six in the first quarter, and five of the baskets came from long range. "I don't want to get into the habit of shooting too many jumpers," he smiled afterward. "But I'll take them when I can."

Duckworth had a productive game against 7-4 Utah center Mark Eaton, dropping eight of 12 shots for 18 points. The Duck had a run-in with Garretson, too, picking up a third-quarter technical after being whistled for his fourth personal foul—all by Garretson. "He said, 'Get out of my face,' but it wasn't like I even said that much to him," a perplexed Duckworth said after the game. "It was a dumb T. It wasn't deserving. I'm going to protest that one. Rod Thorn is going to get a call Monday morning."

Ainge hit six of nine shots to run his field-goal percentage in the playoffs to a saucy .551. He was also shooting .480 from 3-point range and .938 from the foul line. He was averaging 11.1 points and playing more minutes — 22.6 — than he had during the regular season as Adelman went more minutes with a three-guard lineup. Fans, media, and even coaches had a tendency to evaluate Ainge's play primarily on how well he was shooting. It wasn't fair because, even when his shot was off, he was doing other things to help. Ainge was a good passer, a solid position defender and a battler. And he was one of the league's more cerebral players. Not too many players understand the game better than Danny Ainge.

But the fact was, Ainge couldn't get his shot to go down early in the season, and after his first 32 games he was shooting only .389 from the field. Then he began to come on. In the last 49 regular-season games, he shot .468 — even while taking a lot of shots from 3-point range — to lift his season's percentage to .442. His 3-point percentage, .296 in the first half, was .396 the second half of the regular season, and now he was making nearly half his 3s.

To Ainge, part of the reason he hadn't shot as well early was because his minutes were down. It was the old chicken-or-the-egg question. "I'm playing more minutes now," he said after Game 1. "When you get more minutes, you feel more confident. Your confidence soars with every good minute out there."

Adelman prided himself in doling out minutes strictly to those who earned it. In his mind, Ainge was now earning more minutes.

"It could be Danny is playing better because he is getting more time," Adelman said, "but the plain fact is he's playing better, and that's why he is getting more minutes. He is shooting well, and when he is doing that I like to have him in the game with Clyde and Terry. The more minutes for Danny, the better it is for him. It doesn't put so much pressure on him to have to make one or two shots. He knows he's going to be in there for awhile. The way he's been playing, it's been an easy decision to get him into the game."

Oddly, the man who had carried the Blazers through much of the season was the only starter not to have a terrific game. Drexler shot five for 13 and finished with a quiet 11 points, three rebounds, and eight assists in 30 minutes. Clyde, who had averaged 29.1 points through the first nine playoff games, appreciated what amounted to an emotional breather. "That was a total team effort," he beamed. "I'll take a win like that any day."

The only real negative from Portland's standpoint came late in the game. Alaa Abdelnaby, who had fallen into disfavor with Adelman, had been inserted into the game in garbage time. Soon thereafter Adelman called a set and Alaa took his time getting to his assigned spot on the floor. The coach yelled at him and quickly called a timeout. Adelman gave him a piece of his mind in the huddle and Alaa stood up for himself. When play resumed, Alaa was on the bench, and he stayed there the rest of the way.

Adelman wouldn't talk about the incident after the game —but later admitted he didn't like what he perceived as a laissez-faire approach by his second-year forward. Alaa was genuinely stunned at the coach's actions and didn't understand what all the fuss was about. They talked after the game and seemed to have the item resolved, at least on the surface. "He saw it one way and I saw it another way," Alaa said. "But he's the coach, and it's no big deal. Everything is fine now."

Everything wasn't fine with the Jazz. Coach Jerry Sloan, as hard-nosed in his current capacity as he was when he was an All-Star guard with Chicago in the 1970s, managed a sense of humor as he met with the media after the game.

"You guys don't have any guns, do you?" he asked, as if suicide might be the best alternative. Then he shook his head. "That was about the longest game I've ever sat through. Portland was sensational. They were two steps ahead of us in everything we tried to do. They were totally ready for us, and we only had one guy with any life in his body, Jeff Malone. We just didn't have any spark, and I don't know if I've ever seen a team play better than (the Blazers) did."

Sloan was asked what adjustments he planned for Game 2. "We're going to see if we can get David Robinson, Hakeem Olajuwon, and four or five other guys and see if we can play this team," he said stone-faced. He was kidding. The series was a long way from over.

During the off day came news that Drexler had finished second to Michael Jordan in Most-Valuable-Player balloting, as expected. Three weeks earlier, *The Oregonian* had conducted a mock ballot with members of the media from every NBA city, and Clyde had finished as a solid runner-up behind Jordan, and ahead of David Robinson. It wasn't good enough for those Blazer fans with tunnel vision, who complained in the newspaper and on the radio talk shows that Clyde should have won it. But they really had no basis for an argument. Jordan led Drexler in every statistical category except assists, and 3-point shooting, and was on a team with a better record.

It was an easy call, no disrespect to Drexler intended, and Jordan received first-place votes on 80 of the 96 ballots. He totaled 900 points. Clyde got 12 first-place votes and 561 points, well ahead of Robinson with 337 points.

Drexler's finish was the highest for a Blazer since Bill Walton became the only Blazer to win the award in 1977-78. Clyde had finished sixth the previous season and was never a serious contender prior to that, so this was uncharted territory, and he was pleased. "I would like to have won," he said, "but second is pretty nice."

Porter and Drexler continued their two-man terrorization of the opposition, combining for 77 points as Portland claimed a 119-102 win in Game 2. Porter, on the roll of his career, bombed in 41 points, and Clyde had 36 points, 12 assists, six rebounds, and three steals.

Kersey had a new sobriquet for the backcourt pair — "Batman and Robin." That left the question of who was the junior partner on this night.

Probably Clyde. Terry's outburst was his high game in a Portland uniform, either during the regular season or the play-offs, and was the most a Blazer had ever scored in a regulation playoff game. He sank 12 of 14 from the field — including four of five from 3-point land — and 13 of 14 from the line. He also had seven assists, six rebounds, three steals, and only one turnover in 38 remarkable minutes.

Clyde was the sweetheart of Blazer fans, but Terry was deserving of their affection, too. And when he left the game in the fourth quarter, the fans serenaded him. "Terry! Terry! Terry!" they chanted, rising to a standing ovation. Had it been baseball, Porter would have been called out of the dugout to tip his hat.

"I never heard anything like that before," Porter said. "Felt pretty good."

Karl Malone was much more effective in Game 2 than he had been in the opener, collecting 25 points and 11 rebounds, but Williams made him work for everything he got. "Any time you have Karl Malone and Buck Williams on the floor at the same time," Robinson said, "it's going to be physical." But nothing had gotten out of hand, except the score. Much of the reason for that was Porter.

"Terry Porter is a very strong guy," Sloan said, "and this is a time when strong bodies hold up."

Sloan wasn't around to see the whole show. He made an early exit after drawing his second T of the game in the second quarter. It was probably a good thing. Sloan is a tough guy who hates to lose worse than anybody. Had he stayed to the bitter end, he might have inflicted some pain on somebody — anybody.

Porter was doing a lot of that to the Blazers' playoff foes. He was averaging 24 points and shooting a mind-boggling .591 from 3-point range in the playoffs. "That talk about Terry having kind of a down season has been put to rest," Adelman noted. Indeed, it had.

"All I can do is hope the heat leaves his hand," said Stockton, who had a nice game offensively himself, sinking nine of 13 shots en route to a 24-point, 11-assist night. "No question about it, I can't leave Terry Porter (on defense) right now."

Stockton, who played off Porter in Game 1, did his best to get in Porter's face in Game 2. It didn't matter. Several times, Porter stopped on a dime and let fire from afar. . . swish!

"John did a great job defensively," Porter told the media when he finally arrived at his cubicle in the Portland dressing room. "I made four or five shots with him right in my face. When a guy's in a zone like that, you just have to live with it."

Clyde thought he knew what zone Terry was in: "The Twilight Zone."

Porter laughed when told he was 20 for 26 in the first two games. "If I get any hotter than this," he said, "it'd be a scary thought. I don't think it's humanly possible."

As was the case with Kersey, Porter seemed to have the knack to elevate his game at playoff time. The 29-year-old seven-year veteran had cut a higher scoring average during the playoffs than he had in the regular season in each of the last six seasons. That was in contrast to Duckworth, who had not shot or scored well in each of the past three post-seasons.

The one Blazer who was really struggling was Robinson, who was now an almost unbelievable four for 25 in the first two games of the series. And Cliff, he of the all-world scowl, wasn't happy about the way things were going for him. Late in Game 2, after Robinson had complained vehemently to the refs about what he thought was a foul that hadn't been called, Adelman called him over to the sideline. "Maybe you are getting fouled," the coach said, putting an arm around the player's waist. "But you're making things difficult on yourself. Relax. You'll be OK."

It was an example of a player putting his personal situation ahead of the big picture. Things were going very well for the Blazers, and if Robinson was struggling, it was a time to simply shrug it off. Cliff, tightly wound in such a predicament, wasn't that way. Moments later, he had drawn a technical.

But it was an astute move by Adelman, who had a special knack for knowing when to approach a player and when to leave him alone. No coach in the league had more patience with his players. Had Cliff been playing for a Bill Fitch, or a Mike Schuler, or even a Larry Brown, he probably wouldn't have experienced as much success this quickly in his career as he had in Portland under Adelman.

Adelman liked the way Robinson always gave him 100 percent effort, even on the days when he suffered from Juvenile Attitude Syndrome. "The one thing he has done from Day One is play hard," Adelman said. He knew Cliff's shot would come around. And if not, Cliff's defense would make up for it. Nothing was going to bring the coach down on this night.

"When Terry and Clyde get on a roll like that," Adelman said, "we're pretty tough to beat. And we're going to try to ride them as long as we can."

A reporter asked Drexler what he thought about people saying he and Porter are now the best guard combination in basketball. "They should have been saying that years ago," Clyde shrugged. He wasn't being funny. He meant it.

Not everyone was pulling for the Blazers to win a title. Bryant Gumbel, the polished host of NBC's "Today Show" made an offhand remark during a news and weather breakaway for local stations. "Anybody should win except the Portland Cry Blazers," he said. "I mean really . . . Clyde Drexler and Buck Williams are gentlemen, but the rest of that team . . . crybabies."

Portland viewers didn't even hear the statement through the station break — but KGW, the local NBC affiliate, broadcast the remark the next morning. It caused a major stir in the city. It was all over the radio talk shows. One deejay gave out Gumbel's personal fax number in New York, and Blazer fans flooded it with complaints. One report had the network receiving more than 1,000 calls.

To Blazer fans, this was a typical case of no respect. Here was an outsider picking on us again — and, as usual, it's us against the world, so let's circle the wagons and fight back. Though Gumbel had uttered a harmless comment with at least some element of truth to it, it didn't matter. Gumbel was sleeping with the enemy — and the funny thing was, he didn't even know it.

Things were going to be different in Salt Lake City for Games 3 and 4. That much was fact. Both teams knew it. Utah was an NBA-best 37-4 at its brand-new Delta Center during the regular season and was 6-0 during the playoffs. Historically, Portland had been unsuccessful in Salt Lake, winning only seven of 41 games there. The Blazers' plan was to rumple the Jazz's security blanket by stealing one of two games to set up a series-ending victory in Game 5 back in Portland.

The physical matchup Garretson had expected in Game 1 finally surfaced in Game 3, a 97-89 Utah win. Karl Malone, with a cold that had bothered him the first two games finally cleared up, bulled for 25 of his 39 points in the second half. Malone did almost all of his damage inside, scoring nine of his field goals at the basket and getting to the foul line 13 times, making 11.

Williams, saddled with two quick fouls, sat for 10 minutes in the first half, and played only 30 minutes in the game. And afterward, Buck thoughtfully outlined what he saw as an inequity in the way the game was called.

"There's no question (Malone) gets special treatment," he said. "I'd be a fool to say any different. I enjoy the physical play. I just want the same kind of consideration. There's nothing wrong with physical play as long as it's mutual. If he uses his elbow, I should be able to use my elbow. If he gets physical, I should be allowed to be physical. I think he puts the officials in a vulnerable situation because he creates so much contact. They ran that baseline play for him all night."

Yes, refereeing a game with Karl Malone was a near-impossible task. At 6-10 and a good 260, Malone was more powerful than any power forward in the league. Nobody worked harder to get position inside, and he often wound up with defenders draped all over him. Still, his treatment by officials was special on some occasions. Despite Williams' belief Malone had gotten away from his physical game on a consistent basis, he often backed in on defenders and was so big and strong that when he received the ball near the basket, the defender was helpless. Sometimes an offensive foul went uncalled. In Williams' case, he was one of the smallest power forwards in the NBA — 6-8 and only 225 — and while he was a master at using his hands and body positioning to "root" the offensive man out of the paint, he ran the risk of being called for ticky-tacky fouls against a man with the reputation of Malone.

Adelman was angry with the way the game was called. "We need to adjust to the Karl Malone rules," he said. Which are? "He's a very physical post-up player," Adelman said. "If we were able to do the same things at the other end, like with Clyde, I wouldn't have a problem with that. We aren't. The rules changed tonight, and we have to adjust."

Word of Adelman's comments reached Malone in the Jazz dressing room on the opposite side of Delta Center. He held his head in his mammoth hands for a moment, shook it and took a deep breath. "That's a good one. I didn't know I was writing rules now. You know what? I'm not even going to get into it. I'm not going to get into verbal confrontations with anybody."

But the Mailman did have more to say on the matter. "In the two games they won, you didn't hear shit from them. Now you hear something. We won a ballgame, but I'm not going to say everything (with the officiating) was fine. There were times I thought I could have gotten a call, but I didn't. Maybe I went to the free-throw line too much, but I'll just let them do the talking."

Drexler had a decent game with 26 points and seven assists, and Kersey was outstanding with 26 points and nine rebounds. But Porter came crashing back to earth, sinking only three of 13 shots and missing both his 3s. Stockton's defense was superb, but part of it was simply the fact that Terry cooled off.

"Terry was in a different orbit the last two games," Utah assistant coach Gordy Chiesa said after the game. "He's a tough cover, but John has a lot of pride. We tried to really extend on Terry, and it worked pretty well."

"I didn't think I did anything special," said Stockton, who gave credit to Utah's inside people for plugging the middle and preventing Porter's drives to the basket. "The way he was shooting the first two games, I was wondering if he was human. At least that's a step in the right direction.

"We had to make a decision among ourselves, whether we wanted to go on vacation or continue this series. We dug in defensively and made it tough on them, and now we're back in the series."

Said Porter: "John stayed a lot closer to me than he did in the first two games, and I didn't have as many opportunities to be aggressive when I had the ball." That was only partly true. Stockton's defense wasn't that much different than it had been in Game 2. Porter's offense was.

Did this signal an end to Porter's hot streak? "I hope not," he said. "I don't think so. I just didn't get as many good looks. I still feel hot."

The Blazers spent part of their practice session talking about how to free Porter for the shots he was getting in the first two games.

"Guys setting picks have to go down and head-hunt it a little," Kersey said. "Plus, Terry has to be a little more patient, maybe make some backdoor cuts, so they'll loosen up on him."

Porter got back on track in Game 4, going for a game-high 34 points, but the Blazers remained derailed in a 121-112 loss. The folks in the Delta Center — from owner Larry Miller sitting at courtside to the fan in the balcony holding a sign that read, "Jazz Hazz Clazz" — were revved up, and they got a big charge out of both the final result and the way the Blazers became a twelve-car pileup emotionally.

"Tears fall; Blazers, too" read the headline in *The Oregonian*. Indeed, those watching on national television got a heaping dose of the whining and lack of composure that had given the Blazers a crybaby image to many NBA fans throughout the country.

The Blazers waged a running war with referees Joey Crawford, Hue Hollins, and Jack Nies throughout the game. When it was over, they had accumulated 34 personal fouls and five technicals for their extracurricular activities, and Utah had gone to the foul line 55 times, making 48 — both club playoff records. Drexler got the boot from Crawford with a minute and a half left and the Blazers still within shouting distance, down by six.

The national media laid a hammer on the Blazers. Dumb. Their own worst enemies. Inclined to self-destruct.

Somewhere, Bryant Gumbel was laughing and saying, "I told you so."

But on this night, even Clyde wasn't a gentleman.

"We have to control our emotions better," he said after the game. "I think we need to leave the officials alone, because we might be expecting too much of them."

Clyde was saying the right thing, but his honest feeling was he had gotten a raw deal. Clyde was on the rag early in the game and, while he wasn't saying a lot, he was giving the officials plenty of dirty looks. Normally, that's not going to get a player of Clyde's stature tossed. In this case, Crawford decided he'd had enough. When Drexler buried a 3 to get Portland to within 116-110 with 1:30 to play, he thought he was fouled by Jeff Malone on the play. "I was tripped!" Clyde pleaded to Crawford as he ran downcourt, and he continued when they got to the other end. Crawford, who had whistled Clyde for a T in the first half, theatrically gave the Blazers' captain the thumb, and his night was over early.

"He kept trying to disrupt things," Crawford said after the game. "He was aggravated and had been that way for some time. We talked about it. We knew from the second quarter that if they were behind in the fourth quarter, he was going to go. He looked like he was going to take everything out on us. It seemed like he was ticked at everybody. (On the second technical), he wanted to talk and I felt it was better if he went to the dressing room."

Drexler felt strongly that he had been wronged. He felt Crawford's second technical wasn't necessary, that it was done to show him up. "It wasn't like I was in his face," Clyde said. "Maybe he had a short fuse. The refs got uptight, I know that."

Adelman stayed mostly out of the battle with the officials and avoided adding his name to the lengthy technical list. During much of the regular season, he had set the tone for his team's inclination to complain, often waging a steady stream of dialogue with the officials. At some point, he realized the reputation his team was developing and decided he was contributing to the situation. So he had backed away, keeping a tighter handle on his emotions, and had been rather serene during the latter rounds of the playoffs — with the exception of Game 3.

And now, as the series stood tied at 2-2, he seemed to be working on damage control. "I will say I thought a couple (of the Ts) were uncalled for," he said. "Is unsportsmanlike conduct a guy clapping after a call? Buck got a T for doing that. But you have to adjust to the way the game is being officiated. We didn't do a very good job of that. We lost our poise a little bit."

Inside, Adelman was steamed at what he considered an unfair and inadequate officiating job. But he devoted much of his post-game talk to the need for the Blazers to not get carried away with the officiating. He spoke about the need to focus on the task at hand — beating a very tough and, now momentum-driven — Jazz team.

To many fans across the country, those dumb Portland Trail Blazers had gotten themselves into trouble again.

With the series swinging back to Portland for Game 5, the talk again turned to the Blazers' poise, or lack thereof. Clyde, as tightlipped as he'd been all season, didn't want to hear any questions about whether or not the Blazers had gotten too caught up arguing calls with officials.

"I had no thoughts about it Sunday; I have no thoughts now," he said. "My thoughts are on Game 5 and what we need to do better as a team."

Is exhibiting poise part of that? "I thought we showed good poise," he said. "Our aggression was there the whole game. We were right there. We always had a chance. When you lose your poise, you go down by 20 points."

What Clyde said, of course, made little sense. Poise has nothing to do with the score of the game and everything to do with how a team's players collectively handled adverse situations. The Blazers had failed miserably in Game 4. And Clyde, like some of his teammates, was in a state of denial.

Williams thought the focus on the Blazers' complaints was unfair, too, and he made a valid point. "Chicago whined and moaned throughout the whole New York series," he said, "and nobody said anything about it. We get some technicals, and everybody talks about us."

Adelman tried to minimize the issue at hand and to draw the focus back on the court for Game 5. Improved defense, he said, was the real key. He felt the Blazers had a good chance to regain their edge on the homecourt. Utah was a great team at home, but a poor team on the road — only 19-28 away from Delta Center, including the playoffs.

And when the ultimate gut check came along for the Blazers, they answered the bell with pizazz in a 127-121 overtime victory in Game 5.

For the Blazers, the extra session featured the Five Almost Perfect Minutes. Seven of seven from the field. Six of seven from the line. They scored on all 10 possessions and, when the final horn had sounded, they had survived in the biggest game of the season, if only by a whisker.

"They came out very aggressive in the second half and really took it to us, but the thing that was most pleasing to me was we wouldn't crack," said Adelman, sipping at his ceremonial post-game beer. "It was great to see us respond like that with everything on the line."

Utah went into the game without Benoit, the starting small forward in the playoffs, whose father had died. Then Stockton suffered a freak injury at the end of the first half when he was poked in the eye by Drexler on a desperation drive to the basket.

Stockton went down as if he'd been shot and stayed on the floor for several anxious minutes before being helped to the dressing room. He suffered almost immediate swelling around the eye, and experienced double vision and blurry vision. He was held out for the rest of the game, and Jazz officials fretted that he would be lost for the season — however long that was to be.

With Stockton out, the ball was handed to Delaney Rudd, a veteran who had been relegated to third-string point guard behind rookie Eric Murdock for long stretches of the season. But Rudd, the unlikeliest of heroes, ran the offense superbly, and Karl Malone was a terror, and the Jazz, down by eight at the break, led 102-99 with 3:41 to go in regulation.

The Blazers battled back fiercely, and led by three entering the game's closing seconds, only to have Rudd come to Utah's rescue with a 3 with five seconds to go to force overtime and place the Blazers squarely into the biggest pressure cooker of their season.

A loss would all but end Portland's chances to move on to the NBA finals, with Game 6 set for the Delta Center, where the Jazz were darn near unbeatable.

But the Blazers were on the money in the overtime, moving out to a 117-110 lead with 1:36 to play. They found Williams for dunks on successive trips the next two times downcourt and then salted the game away with six straight Ainge free throws in the closing 21.4 seconds.

Kersey, a consistent force in the playoffs, was a whir of constant motion, collecting 29 points, 10 rebounds, five assists, and four blocked shots. He also came through with one of those effort plays that so typified the work ethic he had shown during his career as a Blazer. The Jazz made a steal near midcourt early in the game, and Jeff Malone had clear sailing for an easy basket. Only a handful of defenders in the NBA would have even given Malone a look. But suddenly, here came Kersey, thundering after Malone. And splendidly, just as Malone went up for the layup, Kersey perfectly timed his leap and swatted the ball out of bounds. Malone never saw him coming, nor did he suspect anyone would be foolish enough to try to catch him with such a lead.

Blazer fans had seen it before from Jerome, who many times had run down opponents to prevent what seemed to be a sure basket. They erupted with a tremendous ovation, and his teammates slapped his hand in recognition of one of the most electrifying hustle plays of the season.

"A lot of guys give up on plays like that," Jerome said. At Longwood (Virginia) College, Jerome had been taught to never give up. Coach Cal Luther had a rule called "Put a lid on it." Every player would have to cross halfcourt in every fast-break situation or be sentenced to running sprints. Kersey had carried such a philosophy into the pros and had made it work for him at both ends of the court.

"Never give up," Kersey said later. "I remember seeing Jeff, hesitating for a second, thinking, 'I don't know if I can catch him,' and then I just took off. Just knowing Jeff, I knew he wasn't going to dunk the ball, that he always lays the ball right over the front rim. So I knew if I could get there in time, I'd try to cover that area.

"A lot of guys give up on plays. You have to have some athletic ability to do it, but you have to be willing to bust your gut, too. I've been in a position where I didn't even think I could get to the ball, but I thought, 'Well, I'm going to try.' A lot of times I've gotten there.

"I think guys know that about me. If I'm the guy chasing you down, I'm coming. I might not get there in time, but I'm going to put that in their mind, that I'm coming. A couple of guys call me 'the Rundown Man.' "

Kersey had some shortcomings as a player, but it was that kind of effort that gave him value and made him desirable to just about any front office in the league.

Three teammates scored 24 points in Game 5 — Drexler, Porter, and Duckworth, who had his best playoff game since a 30-point explosion in Game 4 of the Utah series the previous season. The Duck knocked down 11 of 15 shots over Eaton, a man he held in high esteem. "Trust me," Duckworth said, "every shot I take against him is a difficult shot."

Porter also made three of five 3-point shots to run his playoff total to 17, tying an NBA record. It moved the veteran point guard up to fourth on the all-time playoff list with 98 3s, behind only Michael Cooper (124), Ainge (104), and Byron Scott (104).

The Blazers' feeling after it was in the bank? "Relief," Kersey said. "If we'd lost ... I'm not even going to talk about it, because we didn't."

And now they were a win away from returning to the Finals for the second time in three seasons.

Before Game 6 in the Delta Center, Magic Johnson — working as analyst for the NBC broadcast — told Portland radio analyst Mike Rice on his pre-game show he wouldn't be surprised to see the Blazers win the NBA title. "Their decision-making has been so much better," he said. "I like what they're doing. It's the best job I've seen them do of staying focused. They closed out the Lakers — boom! The Phoenix series — same thing. That's the sign of a team that has grown and really wants to win a championship. And they have a great bench. Robinson and Ainge give them a lot more than Chicago or Cleveland has. I think they have a great chance to win it all."

Still, wins by opponents in the Delta Center came along about as often as complete sentences by President Bush. Yet the Blazers could feel it in their bones as they warmed up for Game 6. Robinson and Abdelnaby were fast friends and share the same penchant for a laugh.

"Cliff and I are exact opposites," Alaa said. "He's introverted, I'm outgoing. He looks into people more, I look at them. We're both young and from the East Coast, and have the same tastes in clothes, and cars, and music, and video games . . . but even when we're together we're like night and day. Maybe that's why we get along, why we're so close."

Right before the game, Cliff nudged Alaa. "If we win tonight," he told his teammate, "we're going to do the Uncle Cliffy out of here." The Uncle Cliffy was a sort of dance step with some hand action that Robinson had invented. They'd thought about naming it the Uncle Buck in Williams' honor, but in the opinion of Robinson and Abdelnaby — nearly a decade younger than Williams — Cliff had rhythm, and Buck did not. "He wasn't coordinated enough," Alaa said, winking. They loved to tease the Buckster, and he was pretty capable in the art of dishing it back.

Since Robinson's rookie year in the 1989-90 season, several of the younger Blazer reserves had taken part in a ritual during pre-game introductions. The crowd would rise as one to cheer the starters, who came out of their seats on the bench one by one as their names were called. Meanwhile, with few of the fans paying them any attention, the young guns would do their gig among themselves. The first year it was Cliff and Mark Bryant and Byron Irvin touching elbow to elbow. In Alaa's two seasons it had evolved from the elbow to a low five to touching fingers —

"giving a little sugar," Alaa said — with Cliff and Alaa and Robert Pack taking part.

They would give plenty of sugar on this night, after a slow start. The Trail Blazers spotted the Jazz a 9-0 lead in the first two minutes, then quieted the noisy Delta Center crowd with a 105-97 win that earned them a trip back to the Finals. Portland put on an incredible defensive display in the second half, holding Utah to nine-for-40 shooting. The Jazz front line was relentless in pursuit of its missed shots, out-rebounding the Blazers 54-36 for the game, but it wasn't enough.

"We proved to everyone around the country we have a great team that can win on the road," said Drexler, whose team handed the Jazz its first home defeat of the playoffs. "We stayed poised, our defense was better, and we're thrilled to be going back to the Finals."

Williams was the first to point out that it wasn't the usual, garden-variety win for the Blazers. While Drexler and Porter combined for five-for-17 shooting and 10 points in the first half, Williams and Kersey came through with 20 first-quarter points and 29 in the first half. And the pair paired to sink 17 of 19 from the line on the night.

"This wasn't typical Trail Blazer basketball," Williams said. "We got outrebounded, we shot free throws very well down the stretch, but we won here, and a lot of teams haven't done that."

Adelman threw Williams, Mark Bryant, Kersey, and Robinson at Karl Malone — who finished with 23 points and scored only two points in the final period. Drexler and Porter came on in the second half, and Ainge and Robinson provided important contributions off the bench at both ends of the court.

The Jazz were fighting back late in the game and trailed 98-94, but Drexler rattled Stockton on a layup try, faking a block and seemingly frightening the guard into blowing the shot. Tyrone Corbin got the rebound, but was stripped by Robinson. The Blazers pushed the ball back upcourt and Porter converted a layup to ice the game.

In the end, it was Portland's defense that made the difference.

"Portland did a great job of defending some of the things we were trying to do," Sloan said. "They are a great defensive team. It's tough for us to score against them, and they can also score against us. We knew they were a tough team, and they certainly deserved to win."

After the final horn, Cliff and Alaa did the "Uncle Cliffy," and the rest of the Blazers celebrated in a more conventional manner. The players from both teams met on the court to pay respects. Karl Malone cupped Williams' head in his hands and nodded. "Way to go," Malone said. "You guys deserved it. Now go out and win it all."

Stockton sought out Porter and gave him a hug. "You were great," Stockton said. "Keep shooting it, and go get them in the finals."

Adelman wore a tired smile afterward. He wasn't sure where he stood with Paul Allen and Bert Kolde, and there had been an undercurrent of feeling that the Blazers needed to at least get back to the Finals to put him in good stead with ownership. Adelman didn't think he'd get fired, but he sensed his chances for a contract extension would go out the window if the Blazers were eliminated by the Jazz.

As much as anything, though, he felt his team had proven its mettle. "I felt vindicated," Adelman said. "I felt that way for the players, too. It had been a long season, and a lot of people didn't think we'd make it this far."

There were a lot of smiles in the dressing room despite the foul odor of a stink bomb, evidently planted by an appreciative Jazz fan as a means of wishing the Blazers well in the Finals. Somebody brought out 1992 NBA Finals baseball hats and several of the players put them on. "They sure put these out fast," joked Drexler, mindful that they had been prepared weeks ahead of time.

"We're very excited," Porter said, "but we haven't won anything yet."

"A lot of people said we wouldn't get back to the Finals this year," Kersey said. "We proved a lot of people wrong. Now we have one more thing left to do." Nobody had to ask what that might be.

16

"It's Devastating to Lose Anytime. But To Lose Like This Hurts Even Worse."

The story line for the 1992 NBA Finals was set by the television network carrying the event, as it always is. No longer was this Us Against the World. It was now Clyde Drexler vs. Michael Jordan, a matchup of the top two off guards in basketball and the two men who were among the most exciting players in the game. They had finished 1-2 in the Most Valuable Player balloting and now they were going to settle matters on the court.

And that was the worst thing that could have happened to the Trail Blazers. Drexler is not a one-on-one player the way Jordan is. He isn't a scoring machine like Jordan, either. That's not a knock on Drexler, merely a statement of fact that there is no other player like Jordan—never has been, actually. But the thing that puts Drexler into the elite class of player—the likes of Magic Johnson, Larry Bird, and Jordan—is that he also makes his teammates better.

Drexler had matured into the kind of player any coach would want to have leading his club— a remarkable talent with enough selflessness to maintain a posture of all-for-one and one-for-all. And Clyde tried to avoid sounding cocky, at all costs.

"It's just the way I am," he said. "I just think that's the way to behave. I don't like to brag, I don't like to talk negatively about anyone. Some things are better left for other people to say."

He held a genuine belief the team was more important than any one individual.

"If something happens," he said, "it's the direct result of everyone on the team. It's never just one guy. Basketball is a team sport. That's what I keep stressing to everyone. I don't care what you're doing individually, the other guys are helping you in some way, and you have to acknowledge that. If you think you're doing it all by yourself, you're really being misled. This is not golf or tennis, this is basketball — five guys, the bench, the coaching staff, evern upper management. Everybody has to do his share of the workload."

But Drexler, it appeared from the outset, may have taken all of this Clyde vs. Michael stuff too seriously and regressed to the type of player he was earlier in his career. At times he seemed involved in a game of one-upsmanship with Jordan, a "Can-you-top-this?" matchup that Drexler just couldn't win. The result is that he often seemed to leave his real game, the patient overall team game he played throughout the season, in an effort to, as they say in the commercial, "Be like Mike."

That was the main theme of the Finals, but not the only one. The Blazers, of course, were looking for redemption for last season's flop in the conference finals and the embarrassing five-game Finals loss to Detroit in 1990. They knew that if they lost in the Finals again, all those labels about being dumb and being choke artists would likely surface again. And they knew, if they lost the Big One again, they'd be in danger of being called the Denver Broncos or Minnesota Vikings of the NBA.

The Bulls, on the other hand, were looking to do it back-to-back, thus validating themselves as what qualifies these days in sports as a dynasty. They'd won it easily in 1991, racing through the playoffs with no problem. This year, though, they looked human, needing seven games to get by New York and six to edge Cleveland. At times, it was a struggle for them, and the Blazers took heart in that.

It's not unusual for players to have phone messages waiting for them when they arrive at their hotel, especially the more high-profile players. Many of the callers are young ladies looking to do a little star-tasting.

Kersey, a bachelor at 30, is an old veteran at such games. But he hasn't dealt with many women as creative, or as persistent, as the one who left a message for him on voice mail at his Chicago hotel when he arrived in town before Game 1.

The woman, identifying herself as Vendella, thanked Kersey for sending her flowers and cards and said she was looking forward to telling him in person. Kersey rang the number she left. "I was very concerned," he said. "I figured somebody was using my name."

The woman said she was a 25-year-old swimsuit model who lived in Chicago, but kept a condo in New York, and as they talked it should have become obvious no one had left flowers and cards for her in Jerome Kersey's name. They talked, he hung up and, he said, soon she was back on the phone to him again.

"I put a do-not-disturb on my phone, but she got through by telling the desk she is my wife, my girlfriend, whatever," Kersey said. He was evidently impressed because he gave her a home number.

And soon, "she was calling every day," he said. "She tells me all this stuff about how great we'll be together. My friend talks to her and he said, 'This girl is nuts. She's talking about falling in love with you, and she knows what you're going to do when you get together.' "

Kersey was repulsed enough to give her his mobile phone number, and soon she was calling that, too. Later she sent what she said was a photo of herself to his home.

"She told me she never knew it would be this hard to pursue me," Kersey said, laughing at the thought. "I have to admit, I was really curious about her. I even asked a policeman if he could check it out, but they can't do things like that." And soon, they were arranging to meet while he was on a fishing trip in Vancouver, B.C., late in the summer.

Kersey made it to Vancouver, but his phone pal never did. Jerome was suspicious enough to do some checking and became convinced the woman who was calling him was misrepresenting herself. He had his phone numbers changed, and their relationship ended before it started.

In Game 1, all of the Clyde vs. Michael stuff became a no-contest very quickly in the dingy barn that passes for a sports arena, Chicago Stadium. In business, old buildings with inadequate facilities are usually condemned and replaced with functional edifices that brighten up the workplace. They call these buildings "historic," "storied," and "charming."

In sports, when you see those words, it's usually going to mean the building smells as if the circus just left, and you're going to have to stand in line to buy a hot dog or take a leak. That's Chicago Stadium.

The building does have some character, but it's provided more by the inhabitants than the arena itself. This big house still uses surly off-duty policemen as security guards, who are probably needed to control some of the resident crazies. You never know what you'll see in the Stadium — a guy tired of waiting in line for the bathroom doing his business off the front row of the first balcony, or a local sportswriting legend gulping a Moosehead beer out of a sweatsock he keeps in his briefcase on press row.

The Bulls took Game 1 122-89, and the big one-on-one matchup was a joke. Jordan scored 39 points on 16 of 27 from the floor and had 11 assists. Drexler made five of 14 shots, scored 16 points and had seven assists.

Jordan put on the greatest one-half show in NBA Finals history, making six 3-point field goals and scoring 35 of his points in the first two quarters.

Drexler wouldn't say it, but he seemed embarrassed by the disparity in the statistical matchup, something he needn't have worried about. "It was definitely incredible," he said. "He made some medium-range jumpers, too. But that's actually the shot you want him to take. Those are the shots that are going to be available in Game 2."

Jordan was as stunned by his long-distance shooting — he had made only 27 3-pointers in 100 attempts during the regular season — as anyone else. At one point, he just looked at the bench and shrugged his shoulders, palms up, as if to say, "I don't know what's happening here."

"I tried to stay within the framework of our offense," Jordan said. "The next thing I knew, shots were falling from everywhere. I started running for the 3-point line. It felt like a free throw from that distance. I couldn't miss. I didn't know how to explain it. I just got hot. I was in a zone. I just kept shooting them up there."

Meanwhile, back in Portland, a billboard across the street from Memorial Coliseum was beginning to attract a lot of attention. Paid for by AT&T, a Dream Team sponsor, the sign showed Scottie Pippen dunking a basketball and carried the message, "Barcelona has never seen a Bull like this before."

Ken Croley of San Francisco, a public relations spokesman for AT&T, said the company uses Pippen for consumer long-distance calling advertisements on TV and in newspapers. "Pippen and Portland are on the sports map right now, and AT&T wants to recognize that," Croley said.

But they recognized it the wrong way in the wrong town. This town was edgy enough about the whole world picking on it, without somebody glorifying one of the enemy right there on the doorstep to the battlefield. Under siege a few days later, AT&T relented— when's the last time you heard of these guys surrendering? — and took the billboard down.

Adelman handled the Game 1 loss with humor and seemed much more relaxed throughout the Finals than he had in the regular season or previous playoff rounds. Getting this far had taken the pressure off, and he was finally able to enjoy himself a little.

"We held Michael to four points in the second half," he said. "That's the only good news I can think of tonight. Whether you get beat by four points or 40, it's one loss. I have a lot of faith in our guys. They respond. The second game is usually different.

"It better be different."

Game 2 certainly would be different. But the first game did establish a pattern and provided an important insight. Jordan would be the difference in this series. When he got it going, the Blazers were powerless to do much about it.

Portland unintentionally set a trap for the Bulls in the second game of the Finals. Playing listlessly, the Blazers trailed 92-82 with less than five minutes left in the fourth quarter and Drexler on the bench with six fouls. But playing well together in Drexler's absence, the Blazers pulled off a 115-104 overtime win in Chicago Stadium that vaulted them right back into the championship picture.

It was almost a miracle win, one that prompted *The Oregonian* to gush, "Who's the dumb team now?" in its lead story on the game. The Bulls scored only three points in the final four minutes of regulation and were blown out in overtime. "We had them right where we wanted them," Adelman said. "We got them overconfident."

Jordan scored 39 points, but picked up a technical foul that helped fuel Portland's comeback. He'd told referee Jess Kersey that he'd made a "bullshit call," and even Michael Jordan can't say that. "That was a game we certainly had control of," Jordan said. "We stopped playing to win and started playing not to lose."

Said Danny Ainge: "They got a little bit conservative and we kept them away from the basket. Michael's cape fell off there somewhere down the stretch."

A lot of the post-game discussion on the Portland side was good-natured ribbing of Drexler, who had carried his team on his back through most of the season. And even though it was absurd to think the team could play better without its best player, there was an underlying theme. The Blazers did move the ball better and had better rhythm without him. And only Drexler could do something about that.

"Well," Adelman said with a smile, "we got Clyde out of the game, and finally started to play a little bit."

"I'm going to have to talk with Rick and see if I can get some minutes next game," Drexler said before turning serious. "What did I tell you? It's a team game. That's exactly what happened tonight."

Ainge was sensational in Drexler's absence. He scored nine points in overtime, equalling a Finals record, and scored 17 points in 23 minutes. Ainge made all four of his shots after Drexler fouled out. Terry Porter took over the defensive assignment on Jordan for most of the final quarter and did a terrific job. Jordan managed only two field goals in the final 9:36.

"You noticed his offense," Adelman said, "but Terry's defense was outstanding. He stayed with Michael and forced him to hit some really tough shots."

"I just tried to keep him in front of me and to make him shoot with a hand in his face," Porter said. "He wasn't able to go by me. I think guarding Kevin Johnson and John Stockton in the playoffs really helped me in that respect. But it wasn't just me. Everybody did a great job with help. I can't say enough about the way the guys responded down the stretch."

What really happened down the stretch was two things: First, the Bulls relaxed, as teams often do when the opponents' superstar leaves the game. Second, Portland finally found its rhythm at both ends of the court and returned to the unselfish team game that has been its trademark for most of the past three seasons.

"What happens to every team leading in that situation is you get a little conservative," Ainge said. "That's what happened to the Bulls. The basket got a little smaller for them, and we were able to get back into it."

Ah, but lessons taught are not necessarily lessons learned. Drexler didn't seem to learn anything from what happened in the game, and subsequent appearances continued to show that he was very involved in trying to match Jordan point for point and dunk for dunk. And as far as teams handling huge leads in the fourth quarter, the Trail Blazers would have the same problem the next time they'd play in Chicago, the Finals' Game 6.

The Bulls pointed to the technical foul on Jordan as a big momentum-buster in the fourth quarter —"The momentum swung on that play," Bulls coach Phil Jackson would say — but that was a cheap excuse. Chicago scored on its next possession after the "T" and still led 94-85 with 4:09 to go.

"I guess we got a little too comfortable at the end," Chicago forward Horace Grant said. "And we didn't play the defense we know we're capable of playing. We didn't contest their layups, and we looked at each other and just lost it. I think we got a little relaxed with Drexler and Kersey out and definitely underestimated their bench."

Back in Portland, meanwhile, the city was bracing for the arrival of the Finals — the first event in a unique pro basketball trifecta scheduled over the next month that featured the NBA Draft and the Tournament of the Americas in Memorial Coliseum.

The arena, by now, faced a naked signboard across the street. Scottie Pippen was gone, and the skeleton of a sign remained. "I wanted to burn it down," admitted Pat Hickey, a manager at the AT&T office in Portland.

Take that, world.

Finally, Drexler got the best of Jordan in the individual matchup, outscoring him 32-26 and out-rebounding him 9-7. For all the good it did.

The Blazers, just as they had done two years before, blew a chance to take command of the Finals when they dropped a 94-84 decision at home to the Bulls. It was one of Portland's worst home playoff performances in years, a complete embarrassment on and off the court.

The embarrassment started prior to the game, when the team screened a music video on the board above the court that featured clips of Robinson doing the "Uncle Cliffy" on the sidelines at the tail end of the series-clinching win over Utah. Robinson's victory dance was classless — a bush-league exhibition at the time that would have best been forgotten. They played the video with an accompanying "Uncle Cliffy" song right before the game, much to Robinson's delight. It wasn't Robinson's fault the whole thing surfaced. It was the fault of some dunderhead in the front office who approved the silly stunt. This wasn't some exhibition game, it was the NBA Finals.

Thus inspired, Robinson went out and went two-for-11 from the field in his 25 minutes, while managing to rack up a grand total of three rebounds, one assist, and two turnovers. "The ball came off the wrong side of my hand a couple of times," Robinson said in a classic understatement. "I just didn't finish my shots. I had my concentration. I just missed shots."

Robinson would say later that all the dance stuff got a little carried away. But he didn't see any harm done.

"I think it got a little out of hand," he said later. "But I don't regret it. The fans had fun with it. They were enjoying it. I do regret that every time something happened, the newspaper wanted to talk about it."

With Robinson ineffective, the pressure was on Ainge to contribute something off the bench, and he wasn't up to it. He made only four of 12 shots on a night when the Blazers hit just 28 of 78 from the floor while Chicago was hitting 37 of 78.

A big part of the game, actually, was the schedule forced on the teams by television commitments. The teams had only 43 hours between the end of the overtime Game 2 and the tipoff of Game 3 — with a four-hour flight a part of that 43 hours. And it just wasn't enough rest. This was a game between two tired teams that had trouble executing and concentrating.

It was a huge win for the Bulls, who always seem to recover from a home loss with an immediate road win. But at least one Blazer, watching from the sidelines felt that his team had missed a golden opportunity.

"I think Game 3 was the deciding game of the series," Wayne Cooper said later. "If we had won that game, it would have been a different series. I saw something different in that game than a lot of other people saw. I saw fear in (the Bulls') eyes. I really did. But we struggled so long we let them get into the game. We didn't get it done, and they did."

The Bulls made only five of 17 shots in the second quarter, yet went into the locker room at halftime with a 54-45 lead. All night long, the Bulls blanketed Porter. He took only two shots in the second half, scored just seven points in the game and had but four assists. He played 44 minutes — Adelman couldn't rest him because Ennis Whatley just couldn't get the job done as a backup and Ainge had his shaky moments handling the ball.

"Terry didn't seem to have the same verve he has had," Adelman said.

"It seemed like I couldn't get shots," Porter said. "I thought I was pretty aggressive when I had the ball, but I couldn't always get the ball."

All in all, it was nothing like what an NBA Finals game is supposed to look like. There were too many turnovers and not enough made baskets.

"I don't know how it looked from the stands," Pippen said. "But it was ugly on the floor."

Drexler was terrific in Game 3, but he was even better in Game 4, when the Trail Blazers finally managed to win a Finals game on their home court — something they couldn't do against the Pistons in 1990.

He made only nine of his 22 shots from the floor, but Drexler still had nine assists, eight rebounds, and three blocked shots to go with excellent defense on Jordan. The Bulls star scored

32 points, but went scoreless over the final 10 minutes as Portland again fourth-quartered Chicago. And the Blazers did it with some unconventional tactics.

After spotting the Bulls 10-0 and 18-4 leads to open the game, the Trail Blazers would be trailing most of the way. Chicago still led 80-74 with 7:43 to play before Adelman jerked his taller players out of the game and went with a five-man unit of Drexler, Porter, Ainge, Robinson, and Kersey. The group keyed a defensive resurgence, moved the ball well on offense, and pulled Portland to a 93-88 win that evened the series at two games apiece.

"The last five or six minutes are about as well as we've played defense in a long time," Adelman said. "We were so active, getting our hands on balls and attacking passing lanes. A lot of times we turned it into baskets at the other end."

For the first time in the series, Portland dominated the backboards, pounding out a 45-33 rebound edge that included a 15-7 margin at the offensive end. The Blazers also had edges of 11-7 in steals and 6-1 in blocked shots.

"That's our game," Porter said. "That's what we rely on. Defending, rebounding — the hustle things are the things that have made us so good. The important thing is we played hard for 48 minutes. Guys just kept working."

For the second time in the series, the Bulls had lost a game. And for the second time in the series, they felt they'd gift-wrapped it and presented it to the Blazers.

"This was a game we had," Chicago center Bill Cartwright lamented. "For those who missed the other game, this was just like it."

"Well," added Jackson, "we had this one in hand and let it slip away."

Said Jordan: "We controlled the ball game for 42 minutes. Then the momentum changed. They fed on it a lot more than we did. I felt they did play solid defense down the stretch. We got flustered and turned the ball over."

Drexler made only two of 11 shots from the field in the second half, but he still found ways to help. In the fourth quarter, either Jordan got tired from all the golf he was playing at local courses, or Drexler stepped his defense up a level. Jordan missed his final four shots and was a non-factor down the stretch, when John Paxson did all he could to keep the Bulls in the game.

Drexler got his body on Jordan a little more than usual in the fourth quarter, then got a hand in his face better on the shots. Then when Jordan drove, teammates found ways to help.

"We really wanted to stop Michael's penetration and not let him beat us to the basket," Adelman said. "Clyde wanted to put as much pressure on him as he could, get rotation help early and not let him get within five or six feet. He's so dangerous when he gets inside the paint. He's just incredible. But I thought Clyde did a great job of staying in front of him and trying to bother his shot."

"My shot was not clicking too well," Drexler said sheepishly, "so I tried to do something different."

And he made the biggest play of the game. With the Bulls on top 82-81, Jordan went airborne off a drive, and Drexler cleanly picked his pocket. Drexler fed Porter, who returned the ball to Drexler for a layup that put Portland into the lead. "The biggest play of the game, but I'm used to seeing Clyde do that kind of thing," Adelman said.

"If you play a guy enough, eventually you learn some of his moves," Drexler said. "Michael has about 2,000 of them. It was one of those rare times when I was able to get my hands on the ball . . . just one of those plays you try to anticipate what he's going to do. I got it, and we were off to the races."

The Blazers were miffed heading into Game 5, the final contest scheduled for Portland. They'd read the Bulls' comments in the paper about their two wins and interpreted them as disrespectful. On top of that, Jackson compounded the problem with his remarks a day after the Blazers squared the series at 2.

"We're in control of the series," said the coach of the Bulls. "This series, by all rights and purposes, should be over."

All the way to the Finals, and again the Blazers saw it happen again: They just weren't getting any credit. For Adelman, it was just about the last straw. He may rail against the officiating at times and often questions moves the league office makes. But he never criticizes or belittles an opponent. Earlier in the season, the Bulls had talked about his team's lack of intelligence, and now they were questioning his team's right to be alive in the series.

"Bull," Adelman said when informed of Jackson's comments. "You win games because you go out and do it. And they didn't do it. If they want this series over, they should have gone out and won those two games, and they flat-out didn't do it. If they can't finish a game, it's not my fault. It's a 48-minute game and one was 53, and you've got to play those minutes out if you expect to win. They should know. They've won a championship.

"I just think that's a real cop-out. I don't understand why you have to talk about the other team like they don't have the right to be there and win. If (the opponent) has won two games, you should have done something about that. I think they are a very good team. I give them all the credit in the world. But we've won two games by the rules that they give us. That's all I can do. I'm sorry that they feel that way. That's their own problem. If we can win two more games with them ticked off, hell, I'll take it."

But there was nothing left to take. What happened in Game 5 was almost inexplicable — other than to say the Bulls came out like champs and took complete command in a 119-106 whipping of the Trail Blazers that seemed to leave little reason to return to Chicago.

Portland coughed up 18 turnovers, Jordan scored 46 points, and the Bulls took a 3-2 series lead back to the Windy City. Jordan made 14 of 23 from the floor, 16 of 19 from the line, and put up a career-high scoring total for a Finals game, in spite of foul trouble and a slightly sprained ankle.

"He was phenomenal," Adelman said. "The thing that's so tough about him is he has the ability to shoot the ball from almost anywhere."

Did he ever. He had 27 points by halftime and was scoring from just about every conceivable spot on the floor. And he had help, too. Pippen broke loose for 24 points, 11 rebounds, and nine assists.

It was an overwhelming win, but Adelman kept his poise and kidded a bit with the media afterward. "Obviously," he said, "we gave that one to them." Then he gave the Bulls their due. "They really played a great game," he said. "I think that's the best game they've played in the series — even better than the first game."

Blazer fans, frustrated when their team was behind by 13 after the first quarter and taken out of a chance to win almost immediately, took out their anger on referee Jake O'Donnell, an old nemesis who seemed to want to rekindle his feud with Buck Williams.

Williams got a technical foul from O'Donnell almost immediately. The official had called an offensive foul on Jerome Kersey on Portland's fourth possession, wiping out a layup by Williams. Two trips later, O'Donnell was talking to Williams in the low post — baiting him as only O'Donnell can do. When Williams answered back, he was whistled for the technical.

"As usual, Jake O'Donnell was chewing in my ear," Williams said. "I asked him not to, and he gave me a technical. It's really sad that he's allowed to come in and do that, but that's Jake. Until Rod Thorn or someone puts him down, he's going to keep doing that, because that's the kind of person he is."

O'Donnell, getting well past his years as one of the league's best officials, sees himself as some kind of old western gunslinger who doesn't have to answer to anyone about anything. A reporter bumped into him in the hallway outside the official's locker room after the game and asked him, "Jake, what's the deal between you and Buck, anyway?"

"Why don't you get lost?" O'Donnell screamed.

Certainly the officiating had nothing whatsoever to do with the outcome of the game. Portland scored the first basket, and then watched almost helplessly as the Bulls scored the next 10 points. The Blazers had five turnovers in the first five minutes, seven in the first quarter, and 10 in the first 14 minutes. Chicago scored 15 of its first 18 points off Portland's miscues.

"We're getting killed coming out of the locker room," Ainge said. "I don't know what the numbers are, but the points off turnovers had to be a huge advantage."

The Bulls had an unbelievable 17-0 edge in the points-off-turnovers department after just one period.

"Just some casual passes," said Porter. "The turnovers all led to easy baskets and dunks for them. They really cost us in the first quarter."

After Portland whittled Chicago's lead to 66-54 at halftime, the Bulls charged out and scored the first eight points of the third quarter. In just two minutes, they had the game in hand. "The first five minutes of the first and third quarters have really hurt us this whole series," Porter said. "Chicago comes out busting, and we really don't respond. We can't keep giving them those big leads."

Adelman was left shaking his head in dismay.

"I wish I could answer," he said. "I don't know. It's all we talked about today. We have to come back and come up with some type of solution. They've done an excellent job of coming out aggressively."

The Bulls figured it was just a matter of getting down to business.

"When we need to win, we play basketball," Jordan said.

Portland had opened the game by using Porter on Pippen, hoping to get more defensive pressure on the Chicago small forward. But it didn't work out.

"It was definitely a mismatch," Jackson said. "But we focused so much on mismatches in the previous game we had gotten out of our basic offense. They double-team so well and rotate so quickly. But we were able to take advantage on some cuts to the basket. I thought Scottie Pippen was the difference in the game. He had great energy out there tonight. He played very well early in the game and really helped direct our offense."

Pippen said he had made it a point to get involved early at the offensive end.

"We came out very aggressive from the start," he said. "I wanted to get going early and get Horace Grant involved because it seems when we're both playing well the team seems to do well. We had some momentum and we had guys on the bench ready to step up and contribute."

Said Jordan: "Scottie was really big. Everybody knows what Scottie Pippen means to our team. We work hand-in-hand together, and when we're both playing well, the defense can't really key on both of us."

The only dark moment for the Bulls came in the second quarter. Jordan, falling out of bounds along the baseline under his team's basket, slipped on a camera and sprained his left ankle. He limped off the court and had the ankle re-taped.

"What was going through my mind?" Jordan said, repeating a question. "I thought, 'What are you stupid photographers doing around the court?' I stepped right on a camera. But I just got it re-taped. Once I got back out on the court I didn't even think about it."

Jordan revealed that he'd been hiding a thigh bruise throughout the series, too.

"I've been trying to keep that quiet," he said. "It's showing day-to-day improvement, but I got it hit again tonight. I have to try to protect myself because of all the screens I have to fight through — I don't want to get it hit again."

Jackson had trouble remembering much from what was a very big game for his team. And he couldn't be blamed. It had to be one of the most uninteresting, boring games to come along during the Finals in years. A total of 99 free throws and numerous commercial timeouts made it seem as if the game had gone about 16 innings. It lasted two hours and 43 minutes, an incredibly long game for one that wasn't close enough to require countless late-game timeouts.

"I'm suffering from a case of two-hour amnesia," Jackson said. "I completely forgot what happened in the first hour of this game. It was the longest game I've ever participated in, and it just seemed like it kept going on and on."

But it didn't go long enough for Portland to have a chance to win. But on this night, another three quarters wouldn't have helped the Trail Blazers.

Most of the nation's columnists and sports talk show hosts were counting the Blazers out by now. Sportswriters knew that, because by this time, they felt as if they'd been a guest on nearly every talk show in the country.

All-sports radio is one of the newest fads around the nation, with most major markets now featuring one station with around-the-clock sports. That translates into talk shows in search of guests. Since beat writers' phone numbers are printed in the league's media guide, it's real easy for talk-show hosts and producers to find knowledgeable and — more important — cheap guests for their shows.

Nobody minds helping out once in a while. It gives writers a chance to find out what the fans are talking about. But during the Finals, writers covering both teams were forced to take their phones off the hook in the morning to get adequate sleep. Players and coaches normally won't do the shows, but writers will. Writers for *The Oregonian*, perhaps the only major newspaper in the country that prohibits its employees from hosting their own shows, had little patience by now. Especially when no one would listen when they told people that the Blazers weren't dead yet.

Anyone who expected the Blazers to return to Chicago and roll over for the Bulls just hadn't been paying attention to what Portland had done over the past three seasons. But those close to the team knew better.

The Blazers will have their bad games. They'll make some dumb decisions. They'll get outshot on a given night. They'll even get out-hustled about once or twice a season. But no matter what, they don't quit. They don't give up. And they weren't about to surrender to the Bulls without a fight.

Really, the Game 6 situation at Chicago was one made for the Blazers. They were not expected to give the Bulls much of a game and had already been written off by everyone. That took all the pressure off, and Portland came out in Chicago and played one of its best games.

For three quarters.

Portland led 79-64 going into the fourth quarter, with the Bulls just a basket or two away from running up the white flag of surrender. But it all fell apart so fast and effectively, that the Blazers seemed powerless to do anything about it. And when the game ended, the Bulls were dancing around Chicago Stadium celebrating a 97-93 win that brought them their second straight NBA championship.

It was a devastating loss, a defeat that left the team shaken and in tears in the locker room. "It's devastating to lose anytime," Drexler said. "But to lose a game like this hurts even worse."

The Bulls opened the fourth quarter with Jordan and three other starters on the bench, ready to pull the remaining starter — Pippen — if something positive didn't happen right away. The quarter opened with Chicago getting the ball, and the Bulls appeared to lose it right away. Ainge slapped the ball away from a Chicago player and was headed upcourt on a fastbreak that would have increased the Blazer lead.

But with Ainge already in possession, referee Mike Mathis whistled a foul that he wasn't in position to see — a phantom call that no amount of replays could even find. The call gave the ball back to the Bulls, who worked the ball to Bobby Hansen in the deep left corner. Hansen let fly with a 3-point field goal that hit nothing but the bottom of the net.

One shot. Just three points. But it seemed to light the crowd on fire and turn the entire game around.

"That," Hansen said later, "was the big momentum-shifter."

The Bulls got the ball back quickly after a Portland turnover and Stacey King drove to the basket. Kersey hammered him and referee Hugh Evans jumped on the Chicago Stadium band-wagon to call it a flagrant foul. Two shots, possession. King made one free throw, and Chicago got the ball to Pippen, who drove for a layup.

The Bulls were on their way, and there was nothing that could be done to stop it. Adelman spent four timeouts in the first six minutes of the quarter, but he couldn't shut up the crowd, coax a call out of officials, or get his team going. In just three-and-a-half minutes, the Bulls had whittled the lead to 3 points against the shaken Trail Blazers.

"What can I say, other than we were on a roll?" B.J. Armstrong said. "We were hitting our shots, making some steals, and getting key rebounds. That let us get back in the game and turn it over to Michael. Once we got the flow going, that was it."

Jackson admitted his fourth-quarter lineup was almost a last resort. "As a coach, you just go play by play," the Chicago coach said. "Everything else I had tried hadn't worked. It was on the doorstep for us to lose. We were flirting with disaster. It took a definite drive for us in the fourth quarter. Pippen held them together and scored the points. We held together, and the fourth quarter was magic."

The Blazers looked back on Chicago's quarter-opening run after the game, and then spent a good part of the summer watching it on videotape. Five straight calls went against them during one stretch. Any one of them could have stopped the Bulls' momentum. They were tossup calls, decisions that could have gone either way. They felt they deserved to get at least one of them.

There was the opening call on Ainge, then the flagrant foul on Kersey. Vehemently, the Blazers held that it was a foul, all right, but not a flagrant one.

"That's a dumb call," Kersey said. "How was that flagrant? I fouled him, but I was going for the ball. It was ridiculous to make that call."

Adelman agreed.

"There's no way that was a flagrant foul," Adelman said. "I don't care what anybody says, I can't agree with that. Jerome was going aggressively after the ball. I've watched a lot of tape and seen people tear somebody's head off and not get a flagrant foul. I'm sorry, I have a hard time with that call. It was a killer."

Duckworth was then called for a touch foul on King, who made both free throws. Drexler was whistled for a double-dribble, and Williams was hit with an offensive foul. Then King backed in over Williams with no foul being called.

After this game, it was the Blazers and not the Bulls talking about giveaways.

"We definitely gave it away. Definitely," Porter said in the quiet of the Portland locker room. "They did a good job, but a lot of it had to do with our turnovers in key situations. We didn't get any calls, especially any close calls. We didn't make any shots any time we drove."

Williams was gracious to the Bulls.

"I disapproved of the way they handled the series in terms of the derogatory remarks they made," Williams said. "I'm tempted to use the words Chicago has been using the whole series and say we gave it away.

"But I'm not going to take the easy way out like they did. They deserve credit. They're an arrogant team, and I see why. They executed better than we did. They had control."

After the bench got the Bulls back into the game, Jordan and Pippen took over. The two Olympians scored the Bulls' final 19 points over the last eight minutes. Jordan, a unanimous choice as the Most Valuable Player of the Finals, finished with a game-high 33 points, including Chicago's last six.

"It's different from last year," Jordan said. "Last year there was seven years of emotions built up. This year there's only one year. I can hold back the tears and just enjoy it. I think last year was more for the city and the franchise. This time, I think I can get a little selfish. This year was for myself."

For the series, the Drexler-Jordan matchup was just no contest. Drexler averaged 39.7 minutes per game, shot only 40.7 percent from the floor and averaged 24.8 points per game. Jordan played 42.3 minutes and made 52.6 percent of his shots, averaging 35.8 points per game. Nobody — save perhaps Drexler — expected the Blazer guard to match Jordan's statistics. He shouldn't have tried.

Adelman, shaken by the loss of a game he felt was won, had wanted to get the series to a seventh game. A lot of people in the

Blazer camp felt if they could get the Bulls to a seventh game at home, that the pressure would finally affect them. But that wasn't going to happen, and the Portland coach now worried about how the Finals defeat would impact the fragile mental health of his team. He had to deal with that situation first.

"I knew there was going to be a lot of frustration, especially with the way the game ended," Adelman said. "We had a good chance to win, and let it slip away. My thoughts were twofold. No. 1, there was a lot of disappointment and frustration. I felt it, too. But I knew I was going to have to somehow send a message to them that they were not losers or anything else. That we'd had a heck of a season. More important, I wanted them to remember we were one of the best teams in the league, and that their shot wasn't over. Halfway through the summer they will realize what a great season they had.

"I tried to be . . . maybe not upbeat, but a little reflective. There was a lot of emotion in there. I don't think people understand how much you go through, how much you sacrifice."

And now, in the cruelest of ways, it was over. Just getting the series to a seventh game would have validated the Blazers in many ways. "Anything could have happened in a seventh game," Adelman said. What Game 6 did for the team — or to the team — wasn't immediately clear. Portland didn't quit, didn't give up. The Blazers played some of their best basketball of the season for most of the game, then collapsed. To lose that way, he said, "was the most emotional thing I've gone through since I've been in sports."

At the finish, there were complaints about the officiating and an inner feeling in the locker room — as there was the previous two seasons — that the ride had come to a premature end.

17

"We Were So Far Apart, It Was Useless to Negotiate."

Nobody in the Portland front office was espousing the idea of breaking up the Blazers. Barring a proposed trade that was too sweet to pass up, the starters would all be back for the 1992-93 season. None had passed his 30th birthday except Buck Williams, who was 32 but was still a highly productive rebounder and defender, and was coming off his second straight season leading the NBA in field-goal percentage. And Cliff Robinson, the crown jewel of the Blazers' front-line future, would also return.

But it was quickly evident the new season would hold a new look for the Blazers. And not all of it would come down the way they had planned it.

On July 3, two days after the date that unsigned NBA players became free agents, Danny Ainge signed a three-year contract with the Phoenix Suns valued at $5.2 million. Thus ended a saga that would make the rest of Geoff Petrie's summer more than a little uncomfortable.

While with Boston, Ainge had signed a six-year contract that carried him through the 1991-92 season. That had not been a good move. NBA salaries have escalated dramatically every season, and his $725,000 salary was significantly below the league average.

Ainge went from the Celtics to Sacramento midway through the 1988-89 season, and sometime thereafter was told by King management his contract would be extended to get him a more equitable salary. Before something could be worked out, he was traded to Portland during the summer of 1990. Petrie was involved in contract extension negotiations with the agents of Clyde Drexler, Buck Williams and Jerome Kersey — Drexler would eventually get a deal that will pay him $8 million for the 1995-96 season, Williams will get $4 million for 1993-94, and Kersey was given an additional four years at $11 million. According to Ainge, Petrie indicated if he could wait a year, he would be taken care of. Ainge took that to mean he'd be taken care of in the same manner as the other three, though he didn't expect as much money, with him being only a key reserve, and a little older (32) than his teammates. That seemed reasonable to Ainge, since he was just joining the club and didn't want to cause any waves.

Petrie's recollection was something different. "I told him we'd talk after the season and try to work something out," Petrie said. "We did, and we gave him an offer — a good offer that was a fair one."

Ainge was hoping for a two- or three-year extension that would couple with his final year to give him an average of somewhere between $1.3 and $1.5 million per season. He expected negotiations to commence soon after the 1990-91 season. But Petrie was in no hurry to begin. Finally, after agreeing to a five-year (plus option) extension to Robinson's contract late in the summer at an average of more than $2 million per year over the final four years, Petrie contacted Ainge's new agent, Keith Coe. Ainge had gone through most of his career without an agent, but he was beginning to feel it would be advisable to get some help, so Coe was hired.

Petrie's offer, made about a week before training camp started, was a two-year extension at $1.3 million for 1992-93 and $1.6 million for 1993-94 — but with only $400,000 of the latter season guaranteed. The remainder was incentives largely tied into team achievements, which Petrie said were readily attainable. To Ainge, that was beside the point. Ainge turned the offer down, but he spent $30,000 to take out a $1.5 million tax-free insurance policy — roughly the amount of guaranteed money in Petrie's offer — in case of injury before he became a free agent.

Ainge briefly considered holding out of training camp, but reported on schedule and did not make his contract situation an issue. *The Oregonian's* beat writers regularly asked him if the situation had changed, but it hadn't. Soon, he decided to play out the season and take a look at what the free-agent market would bear. "We were so far apart, it was useless to negotiate," Ainge said. Ainge finished strongly in the regular season, had a nice run in the playoffs, and suddenly his name loomed as the most attractive of all those on the unrestricted free agent list.

After the season ended, Ainge said all things equal, he'd prefer to stay in Portland, but that he was going to go through with his plan to find out where his market value lay. Petrie met with Ainge in his office and told him the Blazers wanted him back. Petrie said he respected his right to entertain offers, but would like the opportunity to match any offer another team might make. Petrie left the meeting with the impression the Blazers would get that chance.

July 1 was the day contracts ran out and players became free agents. Under NBA rules, teams could not contact Ainge until that date. But through friends, relatives, business associates, and the media, Coe and Ainge knew there was interest in acquiring his services in New York, Milwaukee, Phoenix, and with both the Clippers and the Lakers in Los Angeles. Of those, Phoenix was the most attractive. Ainge preferred to raise his four children away from the city problems that a family would encounter in New York and Los Angeles. The Suns had just landed Charles Barkley, they had a team capable of competing for an NBA title, and they needed an off guard to offset the loss of Jeff Hornacek, sent to Philadelphia in the Barkley trade. Ainge, an avid golfer, liked the year-round play the Arizona weather allows. The brother of his wife, Michelle, lives there. So do a lot of Ainge's college buddies.

Ainge sat down with Michelle and the kids and discussed the possible moves they could make. They agreed that Phoenix sounded like a nice place. If things didn't work out in Portland, Ainge was definitely leaning toward Phoenix if the Suns were to make a suitable offer.

On June 29, two days before Ainge's contract expired, Coe called Petrie. Coe faxed Petrie a copy of a one-year offer of $1.8 million from a team in the Italian Pro League. "We've done our research," Coe said. The Italian offer, he said, "is comparable to a three-year offer Ainge would get from an NBA team. An offer of three years at $5.3 million is what it will take for you to keep Danny from becoming a free agent. Let us know as quickly as possible, because in 48 hours, you will not have the opportunity to match another offer."

"We'll evaluate the risk," Petrie said, "and get back to you."

"At that point," Ainge said later that summer, "I really believed Portland would come back with an offer of $5 million, or $5.1 million, or do something to keep me. That would have been enough and I'd have retired a Trail Blazer."

Neither Coe nor Ainge heard from Petrie the next two days. On June 30, Ainge went out to Pumpkin Ridge to play 18 holes of golf and took a mobile phone with him, just in case. The only call he got either day from a Blazer representative was from Brad Greenberg, who had no official responsibilities in the negotiations. Greenberg, whom Ainge regarded as a personal friend, asked if Ainge was insistent on a three-year extension. Ainge said he was.

On the evening of June 30, Ainge attended the Tournament of the Americas games in the coliseum. Ironically, he sat at center court next to Ann-Marie Messano, Petrie's fiancee. They chatted amicably. Geoff was not in attendance. At halftime of one of the games, Greenberg came up to say hello to Ainge. "The clock is ticking down," Greenberg said, smiling. Ainge nodded.

Ainge went home and at about 10:45 p.m. — the deadline had passed at 9 p.m., or midnight eastern time — received a call from Phoenix president Jerry Colangelo. Colangelo threw out a lowball offer of three years at $1.3 million per year. "Thanks, that's a great offer, but we're going to keep searching other teams," Ainge said.

"We want you. We need you. What is it going to take to keep you?" Colangelo asked. "About $5.2 million over three years," Ainge said. "You could structure it any way you want — front-load it, back-load it or whatever, I don't care. But that's the money I'm looking for."

They talked a little more. "We'd have to do some contract-changing to do that, but we can do it," Colangelo said. "But this is a take-it-or-leave it deal. I don't want you shopping the offer around. If you can't decide, this offer isn't in effect when we get off the phone. If you say yes, you got a deal."

Ainge said yes. By the following morning, word was out his two-year reign as a Portland Trail Blazer was over. He agreed to fly to Phoenix to sign a contract and attend a press conference on July 3.

Petrie heard the news reports the following morning and called Coe. "Do we need to talk?" Petrie asked Coe. "You're about 12 hours late," Coe said.

Phoenix reworked the contracts of Barkley and Tom Chambers to get under the $14 million salary cap and clear room for Ainge. On July 3, it was official. Ainge was a Sun.

Petrie said given the chance, the Blazers "probably" would have matched any offer Ainge could land on the open market. "I'm disappointed we didn't have a chance to match," Petrie said. "He said all along he was going to look around, shop, but his preference was to stay here. We were operating under the assumption we'd get a chance to match."

"Why would I weaken my bargaining power by telling Geoff I would let him match?" Ainge asked. "Free agency was my only bargaining power. That would have been the stupidest thing I could do."

The stupidest thing, that is, if he wanted the best contract. If Ainge had wanted to settle for a little less and stay in Portland, he could have done that. He didn't have to give the Blazers any breaks, of course. That's what free agency was all about.

Petrie said later the Blazers actually had more money to work with within the structure of the salary cap than the Suns. He said because the team had high balloon payments to make to Drexler and Williams in years down the road, it would have made sense to give Ainge more money in a shorter-term deal. "We could have given him, say, $5 million over two seasons," Petrie said. "Then he'd have been free to negotiate any contract he could if he still wanted to play a third year. He'd have been in position to make even more money than he did with Phoenix."

Later in the summer, Ainge was miffed about such comments.

"We absolutely had no indication they'd ever do that," Ainge said. "If they were considering doing that, why didn't they start the process at a more reasonable level than $1.7 over two years?"

A native Oregonian, Ainge loved the area and its people. A brother and a sister lived in the state, as did many old friends from his days in Eugene. He liked Rick Adelman and the Blazer players, and he was getting the chance to play for the team he rooted hard for as a kid. His hero in those years had been Geoff Petrie. The irony of that hit him hard now.

"Over the course of the last year," Ainge said, "I got the impression Portland intended to get me for a couple of years, sort of as a Band-Aid measure to be their guy off the bench. They didn't have any long-term plans for me.

"I feel I was deceived by Geoff after I first got here. He said he would take care of me like he did the other guys. 'Play this year, and we'll take care of you next year.' Then the next year, it was like I was backed into a corner. It was like his stance in negotiations was, 'What else are you going to do? If you don't accept our offer, you're throwing away guaranteed money.' I didn't think he was being fair. That's why I rebelled."

The bottom line in the end was the Blazers didn't make Ainge feel wanted. They had gone to great expense to satisfy their first six players. They hadn't with their seventh. A personal phone call by Petrie to Ainge in the final 48 hours before the free-agent deadline might have saved the day.

"What it boiled down to," Ainge said, "was I was disgruntled by our negotiations and very disturbed by no phone calls or conversations from them. And Geoff's comment, 'We'll evaluate the risk and get back to you.' He just wouldn't have said that about a player who was critical to their success."

Teammate Wayne Cooper, a man who has done business internships for several summers during his playing career, saw this as a situation where Ainge let his emotions impact what should have been strictly a business decision.

"I think it got to be a situation where it was personal," Cooper said. "When you take it personally, you really lose. It's business. When you get involved in the negotiations the way Danny did, it's easy to take it personally."

A month after signing with Phoenix, Ainge was still referring to Portland and the Blazers as "us."

"I love Portland," he said, and there was more than a touch of regret to his voice. "I love our team and our fans and the coach. It's a hassle to move my kids to a new school and to sell my house. But when it came down to it, Phoenix came through with a good offer, it was a city my family liked, a team I would be interested to play with.

"I felt they wanted me. I felt they needed me. Every player wants that. The way Portland treated me . . . If Geoff had called me (in the days before the July 1 deadline) and started negotiating . . . if he'd said, 'We'll give you $1.8 million the first year, $1.8 million the second year, $1.0 the third year,' or whatever.

"There was nothing but dollars and cents with them the whole way. I was disturbed by how money was the overriding issue. Obviously money is important, but there is a lot more than money.

"To be honest, I had a great deal of frustration those two days when they never got back to us. I don't hold the organization or my teammates responsible for whatever happened. I've just tried to keep that all in perspective. This is just one guy, not the whole organization. There's no question, at times I felt like, 'I'm outta here no matter what,' because of the treatment. But that would mean I'm leaving Rick, I'm leaving Clyde, I'm leaving Terry, Buck . . . or even Paul Allen for that matter. If there had been any sort of communication indicating, 'We want you, but you're asking for a bit much.' There was just nothing."

Petrie has maintained the public posture he wanted to sign Ainge. Privately, he has held to the same story. Ainge sensed a lack of commitment. "I think he wanted to sign me," Ainge said, "but it was no big deal if he didn't."

That seems fair. In coming to a decision on what to offer Ainge, Petrie kept pointing to negatives. "The first 50 games he didn't play very well," Petrie said. "I took 20 of those games against the better teams and he didn't play very well in those, shooting in particular. And he didn't play very well in the playoffs the year before. You can argue it a lot of ways."

Petrie liked Ainge. He empathized with him in a way. But this was business. A lot of people in the front office had their say on the Ainge situation, but the buck stopped with Petrie. Indeed, it seemed he wanted to sign Ainge, but it was no big deal if he didn't.

It was a big deal to a lot of fans. Many wrote notes to Ainge and called him to express their regrets. Many wrote letters to *The Oregonian* that were published in the following Sunday's *Oregonian*. The Blazers, and Petrie, got roasted. The following week the newspaper printed letters whose authors were taking a different stance: That while Ainge is a good player who had his moments with the Blazers, he was getting old and wanted too much money.

"I got so many notes and letters and phone calls from people around Portland I'd never ever met," Ainge said. "That made me feel good. Even the people who wrote to *The Oregonian* in defense of the club . . . hey, that's kind of the way I feel. I feel like I was a benefit to the team, I played well and I played hard, I had some bad moments, and Portland is going to go on with or without me. They were a great team before I came here, and they'll be a great team without me. People are going to forget about Danny Ainge real soon. Blazer fans are real loyal."

Some are real narrow-minded, too. Petrie got a slug of letters on the Ainge situation. *The Oregonian's* beat writer got a few, too, including one that read in part: "Everyone I have talked to is furious at Jeff (sic) Petrie for letting Danny Ainge go. Next year, when the Suns do better than we do, I hope Petrie gets fired. Danny was our only ballplayer that had the experience we need and could keep it all together . . . And there is one other thing that an awful lot of people are unhappy about, now we don't even have one white ballplayer. It was bad enough before. My little nephews think you have to be black to play basketball already. I am going to root for the Suns next year, and I am not the only one."

Blazer management — and the majority of the team's fans — are color blind. They want the 12 best players they can get, black, white, red, or purple, to help the team win. There obviously are some fans out there, though, who are still counting race among their priorities, which is a sad commentary.

Ainge's words toward Petrie sound harsh, but he says he doesn't mean it that way. He admits he's not sure how much of the decision was Petrie, how much of it was Paul Allen, how much of it was Bert Kolde, how much of it was Rick Adelman.

"I don't feel bitter toward Geoff," he said, "maybe because he was a childhood idol of mine. Maybe that's why I cut him slack. I don't really know who it is who didn't want to pay me. Is it Geoff? Is it Rick? Is it Paul? Is it Bert? I don't get mad at any of them. I don't think Geoff was fair, but was there somebody telling him not to be fair? Honestly, I don't hate Geoff. I idolized him my whole life. Every time we talked one-on-one, we had cordial conversations.

"I have regrets with how it all transpired, but I have no regrets about going to Phoenix. I considered myself the seventh-best player on the team, and I wanted the seventh-best contract. I did what I thought was best for me and my family. I just didn't feel as needed by the Blazers."

Petrie believed the Suns had broken league rules by contacting Ainge prior to the July 1 date and considered filing a complaint with the league before opting not to. Ainge said he was not contacted before July 1. It was no secret in the weeks leading up to the date that the Suns coveted Ainge, and it was no surprise that Ainge and Coe got wind of it.

What happened in the Danny Ainge affair was simple. Ainge played outstanding ball the first half of his first season, but tapered off in the second half and was not much help in the playoffs. Adelman lost some confidence in him, particularly as a backup point guard getting the Blazers into their offense against a quick defender. The Blazers financially took care of all their starters and Robinson, but decided to gamble with Ainge. If he didn't play well in the 1991-92 season, market value for him as a 33-year-old free agent would plummet.

The opposite happened. Ainge finished strong, and his value rose. Even so, had the Blazers gone after Ainge hard, made him feel like they really wanted him, he'd have stayed, even for a little less money. Petrie, for whatever reason, chose not to show much interest until it was too late. Maybe he was lulled into a false sense of security by Ainge's statement that if all things were equal, he'd stay in Portland. Maybe he thought Ainge's ties to the state would keep him a Blazer no matter what their offer. "I think they were counting on those attachments to keep me from going to another team," Ainge said. "They obviously didn't take me very seriously."

When the Blazers signed Ainge, they made a big deal out of him being a part of championship clubs in Boston and knowing what it takes to win a ring. Petrie admitted part of it was to assuage the psyche of the Blazer players. "It's important for your players to see that you're continuing to do things for your team that they believe in," Petrie said. "Danny came in and was a veteran player they thought would help us be better. That mentality of winning was improved." The Celtic aura, and what Ainge had done to help sustain it, was part of the selling point, "and I think the leadership thing was overblown a little bit. Let's face it, when he was with Boston, Danny played a real good role on that team, but McHale, Bird, Parish and Dennis Johnson were the leaders. Danny made a positive contribution for us in his two years here . . . but the emotionalism of his departure was overblown in terms of his importance to our team."

Ainge was asked if he gained satisfaction out of sticking it up the rear end of Blazer management. "I'll get that when we (the Suns) beat them," he said. "I'll get my satisfaction when I help Phoenix have some success. I haven't proven anything yet. If I don't play well in Phoenix, then Portland has done a great job by not signing me."

Reaction by the players to the loss of Ainge was mixed. Some thought his contributions were a little overrated. Some thought he talked too much. None was glad to see him go.

"I'm going to miss Danny," Kevin Duckworth said. "I wish Danny had retired here. He's a great guy and a very good player. He had a sense of humor and he's carefree. I'm sorry they let him go."

"Danny was one of my favorites," Alaa Abdelnaby said. "He always put things into perspective. No matter how bad or how good things were, just for the simple fact he'd been around so long, he had a different angle at looking at things. He's easy to talk to. Not to sound corny, but I hated him when he played for the Celtics, and then I learned to love him as a teammate."

"Danny had a special value to the team," Drexler said. "For the minutes he played we got a lot of production out of him at times. He was good for our team. He's a good guy, and he played well and played hard. His competitive spirit was catchy. But the fact remains, we got to the Finals without him, and don't count us out in the future because we don't have Danny."

Petrie concedes some of the arguments against his stance in the Ainge negotiations carry substance and asks only that things be judged over the course of time.

"Let's let it stand the test of time to find out whether we did blow it," Petrie said. "Whether some of the things we have done will make us a better team, and what happens with Danny down in Phoenix."

Abdelnaby became an ex-Blazer, too, officially even before Ainge. On July 1, San Antonio swapped its No. 1 pick in the 1992 draft, UCLA forward Tracy Murray, to Milwaukee. The Bucks in turn sent Murray to Portland for Abdelnaby, who would never be given the chance to fulfill his promise as a Blazer.

The Blazers said they were willing to give up Abdelnaby only because of their dire need for a shooter. Murray, for sure, was one of the best perimeter shooters in the college ranks, with 3-point capabilities as he matured as a professional player.

But Abdelnaby had just turned 24, and an NBA team simply doesn't deal a young 6-10 player who has shown he can score on an array of shots and on just about anyone in the league.

Abdelnaby was surprised, but since late in the regular season had sensed the possibility he might not be back with the Blazers by the fall. Later in the summer, as he was participating on a Bucks summer-league team in Detroit, he reflected on his departure.

"I don't think anything went wrong," he said. "This is a business and when opportunities arise, you have to take advantage of them. The Blazers needed a backup 3 who could shoot. I think Cliff will play more 4 this year, and they have Mark Bryant. It's a matter of timing."

It was more than that. Adelman was a stickler for strong defense. If a player was a weak defender, he'd have a tougher time getting minutes. Abdelnaby was a decent shot-blocker, but not a consistent defender, and he had a habit of committing foolish fouls, not uncommon for a young player. The biggest thing, though, was consistency of effort, or his lack of it.

"You see the potential, the spark, and then all of a sudden he wouldn't work," Schalow said. "Sometimes he wouldn't get back on defense. That was a thorn in Rick's side. Rick got on him a couple of times about it. I used to tell Alaa, 'The only way you're going to get time is to push yourself all the time,' but he never did. He has unbelievable skills. If he really wanted it and played hard all the time, he could be a very, very good player. I talked to Mike Krzyzewski about him one time, and he said that's the same problem they had with him (at Duke). I think Alaa felt he did work hard, and he probably did work harder for us than he ever did before."

Alaa, indeed, saw himself as a man of labor.

"I don't think it was ever a problem," he said. "I think I worked hard. I've always been the type of person, when you give me an opportunity, I'll work even harder for you. When I first got to Duke, Coach K didn't give me any responsibilities, and I got discouraged. When I get discouraged, people think I'm not into it. But I don't buy the work ethic thing. I worked hard in college, and if I can work hard for Mike Krzyzewski, I can work hard for anybody. The first thing (Milwaukee coach) Mike Dunleavy told me was he liked the way I played against the Lakers and the way I came in early before games and worked."

The famous missing uniform incident didn't help Alaa's standing, but he doesn't think it signaled the beginning of the end for him as a Blazer. "If it did," he said, "that's a bad reflection on anybody who looks at it in a negative way. That's ridiculous. That's something you can't lose sleep over."

Alaa had another mark against him. He and Robinson liked to drive their cars fast. And in the early morning of May 29, hours after they'd polished off Utah to claim the Western Conference championship, both received high-speed tickets as they headed into town from the Hillsboro Airport on Highway 26.

Robinson was ticketed for driving his 1992 Mercedes 500 at 110 in a 55-mile-per-hour zone. A mile or so down the road, Abdelnaby was being charged with driving his 1992 Porsche 928 in excess of the speed limit. His ticket read 110-plus.

Both had poor records since obtaining an Oregon driver's license. Cliff had two speeding tickets, a careless driving ticket, and three citations for driving without a license in the previous three years. Alaa had three speeding tickets and two other citations in the previous two years.

It looked particularly bad for another reason. In December 1989, Blazer rookie Ramon Ramos was driving home from downtown in early-morning hours at a high speed when his car skidded on an icy Interstate 5 and flipped over. Ramos was critically injured and remained in a coma for weeks before gradually coming out of it. His rehabilitation had been a slow and arduous process, and he would never regain his full faculties. It was a painful memory that had not faded easily from the minds of those in the Blazer organization and their many thousands of fans.

Both Robinson and Abdelnaby could have put the issue to rest rather easily by conceding a mistake had been made in the glow of a conference title. Neither showed the least bit of contrition. Robinson was asked by KGW news reporter Walden Kirsch about the incident at the Hillsboro Airport as he prepared to board Blazer One for the trip to Chicago for the first two games of the NBA Finals a few days later. He snapped at the query. "What does that have to do with anything, you . . . get out of my face, asking me about that." Later, when an *Oregonian* beat reporter asked him how he felt about getting the ticket at such a high speed, he asked if the reporter intended to write about it. When the reporter said he thought he would, Robinson grew livid, decorating his language with curse words.

Abdelnaby was more civilized, if less than forthright, in his response. He at first told *The Oregonian* he was not ticketed, that the officer who stopped his car said he should give him a ticket but instead would just give him a warning "this time." Some time later, when a reporter said he had a copy of the ticket that was issued to him, Abdelnaby told a different story. "The cop called me a couple of weeks later and said, 'Would you mind if I gave you a ticket?' " he said. "I said, 'Well, yeah I'd mind, why?' He said, 'because if I don't, I'm going to get fired.' " Abdelnaby said the policeman then wrote out a ticket, predated it to May 29 and sent it to him.

The officer, Sgt. Steve Mathews of the Washington County Sheriff's Department, differed with Abdelnaby's account. "I'd be happy to discuss that with Mr. Abdelnaby in court," Mathews said. "That is not an accurate assessment. It didn't happen that way at all. That's ridiculous." Mathews said he could speak no further on the matter until it had been taken care of in court.

Neither Robinson nor Abdelnaby appeared for a June 12 arraignment date. The court put a sanction on Robinson's license on July 24 and a week later received a check from Robinson for the $278 ticket and a $15 reinstatement fee. Abdelnaby's $278 ticket had not yet been taken care of by late summer and the court had put a sanction on his Oregon driver's license.

Three months later, Robinson was still defiant about the whole incident. "It got overblown," he said. "Sure, you want to put it in the paper, but don't keep trying to bring it up. It might have been poor judgment (might have been?) but this was when we were trying to win a championship and I think the media kept trying to bring up a negative while we were trying to accomplish something positive. We were trying to get something done."

Robinson and Abdelnaby are forever intertwined, because they are good friends, are young, play the same position, and have the potential for long careers in the league. To Petrie, there is an important difference. "Cliff puts it all out there on the court," Petrie said. "Alaa doesn't. You need to be able to count on a guy giving you 65 or 70 good games a season, and hopefully more than that. We got one good game out of every two or three from Alaa."

Alaa was in somebody's doghouse, and the other players knew it.

"Alaa has tremendous talent," Duckworth said. "But I knew they were going to do something (after the season). They didn't want him. Alaa was their whipping boy. He could do no right. I was always in that position before. He played hard. He didn't always play hard defense, but he played hard on offense. A lot of guys do the same thing.

"To them, he had a Mychal Thompson attitude." That meant laid-back, carefree. "There was a point in the season where he got mad and he talked back, spoke his mind. I told him, 'You can't speak your mind yet, you ain't got no clout behind you. You got to wait.' They can deny it, but he was their whipping boy."

The "attitude" claim sticks in Abdelnaby's craw. He thinks he was misunderstood.

"You can't tell me I didn't take things seriously," he said. "When we won, who was the biggest cheerleader on the bench? I could have been a pouter . . . but I wanted us to win. That really bothers me. The defense I had to work on, and telling me to do that is fine, and even telling me a work ethic is something I need to improve on is fine. I heard the coaches would see me smiling and being giddy and that bothered them. Well, that's the way I am. That's my personality. That has nothing to do with how hard I work or how much I want to win."

Alaa had his place in the rotation for more than three months, until he hurt his knee in early March. Then Bryant took his place, and Abdelnaby never got it back.

"Mark was playing better, and we started playing better as a team," Adelman said. "I wanted to cut the rotation down to seven or eight guys and there was only a spot for one of them. I felt we were a better defensive team with Mark coming off the bench. I didn't think we needed Alaa's scoring to win. (Work ethic) is one area Alaa needs to work on. He's a young guy, and it's hard to not play much. But for him to be a successful player he needs to play hard all the time. A lot of guys take a year or two in the league to learn that. Face it, he was playing behind some awfully good talent, and he had to play hard all the time to win minutes away from guys."

Abdelnaby said he had no problem with Adelman, and liked him as a coach. He had only good things to say about the Blazer organization.

"They're a class act," he said. "They treat their players with class. I remember when David Robinson was upset when San Antonio didn't have a team plane. Portland doesn't hold anything back. The Blazers never do anything half-ass. For instance, we'd go on the road and have a day off and have a buffet, just so we could be together as a team. There were things like a function at Geoff's house before the playoffs, and no one was ever excluded . . . I never had anyone to bring, but if I had, I always trusted they would treat her with respect, just like me. Paul Allen, all the way down to the bottom, my memories are nothing but good."

The fans got good vibes from Abdelnaby, whom they enjoyed as one of the most engaging, articulate, likeable players. "I'll really miss them," he said. "I remember having dinner with Christian Laettner in a restaurant during the Tournament of the Americas just after I'd been traded. He's the third pick in the whole draft and on the Olympic team, and in the hour and a half we ate dinner, nobody said a word to him. Everybody came up to me with nice things to say, ranging from, 'We don't think you should be leaving,' to 'We're going to miss you' to 'Good luck.' It put a lump in my throat. They almost made me cry."

Abdelnaby said he was leaving Portland with a positive attitude. "The way to look at it, is they did me a favor," he said. "The month after I was traded was the hardest I've ever had. To be traded does a lot to your psyche. Wayne Cooper told me he was traded five times, and each one affected him. He said you have to look at it as a promotion, because you're going where somebody wants you.

"Clyde is such a class act. He told me before I left it was a great opportunity for me, that I'd be an all-star in two years. I said, 'C'mon, Clyde, do you really believe that?' He said yeah, and that made me feel good, even if it's not true."

Even before Ainge departed, Blazer management was working on adding a veteran point guard. And on July 3, the same day Ainge officially became an ex-Blazer, Rod Strickland was signed to a six-year deal worth about $12.6 million.

Strickland, 26, was a four-year veteran who had played the previous 2 1/2 seasons with San Antonio, all as a starter. He had averaged 13.8 points and 8.6 assists for the Spurs — ranking fifth in the NBA in the latter category — in 1991-92. Normally, a player of such accomplishments would not be available, but the Spurs had renounced their rights to Strickland and he was an unrestricted free agent.

The reason had little to do with his on-court accomplishments. Strickland's reputation throughout the NBA was as trouble. He had been unhappy in New York coming off the bench behind Mark Jackson, precipitating his trade to San Antonio. Once there, he had a few problems away from NBA arenas. He was involved in a late-hour fight in a parking lot outside a San Antonio nightclub that resulted in a broken right hand, which sidelined him for 21 games. He was later charged with indecent exposure after an incident with a flight attendant in the hallway of a Seattle hotel. That charge was eventually dropped. And he had been a holdout the previous season with the Spurs, finally signing a one-year, $1.3 million contract in December.

Strickland would have been a restricted free agent, and the Spurs would have had an opportunity to match any offer, but they evidently decided he was enough of a headache to let him go and wish him well at the next stop on his NBA journey. That would be Portland, where Petrie and Adelman said they felt Strickland would not be a negative influence on his teammates.

"He doesn't have a criminal record, and he doesn't have a drug problem," Petrie said. "I think there are a lot of players around who have done a lot more outrageous things than he has done."

"I don't have any concerns with (his off-court problems)," Adelman said. "I deal with people from the first day they're here. We'll deal with him from this point on."

Strickland's coach through most of his time in San Antonio, Larry Brown, gave him a hearty endorsement. "Rod is really a good kid," Brown said. "He'll be great for Portland. With the kind of guys they have on their team and with his ability, he'll flourish in that environment. We didn't have the greatest guys to be around. David (Robinson) and Sean (Elliott) are wonderful, but they didn't tell you how to act. Buck, Clyde . . . I think being with the guys Rod will be with in Portland, that'll be the greatest thing that could ever happen to him."

At the press conference announcing his signing, Strickland talked as if his troubles were behind him.

"When I went back to the Spurs last season," he said, "they wanted me to do well on and off the court. I did that. I've adjusted. I've had some years in the league now. I don't foresee that as a problem."

Adelman said the Blazers would have pursued Strickland even if they had kept Ainge. The coach said he became convinced during the 1992 Finals there was a need for ball-handling help.

"Once Terry Porter left the game, we struggled to bring the ball upcourt," Adelman said. "Rod was by far the best point guard available on the unrestricted list."

Soon the Blazers were on to their next item of business — Adelman's contract extension. Bert Kolde was handling it, which Petrie endorsed as a good idea. Petrie and Adelman had been teammates and roommates with the Blazers during the early-70s, and though they didn't socialize together anymore, they were still friends. Petrie had made it known to Kolde and Paul Allen he believed Adelman deserved his extension.

And on July 29, Adelman was signed to a two-year extension with a third option year. The option year could become guaranteed, providing the team reached certain goals. Adelman, who was to make less than $400,000 in the final year of his existing contract, would reap an average of $700,000 on his new one, putting him into the upper echelon of the NBA coaching ranks — where he belonged.

The Blazers weren't through tinkering with their roster, either. Mark Bryant was signed to a three-year contract, and Mario Elie, the part-time starter at Golden State, was signed to a two-year, $1.4 million deal as a free agent. Robert Pack was traded to Denver for a future draft choice.

There were other changes in the makeup of the Blazer family. Bill Schonely, by all accounts a living legend as the only radio play-by-play man in the 22 years of the Trail Blazers, made the move over to TV, clearing the way for Eddie Doucette to move into the radio booth. And Wayne Cooper was hired into the front office as a liaison between the coaching staff and management.

The key players remained, but the bottom half of the Blazer roster wore a new look. Out were Ainge, Abdelnaby, and Wayne Cooper. In were Strickland and Elie, and rookies Murray, Dave Johnson, and Reggie Smith. "We've made ourselves younger, we've made ourselves quicker," Petrie said.

Only the future would tell if they had made themselves better.

18

"Deep Down In Our Hearts, We Know Discipline and Attention to Detail Have Plagued Us."

Life went on in Portland, though it took on a more somber mood for a while.

The talk shows, as usual, were alive with criticisms and suggestions. Fans wrote both angry and sympathetic letters to the newspaper. People found excuses, scapegoats, and alibis. Everybody had reasons and answers. Nobody had THE answer or THE reason. One of them reached all the way back to January, when the team decided to cut Danny Young — sentencing Terry Porter to long minutes without a veteran backup during the Finals. But Geoff Petrie, who ultimately takes the rap for personnel decisions, would hear none of that.

"It's an argument that's impossible to prove one way or another," Petrie said. "Lamont Strothers did not play much. How much Danny would have played or how well he would have played will always be subject to debate. We made the decision and did get back to the Finals, which we hadn't done the year before. It's overblown to say if we'd have had Danny Young we would have won a championship. To me, that's absurd."

The Blazers, for the second time in three seasons, had lost in the Finals. They'd come up short, and even though they'd surpassed all but one team in the league, there was an empty feeling.

"It was really disappointing," Cliff Robinson said. "I think there were times in games when we had more in us than we gave.

We just couldn't bring it out. But we let ourselves get down. A year ago, we showed too much emotion and I think this time we didn't show enough. This time we put our heads down.

"We were just so close. But they spurted on us, just like we spurted against everyone else."

"Everything has to be perfect for you to win," said Wayne Cooper, who would quickly find out during the summer that the Blazers had no uniform for him in 1992-93. "I don't think anyone understands what a great run we've had. Frustrating? Well, I would think Phoenix would have to be the team that's frustrated.

"The expectations have been so high in Portland the past two years. I think they've been so high we didn't enjoy ourselves as much as we should have. We should have been sky high. But every win was like a relief. It's not so much fun when you start putting pressure on yourself."

Cooper became a casualty when the team decided it needed his salary slot to sign free agent guard Rod Strickland. Rather than getting a big farewell night and lots of recognition for his distinguished service, Cooper went quietly and without a whimper.

"This is kind of the way I wanted it," he said. "I'd just go quietly. You know it's going to end and you can either be happy with yourself or be sad. You have to keep everything in perspective. I've never been caught up in the glory of this job. It's the least of my worries. I've achieved a lot."

Buck Williams agreed with Cooper in regard to the enormity of the pressure the team felt during the season. Williams actually left the planet during the summer to relieve some of the pressure — he took flying lessons.

"Reflecting back on everything, from Day 1 there was a lot of anticipation," said Williams. "There was a lot of pressure, and a lot of stress. It wasn't one of the most enjoyable seasons. You enjoy winning, but it wasn't as much fun as the previous two years. It just seemed to be ingrained in everyone's mind that it was a do-or-die situation. There was a tremendous amount of pressure on us. But winning a championship isn't just something that falls out of the sky.

"That first year, there was nothing expected of us. It changed after that. We weren't having fun last year. There was pressure from management and from ourselves. Every move all year seemed so calculated. You need to have fun. It was like every game was a playoff game all year."

Williams has some definite opinions on what he can do to improve his team's chances to win a championship in the coming season.

"I think I was too unselfish, offensively," Williams said. "When you play that unselfishly, you get taken for granted. I'm as much responsible for that as my teammates and the coaches. I'm not going to shoot bad shots, but I'm going to look to score more often next year."

Williams did some deep soul-searching after the Finals and faced a reality that a lot of his teammates have run from. This is a club that still has a ways to go before it gets the most out of its ability.

"It was real saddening," he said. "We felt we had a better team than Chicago. Deep down in our hearts, though, I think we know that discipline and attention to detail has plagued us. We're going to have to get better at that. What set the two teams apart in the Finals was attention to detail and discipline. They took some things away from us in our offense and the coach gave us some things we could do to counter it. But we didn't take advantage of what was there.

"We have to change. We have to get more disciplined. When you change, there's always going to be resistance to it. People resist change. But we're going to have to do it. It's not just some of the players, it's all of us.

"Rick has done a phenomenal job the past three years. This year in the playoffs he was more professional and more focused than I've ever seen him.

"He was like a different coach. I think we as players need to be a little more responsible. It starts with a player like myself. I've got to get to practice earlier next year. That's going to be very, very difficult for me to do. But other players will see me at practice early, and I think it will send a message to them.

"I've got to do that. I've got to make that commitment. And I think we've got to make a commitment to discipline. If Michael Jordan can run that system in Chicago, then Buck Williams can stay within this system. If Buck Williams can deviate, then other players can deviate, too."

Terry Porter was hitting at the same theme when he pointed to the team's 102 turnovers in the six-game series.

"Give Chicago credit, but our turnover ratio was terrible," he said. "Not being able to move the ball the way we had in the previous two series hurt us a lot. It hurt my game, and it hurt Jerome's opportunities. You can't play the way we did against Chicago. Without a doubt, come the Finals, and it's at another level. You have to be willing to turn it up.

"But maybe it just wasn't meant to be. It's an old cliche, but we just didn't play well enough to win. Chicago's not a great team. They have a great player and a lot of good role players. Pippen wouldn't be as good a player on another team — without No. 23 next to him."

Kersey felt much the same as Porter — that the Bulls were a team the Blazers should have whipped.

"It was the best opportunity we've had to win it," Kersey said. "They had the homecourt advantage, but I felt Chicago was a team we should have dominated. They're the world champions, but I felt our team was much better than theirs. To not play to the level we could have was very frustrating. When we were at the top of our game — like the first three quarters of the sixth game — there was no way they could stay with us.

"I thought about my family, talking to them earlier this year and knowing how much they were pulling for us — my family and friends. That hits another part of you inside, that you let down so many people. You feel as though it's just you, not 12 guys. You can only do as much as you can do. But I still felt as if I didn't leave everything I had on the court."

Kersey had a bad taste in his mouth, thanks to all the talking the Bulls did during the series and a remark Jordan made afterward, telling the Chicago fans he was glad he wasn't drafted by Portland.

"That was a little uncalled for," Kersey said. "I think they're an arrogant bunch of guys, I really do."

Danny Ainge, now a Phoenix Sun, also talked about the value of Jordan to the Bulls.

"I thought we had a good shot at winning," he said. "I know we were playing a great team, but I felt Chicago was vulnerable. There's a lot more to it than Jordan, I guess, but he's incredible. Whenever they needed something, he was there. He was unconscious in that first half. Those kinds of things happen. We were ready to play and Jordan just went crazy.

"Game 3 was the most disappointing loss by far — even more than Game 6. For some reason, we didn't respond. Games 3 and 5 were the most discouraging. If we'd put forward the effort we did in Game 6 in those games, we would have won."

But the Bulls played at a much higher level than the Blazers for much longer periods of time. That's fact, not speculation. And perhaps facing up to that is the only avenue for improvement.

"We made big shots in the Utah and Phoenix series," Adelman said. "Same thing two years ago against San Antonio and Phoenix. But in the Finals, Detroit and Chicago made big shots against us. We got beat."

By a better team.

"I think Chicago was playing at a real high level," assistant coach John Wetzel said. "They defended us real well. One of the reasons we didn't shoot well was they forced us into some tough shots. We had a good game plan, they just took us out of some of the things we were trying to do.

"They're awfully good and awfully quick. I think Scottie Pippen is a superstar. We have to be more determined to set picks to free our shooters. We allowed them to overplay us. We didn't handle their pressure as well as we should have, but part of that was because Terry played too many minutes. We were forced to play him too many. One of the reasons he didn't shoot the ball well is that he got leg weary from playing too many minutes."

Wetzel escapes each summer to a condominium in the Hawaiian Islands. Nobody talks basketball there much. They don't even have a sports talk show on his little island.

"I think the expectations in Portland have become so doggone high," he said. "That's good because it motivates us. But on the other hand, sometimes there's no relief from it. You read the newspapers, watch TV, it's Blazers all the time. There was a great letter to the editor the other day where some guy just said, 'Hey, let basketball rest.' Give us a break. But it's a year-round thing. And people just want to be a part of it."

It was really a year-round thing this season, because of all the things that went on after the Finals ended. First, there was the NBA Draft, a sellout in Memorial Coliseum with all the top picks on hand. The Blazers took Syracuse's Dave Johnson, then spent much of the summer before negotiating a contract with him. Within a few weeks after the draft, they lost Ainge to Phoenix, signed Strickland and Mario Elie, traded Alaa Abdelnaby to

Milwaukee for Tracy Murray, and played host to the Tournament of Americas.

At summer's end, the team's proposed new arena still hung in the balance, the result of negotiating problems between the Blazers and various local government agencies. Paul Allen, who is going to pour approximately $170 million into the project, was doing a slow burn because he couldn't get moving on the project. Several sources inside the team said he was close to pulling the plug on the whole thing and going elsewhere.

Elsewhere in this case would likely have meant Vancouver, Washington, or other suburbs of Portland. To move one of the most financially successful franchises in pro sports would not be a smart decision. What it would do, though, is remove all the financial advantages of that team into another marketplace — one more appreciative, perhaps, of its impact on an economy.

Allen, by the way, is an unusual person. Some outsiders figure him for a fast-moving man of action, since he's so deeply involved with the quick-changing computer software business. But that's not the case. Allen is actually a man who frustrates those around him sometimes because of how deliberate he is in making important decisions.

Most billionaires are perceived as people capable of making monetary decisions quickly, too. But that's not always the case. Those people agonize over money just the way everyone else does — sometimes even more so. Perhaps that's how they accumulated all that wealth in the first place.

Even though Memorial Coliseum is becoming woefully out of date, it was probably the ideal home for the Tournament of Americas. Its coziness seemed a perfect atmosphere for what turned out to be a fun-filled U.S. romp through the Western Hemisphere.

The Dream Team was a big item in Portland, especially because of Drexler's presence. As expected, the team came back from Barcelona with gold medals — and some warm memories. He'd been a member of a team that will probably find its place in history as one of the most talented and storied teams of all time —in any sport.

"I really enjoyed the whole atmosphere," Drexler said upon his return. "From start to finish, it was a class act. Winning the gold was our focus. Everything else was not important. We wanted to enjoy the companionships and friendships we shared, and have a good time. You get to know them much better than you did previously, because you get to spend time with them.

"They're quality guys. I was not surprised at that at all. I got to know David Robinson much better . . . John Stockton, Karl Malone. They're great guys."

Drexler played very well in the Olympics but made himself even more famous for an incident that Magic Johnson later related on the Arsenio Hall show. But Drexler tells the story even better than Johnson.

"It was human error," Drexler said with his shy smile. "I was in our hotel, about 10 in the morning, but it felt like about 6 a.m. My wife and kids were asleep, and I'm getting out of bed trying to make this 10:30 practice. I put on my slippers and shorts and put two shoes in my bag. The two shoes were both for the right foot.

"The thing I learned from that is, you never want to keep two of the same shoes right next to each other."

Drexler arrived at the practice and had a decision to make, once he pulled the shoes out of his bag.

"You could either sit there with no shoes or you can put them on," he said. "I wanted to see how it felt, so I put it on the other foot and it didn't feel bad. I could run around on it. I figured I'd make it through without anybody heckling me, but lo and behold, Charles Barkley noticed.

"It was comical and they all talked about it for the next couple of days. What else can you do but laugh? It was one of those comical mistakes."

Drexler's appearance on Arsenio Hall was lighthearted, and he did a nice job until he was asked about the "dumb" label that had been put on the Blazers. "To me, that's nothing more than a racist statement," he said, ignoring the fact the theory had been perpetrated by the likes of Magic Johnson, Michael Jordan, and Scottie Pippen, among others.

Duckworth spent much of his summer playing softball and working out six days a week with a personal trainer he hired out of Gold's Gym. But much of the old persecution complex had not yet been exorcised.

"I want to be toned up and a little lighter," he said. "But I'm not going to be skinny. My weight is always going to be there. I'm not going to look like Buck Williams. It's not going to happen, and I have to face reality. Maybe I should have played another sport, because when you wished you'd never played professional basketball, that's terrible.

"People want to punish me for my size. I'm not obese, I'm just big. My stomach's not hanging out over my pants. My weight is always going to be a sensitive subject, but I'd appreciate if people would take everything into consideration."

In a summer interview at his Beaverton home, Duckworth said he has undergone a personality change as a result of the past two seasons.

"Want me to be honest?" he asked, hopping onto Freud's couch. "They changed my whole personality. I'm a totally different person than I used to be. I'm colder. I tell people to kiss my ass in a minute. I used to try to please people, but people don't really care about you. I'm not an outgoing person no more. I'm more to myself. With my friends, I enjoy things, but I'm not a laughing person like I used to be. The bad part about it is loved ones who know how you used to be tell you you've changed a lot, that you hold so much in. It bothers me that I hurt them a lot of times, but what can a person do?"

Duckworth bore the brunt of criticism after the Blazers' loss to the Lakers in the 1991 Western Conference finals and feels Blazer management should have deflected the criticism.

"Everyone put the blame on me," he said, "and I never saw nobody from the Blazer office say it wasn't Kevin's fault. It's like, 'Well, Kevin, somebody's got to take the blame, sorry it's you.' I'd have said it's a team game, and we lost. But no, they point the finger at me. I was so bitter and pissed off at the end of last year, I could have punched everybody in the face in the whole organization." Fortunately for him and everyone else concerned, he doesn't still feel that way. "I can talk to anybody in the organization now," he said.

In a warped sense of perception, Duckworth — forgetting he had thousands of loyal fans and many who admired him and regarded him as a friend — felt as if he were waging battle with the whole state.

"I was not fighting just the Trail Blazers," he said, "I was fighting Oregon itself. It got so bad during the season that my agent asked me if maybe it would be best for me to be traded. But I'm not bitter. It helped me a lot. I know who I can count on now. I know who is sincere, and who is phony. I enjoy my teammates, because I tell you what, I've got the best teammates in the world. My teammates are my family here."

Ironically, Duckworth still loves the state and its natural beauty, and he intends to stay. "I love Oregon," he said. "Hey, they can trade me to Timbuktu, but when summertime comes, this is my home. I bought this house to stay. I'm not moving anywhere."

Drexler will head into the next season more confident than ever that his team has what it takes to go all the way.

"We have more talent this year than last year," he said. "With Tracy, Strickland, and Mario Elie, we're much more talented. We'll miss Alaa and Danny. But it's a question of us getting better. It's just a matter of getting over the hump. We need to do everything better. We need to cut down on the turnovers and shoot free throws better."

Cooper, the elder statesman, believes the window of opportunity for the Trail Blazers will be open for a few more years.

"I think they'll get a couple more shots at it," he said. "Strickland gives them a dimension they haven't had in a long, long time — a point guard who can penetrate and create.

"Rick has done an outstanding job here. He'll never get the credit he deserves. This team could have taken a U-turn. He's just always had a sense for this team. And there have always been stable guys on the team who wouldn't let nonsense happen here. This year was Rick's best coaching job. There was nothing more he could have done."

Perhaps there was nothing more anyone could have done. Most of the time, when it's you against the world, the world wins.